## PRAISE FOR *FOR THE CU*

"An engrossing book that will make you better at any job involving money. Warning: you might be up all night reading it."
—SCOTT GALLOWAY, NYU professor of marketing and author of *Adrift*

"A must-have for any leader, marketer, or simply any person who wants to understand how culture impacts the world around us and how they can [create] impactful contributions to the tapestry of what shapes human connection."
—GOD-IS RIVERA, VP of inclusive marketing,
Disney Media & Entertainment

"Marcus Collins does much more than identify potent drivers of human conduct such as values, ideologies, norms, and trends. With compelling prose and vivid accounts, he locates their common source in the concept of culture—which he beautifully dissects and knits back together for readers like a skilled surgeon."
—ROBERT CIALDINI, author of *Influence* and *Pre-Suasion*

"This book is insightful, enlightening, and sure to challenge any preconceived notions about communicating with the world. Talk the talk, walk the walk, and always do it for the culture."
—JAY NORMAN, global head of music marketing, Spotify

"Collins provides an insightful blueprint for harnessing the power of identity and culture to build brand love and inspire action. After reading Collins's well-crafted gem, you will never go about marketing, advertising, or building communities quite the same way."
—KENNY MITCHELL, global chief marketing officer,
Levi Strauss & Co.

"We all know culture can be a vehicle for influence, but in *For the Culture*, Collins shows us how. He provides fascinating deep-dives into the power of cultural community and illustrates how we can use it to change minds and inspire action."
—JONAH BERGER, bestselling author of *Contagious*

"Some people seem to intuitively 'get it.' Most do not. Collins articulates 'it' for the rest of us and provides not just an understanding, but a guide for how to actually engage and influence culture."
—STEVE HUFFMAN, cofounder and CEO, Reddit

"Creating a brand that meets customers at the intersection of the cultural and commerce is the key to connecting with customers in a more authentic and meaningful way. *For the Culture* shows how companies can build brands that resonate with their market on a deeper level and create a strong emotional connection that will reward their business in the fight for their lifetime value."

—TARIQ HASSAN, chief marketing and
customer experience officer, McDonald's USA

"While great brands have always tapped into culture to deliver massive wins for themselves and their stakeholders, the idea of culture, and how to consistently and appropriately leverage it, has remained a mystery to most. With *For the Culture*, Marcus Collins not only makes the definitive argument for why engaging in culture is critical to commerce and anyone who wants to influence behavior, but he also removes the mystery behind how it's done without misusing or appropriating it."

—DETAVIO SAMUELS, chief executive officer, Revolt

"I can confidently say this book is a game changer. Collins's insights on the role of culture as the kindling to the brushfire of public opinion are absolutely powerful and necessary. This book is a must-read for anyone looking to deepen their understanding of the catalytic power of culture as a force for growth and for good."

—TRISTAN WALKER, founder and CEO,
Walker & Company Brands

"Collins is a comet moving effortlessly through branding, marketing, engagement, advertising, social media, and meaning making, giving new life, clarity, and purpose to them all. My advice: read this book! It will transform you, your career, and how you see the world."

—GRANT McCRACKEN, anthropologist
and author of *Chief Culture Officer*

"*For the Culture* explains the profound influence of cultural perspectives on consumer worlds like never before. Collins's beautifully written book is a must-read for anyone who wants to understand today's trillion-dollar dance of brands and culture."

—ROBERT V. KOZINETS, Jayne and Hans Hufschmid Chair
of Strategic Public Relations and Business
Communication, University of Southern California

"This is the new Bible for anyone who wants to understand how to influence behavior through culture. A uniquely compelling interpretation of humans today and how we see the world, brought to life with brilliant examples and stories along the way."

—LORRAINE TWOHILL, chief marketing officer, Google

"What is culture, exactly? Mr. Collins calls it the operating system by which we live, and includes identity, shared language, social norms, and cultural production—art, movies, fashion, and branded products. To help develop this picture he hauls in the big guns of social psychology, anthropology, and even French philosophy, marshaling such forces in an elegantly friendly writing style."

—*Wall Street Journal*

"Perceptive.... Collins has a knack for delivering his smart ideas in accessible prose. This is a superior program on how the business world can use the interplay between culture, consumption, and identity to their advantage."

—*Publishers Weekly*

"Collins offers plenty of food for thought about how the social landscape is evolving.... With personal stories and a dry wit, he bridges the gap between cultural theory and marketing practice."

—KIRKUS

"Fascinating and fun.... This eye-opening book arms readers with a wealth of knowledge about how we make important choices and how to mobilize others using innovative tactics and tools."

—*Shelf Awareness*

"*For the Culture* is a highly accessible, smart, and well-written book."

—*Hour Detroit*

"Collins is uniquely qualified to deconstruct this elusive topic."

—*Inc.*

# FOR THE CULTURE

### THE POWER BEHIND WHAT WE BUY, WHAT WE DO, AND WHO WE WANT TO BE

## MARCUS COLLINS

**PUBLIC**AFFAIRS

NEW YORK

PublicAffairs
Hachette Book Group
1290 Avenue of the Americas, New York, NY 10104
www.publicaffairsbooks.com
@Public_Affairs

Printed in the United States of America
First Edition: May 2023
First Trade Paperback Edition: September 2024

Published by PublicAffairs, an imprint of Hachette Book Group, Inc. The PublicAffairs name and logo is a registered trademark of the Hachette Book Group.

The Hachette Speakers Bureau provides a wide range of authors for speaking events. To find out more, go to hachettespeakersbureau.com or email HachetteSpeakers@hbgusa.com.

PublicAffairs books may be purchased in bulk for business, educational, or promotional use. For more information, please contact your local bookseller or the Hachette Book Group Special Markets Department at special.markets@hbgusa.com.

The publisher is not responsible for websites (or their content) that are not owned by the publisher.

Print book interior design by Linda Mark.

Library of Congress Control Number: 2022037760

ISBNs: 9781541700963 (hardcover), 9781541702783 (ebook), 9781541700970 (paperback)

LSC-C

Printing 2, 2024

*To Georgia and Ivy:*
*I pray that you see the world more vividly than I ever did*
*and that you make a bigger impact on the world than I ever could.*
*I love you.*

# Contents

# INTRODUCTION

*I do this for my culture.*

—Jay-Z

T HE 1960S WERE A DECADE OF SWEEPING SOCIAL CHANGE.
From civil rights to gay rights, the Hispanic movement to the
second wave of feminism, America experienced a decade of culture
shock. These changes brought with them new ideas and new identities, which in turn led to new behaviors and new norms. Take, for instance, the rise of "hippies," a countercultural collective that was born
out of the "Beat generation" the decade prior. Like Beats, hippies re-
belled against the conventions of the status quo. They adopted a bo-
hemian outlook that challenged capitalism and traditional norms in
favor of egalitarianism and free thought. The cultural characteristics
of hippies were obvious, and those who subscribed to their beliefs
adopted them in droves. They donned the look—long hair, tie-dyed
clothes, bare feet—and adhered to the traditions of free love and

1

(ironically) anticonformity. Over time, their way of life spread across the country and amassed legions of new community members.

In 1965, at least a thousand hippies lived on Haight and Ashbury Streets in San Francisco, California. By 1966, that number had jumped to fifteen thousand. A hundred thousand people attended the 1967 Summer of Love festival in San Francisco, and five hundred thousand people attended the Woodstock music festival in 1969. Before long, millions of people had adopted the hippie cultural characteristics. Soon the counterculture had become the mainstream culture, but by the end of the decade, the allure of the hippie generation had faded— only to be reborn, just shy of forty years later, as twenty-first-century urban hipsters.

Like hippies, hipsters challenged the ideals of capitalism and bought in to the beliefs of egalitarianism. But instead of the tie-dye and bare feet of their predecessors, hipsters wore plaid shirts with suspenders, "ironic" facial hair, and dark-rimmed glasses. And their adult beverage of choice? Pabst Blue Ribbon beer, also known as PBR. There was nothing in particular about the liquid that endeared it to the hipster community. No proprietary brewing filtration system or special hops that gave it a unique taste. No, there was nothing intrinsic to the beer itself to which PBR's magnetic pull on urban hipsters could be attributed. Nothing inside the can, that is, but everything outside of it. Everything about the brand.

As a brand, PBR represented autonomy and freedom of expression, both of which were core tenets of hipsters' shared beliefs and ideology. While other beer brands with enormous marketing budgets spoke to the masses through splashy television ads, PBR strategically used its modest resources to speak to the fringe with off-kilter tactics such as sponsoring bike messenger rodeos and opening artist galleries in hipster havens like Portland, Oregon. PBR eschewed celebrity endorsements and refused to run commercials during the Super Bowl because these tactics seemed out of step with its countercultural beliefs. The brand's intentional rejection of mainstream sensibilities felt more like a social protest than marketing communications, and this posture fit the rebelliousness of hipsters. PBR didn't use its marketing resources to convince consumers that the brand was cool. Instead, it actively lived out its beliefs as an outsider brand that deviated from the norm of its more traditional competitors. This made PBR seem cool to hipsters who themselves were outsiders to mainstream America—much like the hippies and the Beats who preceded them. Furthermore, PBR didn't "market" to hipsters. It was "chosen" by hipsters who shared a penchant for dissent with the brand. And these fellow dissenters consumed PBR as a symbol of protest.

PBR was more than a beer for the hipster community. It was a badge of identity, a receipt of hipsterdom—a lifestyle of dissent and autonomy—that transcended the functional utility of the product and elevated it to an artifact within the hipster culture. Subsequently, those who subscribed to this identity naturally drank PBR, and it spread to other like-minded communities as well—to the tune of roughly two hundred million liters over the course of five years. While category leaders such as Bud Light and Busch were declining, PBR was experiencing hockey-stick growth. Within a matter of four short years, the 150-something-year-old company had become a $1 billion business, thanks in large part to the hipster community and its cultural consumption.

We see this kind of relationship everywhere. Like skaters to Supreme, early hip-hop to the LA Raiders, and Republicans to Fox News, people gravitate to the entities that are representative of their identity and corresponding beliefs. We have seen this phenomenon play out in the acceptance and adoption of fashion (Yeezy sneakers), music (Cardi B), cars (Tesla), smoking (Marlboro), dieting (Atkins), and political affiliations (MAGA). They manifest in collectives like the Harley-Davidson Owners Group (affectionately known as H.O.G.s), Apple fanatics, Patagonia loyalists, hypebeasts, QAnon members, and Bernie Bros. The actions of the people in these groups extend far beyond a commitment to a shared consumption behavior or voting allegiance. Their identity is intentionally reflected in and projected through these brands, so strongly that the brand, product, or organization transcends its categorical label and becomes a part of their cultural practice.

If you look at photos taken before the twentieth century, there is a 99.99 percent chance that no one in the picture will be smiling (the academic in me must allow for at least a 0.01 percent margin of error because . . . science). Why is that? Deductive reasoning might propose that this phenomenon is due to the limitations of technology at the time. When I first pondered this question, my mind immediately went to portraits that were painted of royalty, dignitaries, and notable families. It took a great deal of time for painters to portray their subjects. One sitting alone, of the many sittings necessary before a painter could render a completed portrait, could take hours. Sustaining a smile for these long durations would be terribly taxing on the facial muscles of a posing subject. Therefore, the subjects for these paintings would don a solemn facial expression, which resulted in pictures with no smiles.

While that may have been the case for paintings, photographic portraits required far less effort from their subjects, which undermines this hypothesis about why people didn't smile when their pictures were taken. In fact, what is believed to be the first photograph of a person was taken by accident in 1838 when Louis Daguerre, a photography enthusiast, snapped a picture of what appeared to be an empty street in Paris, France. Unbeknownst to him, according to reports, his photo also captured a nondescript man getting his shoes shined, which goes to show that it didn't take much to have your picture taken—and debunked the "facial muscle taxation" argument I had begun to ponder. Interestingly, a year later, the first self-portrait was taken by Robert Cornelius, an amateur chemist who set up a camera, removed the lens cap, and ran into frame while the shutter snapped. It is said that he sat in front of the camera for about a minute before he produced what would be considered the first "selfie." Again, it didn't take much effort to be photographed. So what was going on here? Why were people so averse to smiling in photos?

There is a case to be made for dental hygiene, a practice that wasn't established until 1913 by Dr. Alfred Fones in Bridgeport, Connecticut. Before then, the negligence of dental care did not boost people's confidence to show their (less than) pearly whites in a photo. However, according to Today's RDH, a digital media publisher for registered dental hygienists, it wasn't until the 1950s and 1960s that access to advanced oral care became more widely available to Americans, thanks in part to the Civil Rights Act. Yet, as evidenced in a study by a team of researchers from the University of California, Berkeley and Brown University, the transition from stoic faces to smiling faces in photos had begun decades before this moment in time. Their research examined thirty-eight thousand high school yearbook photos taken from 1905 to 2013 and measured the lip curvature in those photos due to the zygomatic muscles in our faces that are engaged when we smile. According to their findings, photographed smiles were on the rise around the 1920s, some twenty years after the first smiling photo of a US president—Theodore Roosevelt—was taken and almost a century after the first-ever photo of a US president—John Quincy Adams, who of course was not smiling—was taken.

What I came to learn about this mystery is that it had almost nothing to do with the technology of cameras and little to do with the advancement of dentistry but everything to do with culture. In those days, practitioners of the fine arts considered smiling to be a practice saved for peasants, dimwits, drunks, or children. Essentially, to smile in a photo meant that you were of a lower class; therefore, people wouldn't smile in photographs as a strategy to project their desired social status. This shared belief fortified what would become a ubiquitous cultural norm in society at that time, much to the dismay of Eastman Kodak, the New York–based company that dominated the amateur film market. Since photos were seen as a serious endeavor, used for artistic expression and archival documentation, people weren't taking a ton of photos. In response to this challenge, Kodak invested its resources and energy to reposition photo-taking as a way to capture joyous moments.

Fittingly, the people represented in Kodak's advertising material were all happy—and, of course, smiling. It wasn't long before we went from saying "prune" before the camera snapped, to mitigate the possibilities of a grin crossing our faces, to saying "cheese" in hopes of maximizing our smiles. This conclusion is further substantiated by the high school yearbook study's findings.

People's beliefs about photos had changed, and consequently, their behaviors changed in a systematic and predictable fashion. Through its marketing efforts, Kodak was able to turn the tide of consumption, not because of any specific product advancement alone but rather because of its understanding of culture. Oddly enough, though Kodak went on to become a multibillion-dollar business decades later, the company faced ruin in the late 2000s because it had missed another cultural shift: digital media as a means of connecting people through photos as relationship currency. The company's leadership misread the cultural cues, and what was once a category-defining business was ultimately forced to file for bankruptcy by 2012.

This is the power of culture. It's contagious, and it influences people to move in predictable ways. Whether we are aware of it or not, this influence is happening all around us all the time. And those who understand the dynamics of culture are more likely to have influence, while those who do not are almost always influenced by those who do. It doesn't matter if your product is better or your cause is more noble. The ones who lead culture—who contribute to the cultural characteristics of a community—tend to be more successful than those who follow trends.

For years, Bose was considered the trusted category leader in the consumer audio electronics space. But when Beats by Dre came to market in 2011, it rapidly overtook Bose's standing. Was Beats a better product? Sonically speaking, it empirically was not. But Beats was more than just a device for listening to music. It was a symbol that signaled to the world who you were and, perhaps, even who you were not. People walked around with Beats headphones around their neck as an accessory, a cultural artifact, that just happened to play music. As the cultural scholar Douglas Holt put it, "Culture side-steps conventional value propositions, functional or category benefits, and mind-share marketing." It moves beyond a brand having the sharpest razor, the fastest car, or the longest-lasting battery. Culture supersedes all these product differentiators because it does not revolve around what the product is. Culture focuses on who we are.

All of this begs a series of questions. What is culture exactly? Why does it have such a powerful effect on people? And finally, how might a marketer, manager, leader, or entrepreneur leverage the power of culture to influence collective behavior and inspire people to move? Well, my friends, that's exactly what this book aims to address. So let's get started.

Culture is one of those words that is often used but seldom understood. We think we know what it is, but we almost never do. This is not surprising considering both the intangible nature of culture and our relatively loose use of it in our everyday conversations. The irony is that culture *is our everyday life*. It's "how we do things around here," and its omnipresence in our lives makes it very difficult to comprehend and, subsequently, hard to define. It's like explaining water to a fish—we live in it, we navigate through it, and it encompasses everything around us. My frequent collaborator and thought partner John Branch, a marketing professor at the Ross School of Business, University of Michigan, refers to culture as the program for everyday living. Like the programming code that makes up an operating system, providing a navigable user experience and running applications, culture is the programming code that informs where we go, what we do, and how we do it for just about every facet of our everyday lives.

Take, for instance, what you ate for breakfast this morning. If you live in the United States, it is likely that your breakfast consisted of some combination of eggs, bread, cereal, milk, and/or coffee—that is, of course, assuming you did not skip breakfast altogether, which is quite common here. In China, however, breakfast typically consists of dumplings, noodles, or maybe a rice-based dish or drink. Meanwhile, in Saudi Arabia, breakfast might comprise dates, bread, cheese, yogurt, and coffee. Each of these societies has its own program for everyday living, a code for what is considered normal. We know this intuitively when we visit other countries. We ask about the food, the dress, the music, the customs, and all the other codes that make up people's everyday life—the characteristics that make up their culture.

The metaphor for culture as a programming code lends itself nicely to a Durkheimian view of culture. Émile Durkheim, widely considered one of the founding fathers of sociology in the 1800s, referred to culture as a system of symbols, beliefs, and values used by groups of people to establish norms and roles. Durkheim underscored the complexity of culture, as a "system" that defines a group of people, while also providing some elemental codes that collectively make up the system—shared beliefs (values and principles, a way of thinking), rituals (traditions, social norms), artifacts (symbols, clothes, decorations, tools), and, of course, language (dialect, lexicon, songs, poetry). Durkheim called these elemental codes "social facts," a manner of thinking, feeling, and acting that is constructed by society at large. In this way, social facts are the collective representation of social behavior for a distinct group of people.

Though these social facts are external to the individual, they put pressure on each of us to behave in a particular—and predictable—manner. For instance, in the United States, if someone extends their hand upon greeting you, it is customary to mimic the gesture and interlock hands for a few brief seconds. Why? Because shaking hands is a social fact here, much like bowing is in Japan or air kisses on cheeks are in France. To do otherwise in this scenario, within these respective societies, would be considered at best socially odd and at worst an offense. Therefore, members of a given society adhere to these norms so they don't experience the social consequences that follow if they don't. It's a societal instinct to maintain orderly living, and adherence to these social facts is a large part of how that is achieved.

## A WHOLE NEW WORLD

All this talk about social facts, Durkheim, and behavioral adoption may be new to many of you reading this. At least, it was for me. I studied materials science engineering as an undergraduate student, and the only humanities course I took was Sociology 101 during my freshman year. I was a latecomer to this world of human behavior and the social sciences. In fact, I was almost a decade into my career before I was even introduced to this world—or, more accurately, thrust into it. As a newly hired executive at a cutting-edge advertising agency called Translation, cofounded by Steve Stoute and Jay-Z, I was tasked with building and leading the company's social media marketing practice. However, my understanding of "social" was primarily technology centric. I had a deep knowledge of the social networking platforms that dominated at that time, like Facebook, YouTube, Twitter, and Foursquare. But I didn't understand people, which was problematic because "social" is people.

Think about it for a moment. What do "social work," "social action," and "social welfare" have in common? They each pertain to people. "Social work" is the practice of enhancing the lives of people, "social action" is a commitment to the empowerment and advancement of people, and "social welfare" is concerned with assisting people. "Social" is all about people, and culture is the governing operating system of people. I didn't know much about culture at that time because I didn't know much about people, despite my past experiences working on social media campaigns at Apple, running digital strategy for Beyoncé, and leading a handful of accounts at a pure-play social media agency. To rectify this lack of knowledge, I began to investigate the social sciences, reading everything I could get my hands on in order to learn more about people—and, subsequently, to learn more about culture.

I started with Dan Ariely's *Predictably Irrational*, and it rang a bell inside me that I couldn't unring. I found its exploration to be nothing short of fascinating. I read the book twice. In my second pass, I highlighted the research and researchers that I thought were most interesting and started studying their work, too. Ariely led me to Loewenstein, and Loewenstein led me to Kahneman. I detoured to McLuhan and then turned to Berger, who led me to Watts and Thaler, and soon after, I moved on to Asch and Milgram. My curiosity was insatiable and, as a result, I read broadly and deeply. It wasn't long before my self-directed research began to manifest in my own work, and I started to get really good at my job.

With a new perspective on "social," I found myself challenging the long-standing conventions of traditional advertising and began applying my newly acquired repertoire of academic theories to brand marketing. If a client expressed interest in creating an influencer program, I relied on network theory, whose dynamics inform the diffusion of influence, to guide my approach. If another client inquired about getting people to adopt a new behavior, I recounted the importance of creating defaults in the environmental design to act as a nudge. The more I applied theories from the social sciences to my marketing practice, the better the outcomes were. This was evidenced in my work that helped conceive and launch the Cliff Paul campaign for State Farm, where I leveraged Loewenstein's "gap in knowledge" theory. Likewise, when I helped move the New Jersey Nets to New York to become the

Brooklyn Nets, I borrowed from Bernays's propaganda theory. Since I started this exploration over twelve years ago, I have embraced the world of academia to better understand people and the governing operating system that influences our collective behavior—culture. And, boy, did I ever embrace academia. Not only did I begin teaching at schools like NYU, Boston University, Harvard, and now the University of Michigan, but I also went on to study cultural contagion and earned my doctorate in marketing at Temple University.

The marriage of academia and practice has been the biggest cheat code in my career because it unlocked an unequivocal truth: if you want to get people to move, there is no vehicle more powerful or more influential than culture—full stop. Why? Because if a product, idea, behavior, or institution is adopted into a community's cultural practice, not only will people take action, but they will also share it with people who are like themselves. And those people will tell other people, and eventually, that product, idea, behavior, or institution will be adopted into their cultural practice. This isn't just about marketing or technology, category, or business model. This is all about people and the governing operating system that informs what we do and with whom we do it. I have seen this in my work with tech firms (like Google), telecom companies (like Sprint), automakers (like Ford), quick-service restaurants (QSRs) (like McDonald's), consumer package goods producers (like Kellogg's Eggo), retailers (like Champs Sports), health care providers (like Kaiser Permanente), clothing outfitters (like GORE-TEX), artists (like Beyoncé), educators (like Harvard), and nonprofits (like Big Brothers Big Sisters of America). This truth is category agnostic, and it does not depend on the business model of the company or organization. Whether it be B2B (business to business) or B2C (business to consumer), it makes no difference because it's all P2P (person to person). And no force influences people more consistently than culture.

It took me what felt like a lifetime to come to this realization. It wasn't just knowing about culture that made such an impact on me, it was understanding the nuances of culture—with the level of concreteness necessary to actually impact it—that made the difference. Today, I operate as one part practitioner and one part academic. I work in advertising as the head of strategy at Wieden+Kennedy New York, the biggest independent advertising agency (and arguably the most celebrated creative agency) on the planet, where I help "blue-chip" brands put ideas into the world that leverage the influence of culture to get people to take action. I am also a marketing professor at the Ross School of Business, University of Michigan, where I help some of the brightest minds in the world leverage what we know about culture to use business to better society. This duality has uniquely shaped my perspective and, ultimately, my practice as a marketer. But that's not nearly enough. The research I've done over the years with regard to the mechanisms that shape collective behavior goes far beyond "marketing" as a discipline. Rather, it reaches further into the ambitions of getting people to move writ large—whether you have "marketing" in your title or not. Whether you have a traditional product, a nonprofit organization, or political aspirations, my work aims to get people to move.

## CULTURE AND MARKETING

What is marketing, after all? The traditional definition, according to the American Marketing Association, is "an organizational function and a set of processes for creating, communicating, and delivering value to customers and for managing customer relationships in ways that benefit the organization and its stakeholders." Huh? This is in my area of expertise, and even I struggle a bit to parse this definition. Could it (in my best Chandler Bing impression) *be* any more opaque? In the search for a better definition, I found frustrating abstractions everywhere—even from Philip Kotler, the man who basically wrote the book on marketing. (I don't mean that as an idiom, by the way. If you have ever taken a marketing course in college, it is highly likely that your assigned textbook was written by Philip Kotler. He's "the" marketing guy.) He called it "the science and art of exploring, creating, and delivering value to satisfy the needs of a target market at a profit. Marketing identifies unfulfilled needs and desires. It defines, measures and quantifies the size of the identified market and the profit potential. It pinpoints which segments the company is capable of best serving and it designs and promotes the appropriate products and services." What in the world is going on here? Can someone—anyone!—define marketing as if they were explaining it to a five-year-old? Turns out someone could and did—nearly six hundred years ago.

According to the *Oxford English Dictionary*, the earliest instance of the word "marketing" dates back to 1455, which defines marketing as "to bring to market." Finally(!), some simplicity. If marketing is "to bring to market," then it begs the question: What is the market?

At a glance, most people might think of the market as the place where people exchange goods and services. You might imagine a farmers market or even a Turkish bazaar where people buy garments, fruit, crafts, and the like. However, economists think of the market as an abstract idea rather than a physical location. For economists, "the market" represents the decisions and behaviors of product producers, intermediaries, consumers, institutions, and stakeholders. This is more than a geography. Business folks, on the other hand, refer to "the market" as the dynamism between people, institutions, and organizations.

In both cases, we see that "the market" is more than the area in which commercial dealings are conducted. The market represents a set of players who interact in pursuit of exchange. It consists of groups of people who work in companies and make decisions on behalf of their stakeholders, people who represent organizations and institutions, and people who seek to identify solutions that satisfy a particular need—be it functional, emotional, or social. Consider this intellectual exercise: If there were no people in that farmers market you conjured in your mind a few lines ago—no one selling fruits or crafts and no one there to buy them—would it still be a market? Of course not. It would merely be a geographic site, an open space of nothingness, until, of course, people showed up to buy and sell.

Suffice it to say, people make up the market; we are the market. When you hear talk of market demand or market behavior, it means people's demand and people's behavior. "Market response" is code for "people's response." The market is the people, and the marketplace is where people go to exchange. And as Professor Branch would say, marketing is the act of going to market—going to the people.

But this begs an even bigger question: *What is the core purpose of going to market?* Think about it for a second. Why do we engage people? What is the aim of a marketer? If I'm doing marketing for a company that sells widgets, it's likely that I am going to market to exchange widgets for money. But what if I'm a political candidate running for mayor of Detroit, Michigan? Am I trying to get money? Perhaps, but in service of what? I don't become mayor from financial contributions, I need votes. Therefore, I go to market as a candidate to inspire people to vote for me. Or, say I want to market my new company website. What would be the purpose of my marketing activity? I am motivated to get visitors and clicks on my content.

This line of thinking makes the pathway of understanding marketing quite clear. As marketers, we go to market to *influence behavior*. Everything we do is in service of this imperative—buy this, not that; go here, not there; drink this, not that; support her, not him; join this, not that; use this technology and not the other. We are in the business of behavioral adoption. This is the destination for all marketing activity—the campaign tactics (advertising, communications, sponsorships, etc.) are merely a bunch of different routes to get there—and no vehicle is more powerful than culture when it comes to influencing human behavior.

Now, if you buy that, then hold on to your seats, folks, because this is where things get good. Every single one of us goes to market to influence people to take action. Whether you are a manager trying to motivate your team, an activist staging a protest, an organization trying to get people to adopt a policy, a teacher trying to encourage your students to study for an exam, or a father trying to convince his daughter to try just one bite of peas (just one bite, Georgia, for Pete's sake! It's not going to kill you), we are all marketers. Every day, we all try to get people to adopt behavior, and this, my friends, is the essential function of marketing and, thus, the focus of this book.

However, this is not a marketing book. It's a people book—a book that explores what happens when people who share a similar worldview are activated and how anyone with an idea, product, or cause can leverage the influence of culture to inspire these people to act in concert. It's the book I wish I'd read much earlier in my career, an aggregation of a decade-long investment in the applied social sciences. It's a book that bridges the rigor of academia and the pragmatism of practice based on everything I've learned and everything I've done throughout my career.

Fittingly, this book is meant to teach as much as it is meant to empower you with the ability to inspire collective behavioral change. It's one part perspective and one part guide, giving you the tools you need to leverage these lessons in both your work and your day-to-day life. This duality of "perspective" and "guide" is also represented in the structure of the book, where each chapter will provide a theoretical foundation that relates to the influence of culture—to help you understand the underlying social physics of why things are the way they are—and conclude with takeaways for how to apply the theory— moving from "know-why" to "know-how."

I will begin the book with an exploration of why culture is the most predictable vehicle for influencing behavior at scale. We'll unpack the origins of culture and why it holds such compelling sway over what we do and why we do it. Then, we'll dive into how we might leverage the power of culture to get people to move. Finally, I'll close with a call to action: today's technology offers an unbelievable opportunity to better observe, understand, and harness the power of culture to get people to take action. However, readers and leaders must consider not only what culture can do for them but also what they can do for culture.

I can think of no better time than the present to write this book. Among the many changes that the COVID-19 pandemic thrust upon us, it forced us to completely rethink how we engage with people— in business, in education, in politics, in religion, in technology, and in just about every other facet of life. It forced us to reconsider how we persuade people to consume, study, worship, vote, wear a mask, recycle, and everything in between. Simply put, it made us rethink: How do we inspire people to act?

With a deep perspective based on a century's worth of data and a keen understanding of today's hyperconnected world, this book will tackle this question head-on. But it will do more than that: it will remind readers of the power of communities and the reverberating impact wielded by people acting in concert. After two years of social distancing, videoconferences, stay-at-home orders, and travel bans, we desperately need to restore that sense of community in our personal and professional lives before we lose it altogether. In the words of the late, great jazz saxophonist, Charlie Parker, "Now's the time." So let's get into it.

## CHAPTER 1

# UNPACKING CULTURE

R EWIND THE CLOCK WITH ME TO 1999. CHARLES STONE III was a music video director with aspirations of making full-length feature films. His work had been most prominent in hip-hop circles, where he had directed videos in the early '90s for artists like A Tribe Called Quest and Public Enemy. These were still the early days of hip-hop, when budgets for music videos were not as massive as they would come to be by the end of the decade, and the production budgets for Stone's videos were modest. But Stone had greater ambitions. He wanted to make movies, not music videos, yet he could not get his foot in the door at the major motion picture studios. So in 1999, he decided to take matters into his own hands. With a $1,000 budget, he enlisted his closest buddies from his hometown of Philadelphia to costar in his directorial film debut, a three-minute short simply titled *True*.

To say that *True* was light on dialogue would be an understatement. The short film followed a series of exchanges between Stone and his friends—Kevin Lofton, Fred Thomas Jr., Paul Williams, and Terry

Williams—that could be summed up in one word: "wassup," a colloqui-alism for "what's up." It was a common greeting among young urban dwellers, particularly those from the Black community. "Wassup" had found an even larger audience in the '90s thanks to the meteoric suc-cess of Martin Lawrence's television show *Martin*. As star of the show, Lawrence, one of the biggest stand-up comedians at the time in real life, played a Detroit radio personality for a fictional radio station with the call letters WZUP, pronounced "wassup." His signature on-air salute was a high-pitched repetition of "wassup," which would become one of the many memorable catchphrases of the show. But that would be eclipsed by what happened next.

According to the lore, a creative director from the advertising agency DDB Chicago saw Stone's short and thought it was perfect for one of his clients, Budweiser. It didn't feel like advertising to the ad exec. It felt like something altogether different. The short features a twenty-something man on the couch, watching sports. The phone rings. His friend on the line asks, "Yo, what's up?" The young man responds, "Nothing, man. Just chillin'," to which his friend responds, "True," as if to say, "I hear ya." Just then, another friend of the young man enters the apartment and gregariously asks, "Wassup?" in an exaggerated, elongated fashion. The two re-spond in kind with their own exaggerated exclamation, "Wassup!" Before long, two additional friends join the exchange of "Wassup." The film ends in a fashion similar to how it started. The original friend asks the twenty-something man, "What's up with you?" The twenty-something responds, "Nothing, man. Just chillin'," to which the friend responds, "True."

The creative director's instincts were spot-on. At the time, Bud-weiser positioned itself as a champion of camaraderie, the social lubricant among close friends—your buddies—as signified in its his-toric tagline, "This Bud's for You." From its heights in the 1950s and on throughout the decades, Budweiser had been synonymous with

American culture, sponsoring popular shows and sporting events. However, its relevance had begun to wane in the 1990s because it was no longer representative of the cultural zeitgeist. However, *True* captured the essence of contemporary friendship. You don't need many words when you're talking with your closest friends. Friends speak in code, and everyone who understands the code just "gets it." Stone and his "buds" demonstrated that perfectly in the film, so much so that DDB simply recreated *True*—with the original cast and all—for the Budweiser campaign. Budweiser's "Wassup" ad hit the airwaves later that year, and the rest, as they say, was history. Within a matter of months, "Wassup" had been imitated by talk-show hosts and radio personalities, parodied by movies, memed and proliferated by online content creators in the early days of the Internet, and adopted into the cultural lexicon of the masses. America got a new catchphrase, and Budweiser was legitimated as a culturally relevant brand once again, which led to millions in beer sales and major motion picture gigs for Stone—along with a ton of advertising awards.

Budweiser's "Wassup" commercial was more than an advertisement; it became a part of culture because it understood culture. Like sitcoms and movies that depict the norms of social living in which people can see themselves and relate, the "Wassup" commercial accurately depicted the nuances of what people—particularly young Black people—just did in their everyday lives. And, upon seeing the commercial, we saw ourselves in it. Folks were already using "wassup" as salutatory language years before Budweiser leveraged the phrase for its campaign. The context for "wassup" had already been negotiated as an everyday phrase among peers, not formally between employees and bosses or something I'd say to any other authoritative figure, like my parents or professors. "Wassup" was one of our social facts. By integrating the phrase into its campaign as it did, Budweiser turned something that was typically used to talk *to* us (advertising) into something that helped us talk to each other and express who we are—both individually and collectively. And we subsequently used the campaign as a way to project our identity and connect with people like us. In this way, the thirty-second film transformed what would normally be considered advertising into what scholars would call a cultural product, the tangible or intangible creations that reflect the shared perspectives of a group of people. Culture has this transformative effect on almost everything it touches. Understanding the underlying physics of culture and its impact on human behavior, therefore, will allow leaders, managers, marketers, and entrepreneurs to leverage its influence, much as Budweiser did here.

The cultural scholar Raymond Williams provided a useful and contemporary perspective on culture that helped me understand the concept better than I had before. Williams is considered one of the founding fathers of cultural studies, and his work on culture widened the aperture of how theorists framed what is thought of as culture and how it relates to society. Williams mapped the genealogy of the word "culture" and its associated meaning, which for me fully revealed the impact of culture and how it can be used to catalyze collective behavior and inspire people to move.

The word originates from the Latin term "colere," which means to cultivate, to tend to something in a nurturing way. Fittingly, the early usage of the word "culture" occurred within the word "agriculture," which refers to cultivating soil to grow uniform crops. Farming and growing crops were the economic activities of the agricultural society that persisted for thousands of years. The eighteenth century ushered in the Industrial Revolution, which not only changed the economic landscape of society from harvesting to machinery but also changed the context and usage of the word "culture." Still keeping its Latin roots, the meaning of the word expanded to include the intellectual, moral, and expressive development of children in an industrial society. Just as farmers, centuries earlier, had tended to the growth of their crops, ensuring uniformity in their optimum flourishing, culture became the means by which parents tended to the growth of their children to ensure predictability in their upbringing within this new society. Like Durkheim, Williams suggested that culture implies social forces—both subtle and overt—that govern the beliefs and behaviors of everyday life.

Williams defined culture as a realized signifying system, a system through which we interpret the world and make sense of it. This system, as Williams argued, is a whole way of life for people—a program for everyday living. It is through this system that we translate our daily experiences to inform how we respond to them because of what they mean. Culture is a realized meaning-making system. More accurately, it is a system of systems—a set of interdependent principles and mechanisms that all inform each other—which, collectively, influences practically everything that we do because of who we are and how we see the world.

Therefore, our cultural affiliation is anchored by how we self-identify—the categorical labels we use to tell people who we are and to associate with other people based on who they are. These labels range from geographical in nature (like where you're from) to institutions (the college you attended), activities (sports), consumption behavior (anime enthusiasts), and a host of seemingly endless designations that make up our identity. Identity is the cornerstone of culture. Once we take on an identity marker, either by choice (subscription) or endowment (ascription), we implicitly inherit the cultural characteristics of the community through the interworking of the meaning-making system. Let's explore this further by unpacking the systems.

## SYSTEM ONE: HOW WE SEE THE WORLD

Understanding who we are is a fundamental human drive. This designation, our identity, acts as a compass that guides how we see the world. Over seven decades of research on identity-related concepts has shown the critical role that identity plays in shaping the shared attitudes, values, and ideas of a group of people, which, in turn, informs how they make meaning and go about their daily lives. Whether based on socially constructed references (like the familial role of "mother"), an individual reference (like a person we want to emulate, be it a pop star or mentor), a group affiliation (like our religion), or a combination of them all, our identities help provide a lens through which to see the world based on the shared beliefs of the people who subscribe to the same identity. For instance, if you're a Christian, you see the world one way. If you're Hindu, you see the world another way. If you're an atheist, you see the world in an entirely different way, which subsequently influences how you live your life from day to day.

It's no coincidence that I use religion as an example to illustrate the relationship among identity, worldview, and behavior. Religion is an institution that exists in every known human society. It shapes collective beliefs and powers societal coordination. Members who subscribe to a religious identity also take on a collective consciousness that unifies them within a society. These forces make religion a very useful proxy for understanding the dynamics of culture. In fact, the academic field of sociology itself started with the study of religion for this very reason. Durkheim explored contagious behavior due in part to the social cohesion of religion. Max Weber, another founding father of sociology, explored religion's role and influence on institutions like the economy and politics, while Karl Marx critiqued the oppression that religion exerts on social classes. The investigation of religion as a means to understand culture has been an ongoing project ever since. Modern scholars have even expanded the remit of religion to encompass cults, fandom, and consumption. From an academic view, religion and culture are inextricably linked.

Whether you're "religious" or not, you understand the gravitational pull that religion can have on people, which makes religion a helpful tool to explain the power of culture. Throughout this book, you will see religious references used here and there to explain a concept or illustrate a point.

On its surface, the concept of a shared belief is fairly straightforward. It is the collective acceptance of a truth, the communal view of reality. Is there a God? Are there other life forms throughout the galaxies? Was the moon landing a hoax? Should there be a separation of church and state? Are all men created equal? Is there no place for politics in sports? These held beliefs help us frame the endless amount of information that is transmitted from our senses to our brains so that we can make meaning of the world and know how to operate in it. Anaïs Nin is famously quoted as saying, "We don't see things as they are, we see them as we are." That is, the *truth* is not as objective as we would like to believe. The truth is culturally mediated and socially negotiated and constructed based on our communal view of reality—our beliefs.

Shared beliefs and ideologies are the least tangible system of culture but arguably the most important because this system precedes all others. It's because we hold certain beliefs—deeply and emotionally— that we commit to certain behaviors, not the other way around. Although our beliefs and ideologies are not easily seen, they are reflected in everything we do. The anthropologist and culture scholar Grant McCracken wrote about how our everyday experiences are culturally constituted, shaped, and mediated by our beliefs and assumptions of right and wrong, just and unfair, acceptable and undesirable. It's our system of shared beliefs and ideologies that dictates what seems "normal" and what seems "out of place," and therefore, it's this system that determines what gets adopted and what does not. So appealing to someone's beliefs and ideologies could have a material influence on their behavior. And the more indoctrinated a person is with those shared beliefs, the more influential that appeal can be.

You probably read that last line and got some serious "cult" vibes, didn't you? I wouldn't be surprised. Culture and cults share a lot in common beyond a four-letter root word. Cults are organized groups of people who have devoted themselves to an idea or person. Derived from the French word "culte," which means worship, "cult" provides a metaphor that captures the seemingly religious devotion of a group of people to a shared set of social facts that govern the group and the worldview in which they are indoctrinated.

I am fascinated by religious cults like the Peoples Temple, Heaven's Gate, and NXIVM. I read the stories and watch the documentaries about people who found themselves completely consumed by an organization and its ideas. Like most people, I hear these cautionary tales and ask myself, "How could people be so gullible?" I'm just amazed at how seemingly easy it is for people to be swept up in something so obviously "crazy." But one must wonder, just how crazy is it, really? No one entered these cults thinking they were joining a cult. Yet, over time, they looked up and found themselves firmly planted inside one. This phenomenon can be partially explained by what the French philosopher Louis Althusser refers to as interpellation, the process by which powerful ideas are repeated and begin to weave themselves into our lives to the point that they begin to feel like our own.

According to Althusser, starting at birth, we are raised with the ideas and values that are a part of the family's belief system and shared among family members. From a very young age through our adolescence, we are conditioned to see the world through this framing and to behave in accordance with it. Naturally, this is a part of a wider societal belief system with which the family self-identifies—be it nationality, religion, or trade. For instance, if your family is a member of a conservative church, then it is likely that you were raised with conservative ideas that you accepted as your own beliefs. This is what it means to be fully indoctrinated into a belief. We are interpellated. While it is convenient to dismiss the people who have fallen victim to the wiles of a cult as "crazy," we, too, have been indoctrinated into our own cults. We just happen to call them by a different name: culture.

During the summer of 2008, after my first year in the MBA program at the University of Michigan, I had the opportunity to intern at Apple in Cupertino, California. I worked in the partner marketing group of iTunes, Apple's online music platform, managing our partnership with Nike Sport Music and a major college marketing initiative that I championed. By the end of that summer, my internship had turned into employment, and instantaneously, I felt like I was officially a part of the Apple community. I was, in my mind at least, an "Apple guy." I had worked this designation into my identity, and I wore that moniker with pride. I would find myself espousing ideas that were commonplace within the walls of the company as if they were my own (i.e., "We say 'no' to the thousand things we like so we can say 'yes' to the one thing we love" or "That experience isn't user-friendly") and unconsciously doing my best Steve Jobs impersonation every time I took the floor to give a presentation. I had become successfully interpellated into the *culture* of Apple. Of course, it wasn't just me; it happened to all of us—employees and fanboys alike. Our identities were defined by Apple, and our worldview was shaped by it as well. It's probably no wonder that companies like Apple, Google, Nike, and Tesla have what many consider to be a "cultlike" following. Their system of shared beliefs and ideologies are salient among those who self-identify with them and are represented in how these people conduct themselves, which leads us to the second system: a shared way of life.

## SYSTEM TWO: A SHARED WAY OF LIFE

The second system of culture is a shared way of life. This refers to the way a group of people behave and live in accordance with their shared beliefs and ideologies. Take, for instance, shared faith and patriotism. They both have a fixed set of values and ideas attached to them that influence the way people who subscribe to them live. Christians believe that Jesus Christ is the son of God and, therefore, live their lives according to his teachings. However, the way his teachings are internalized and exercised varies depending on the type of Christian you are.

After the death of Jesus Christ, his disciples—his most fervent followers at that time—carried on his teachings (the beliefs and ideologies of Christianity) and began to propagate these ideas to more people across distant lands. In 325 AD, a conference of Christian clergy met as an ecumenical council to address some of the growing questions and disagreements about the nature of Jesus himself. Was he a man? Was he the son of God? Was he both? Though they reached agreement, questions still lingered. A century later, the church began to splinter, and some groups broke away to practice their own understanding of Christianity, with their own systems of shared beliefs and corresponding collections of norms, artifacts, and language. This birthed denominationalism in the Christian faith and new religions altogether, like Islam. In 1054, the church experienced the Great Schism and formed the Roman Catholic Church and the Eastern Orthodox Church, each with its own nuanced system of beliefs and corresponding cultural practices, or way of life. Centuries later, a German priest named Martin Luther voiced his ideological issues with the church in protest and recruited others to form a completely new Christian sect known as Protestants—with the Latin etymology "protestari," or protester. But even the Protestants could not fully agree on their ideological views, so they, too, splintered into different sects, like Lutherans and Calvinists, each with its own nuanced system of beliefs and way of life.

As we see in the history of Christianity, shifts in beliefs inform how people see the world and, ultimately, how they behave in the world. If you identify as an Orthodox Jew, you see the world differently than a Reformed Jew or a Hasidic Jew, and, therefore, you behave differently. Our identities and corresponding belief systems help us make meaning of the world, and our way of life is how we realize those beliefs. Our beliefs are exercised by the artifacts we employ, the behaviors that we normalize, the language that we use, and all the other forms of cultural practice that are incorporated into our daily lives.

Let's look at the idea of patriotism in America. Our shared beliefs tend to revolve around the notion of freedom: "land of the free and home of the brave." Freedom is very much part of the ideological fabric of the United States, even though the country continues to fall short of providing the same freedoms to all its inhabitants. This inequality has been evidenced from the early existence of the United States, with slavery, to our present-day prison industrial complex. Be that as it may, freedom is still held to be a bedrock of the country's belief system, and it is exercised in our way of life, from free speech to the right to bear arms. For many, any form of rule or law could be perceived as an infringement on their liberty, which would be met with great opposition. Therefore, it should have come as no surprise that when COVID-19 ran rampant across the globe and individual states in the United States began to enforce mask mandates on their citizens, a broad swath of Americans pushed back. Many said that they would rather die than give up their liberty. Why? Because that's just the American way. Our ideologies inform our way of life.

Surely, this does not apply to everyone in the country. Plenty of Americans wore masks, as was mandated during the pandemic, and abided by the rules laid out by public health officials because they believed it was the right thing to do. Both groups identify as "Americans" and share the same affinity for "freedom." However, their interpretation of "freedom" differs, and, therefore, they exercise their freedoms differently. Not all people make meaning in the same way, so we tend to gravitate toward those who share a similar worldview and, collectively, self-identify with them. Those who interpret the world the way we do, we call "our people," and those who do not, we call "crazy." This difference in interpretation represents a microcosm of the many fractures in American culture that make "what we do around here" so heterogeneous. In the case of wearing masks, some people call this particular fracture the difference between being a liberal and being a conservative. Others might refer to it as "coastals" versus "Middle America" or America versus 'Merica. Whatever the naming convention, they all help us assign identity to people who hold a certain interpretation of the world—a set of beliefs and ideologies— that is manifested through their way of life. The artifacts that we wear, the behaviors we adopt, and the coded language that we use are outward representations of our worldview.

The relationship between our shared belief system and our shared way of life loosely equates to the way our genes make up our physical appearances. It's what's inside us that determines our height, skin tone, and facial features. Similarly, it's because of the beliefs that we hold in our minds that we are the way we are and do the things we do. A deep understanding of the meanings associated with our artifacts, behaviors, and language can reveal much about the beliefs that inform them and empower marketers and leaders to influence them. Let's start by unpacking artifacts.

Artifacts are human-made objects that people use to signify their cultural affiliations. These objects take many different forms—clothes, tools, decorations, symbols, etc.—but they are all used as a way to exercise the beliefs that people hold and their ideologies about the world. If you are a devoted Catholic, then you might wear a rosary—a wood or metal crucifix that hangs on a string of beads for the purpose of counting a series of prayers—to exercise your faith. However, in the Islamic faith, women don the hijab as a way to exercise their beliefs. The hijab is best known as the head wrap that Muslim women wear to cover their hair. However, the term "hijab" actually refers to any covering as an act of modesty, whether it covers the hair, head, face, legs, or body. The beliefs and ideologies of the Islamic faith are exercised by the meaningful (as in "full of meaning") artifacts that Muslims use and wear. This is the power of artifacts. It helps us make our culture material by making the abstract beliefs and ideologies that we hold within our cultural subscriptions more tangible. Furthermore, artifacts allow us to express our cultural identity to the world so that we can demarcate our place in the world and identify "people like us."

Artifacts make the intangible tangible and send a signal to the world that says, "This is who I am." They also serve as a mnemonic for members of the community to help them live their lives in accordance with the beliefs and ideologies of the community. As my mother would say, "If you look the part, you will act the part." The garbs, symbols, and adornments we wear and use act as cues to help us stay within the acceptable boundaries of our cultural subscriptions. These cues can be very influential in how people behave because of the artifacts' associated meaning. More on this in Chapter 5. In the meantime, let's consider war-torn Afghanistan as an example of how the significance of artifacts can lead to desired behavioral outcomes.

Afghanistan has the world's worst infant mortality rate, much of which is due to the challenges that doctors in the region face with regard to maintaining an accurate record of a child's immunizations. These historical records help doctors know what vaccinations are due for a certain child and when said vaccinations should be administered. Without them, doctors are left in the dark as to the medicines a child might need to live. To compound these challenges, Afghani physicians serve a community with a high level of illiteracy and suspicion about vaccinations. Muslim fundamentalists have created resistance within the region by positioning vaccines as an American ploy to sterilize Muslim populations and potentially subvert the will of the god in Islam, Allah. With such hurdles to overcome, the Ministry of Public Health in the Islamic Republic of Afghanistan turned to a cultural artifact.

When Afghani babies are born, it is a tradition to tie a beaded bracelet onto their wrist that serves as a charm to protect the newborn from evil forces. With the help of the advertising agency McCann Health India, the Ministry of Public Health reworked this artifact to serve as an immunity charm, where color-coded beads were placed on the bracelets as a way for doctors to communicate with each other about which vaccines had been administered to the child. Each colored bead represented a different vaccination: yellow for the hepatitis B vaccine, blue for the flu vaccine. With every vaccination, the doctor would add the corresponding bead as a charm to the child's bracelet, turning a cultural artifact into a medical record. Afghani parents didn't change their behavior per se. They merely exercised their beliefs and ideologies through the use of the charms to protect their children from bad spirits. However, the ministry was able to save thousands of children's lives because infants completed their vaccination schedules.

Of the three elements that comprise our way of life (artifacts, behaviors, and language), artifacts are the most easily identifiable because they are overtly visible. Symbols, patterns, pins, buttons, hats, clothes, tools, and technology of all kinds of variety make up the many forms of human-made creations that reveal information about the values and customs of the people who use them. We know what we know about ancient civilizations because of the artifacts that archaeologists discovered from the past that divulged information about those societies. These artifacts of the past are remnants of the material world that members of society at the time modified with embedded meaning to serve both functional and social needs, just like the artifacts we use today. Consider braces, for example. Legions of teenagers around the country wear braces to straighten crooked teeth. While braces provide a tangible function, they also reveal information about society's aesthetic standard and the lengths to which people will go to achieve it. I wore braces for three years, as did over half of my classmates growing up. Like braces, artifacts are more than material; they are also conceptual, as we saw with the Afghani bracelet.

The American psychologist and philosopher John Dewey described artifacts as natural things that have been reshaped and reworked for the sake of human engagement. They serve a practical function and a social function, each of which has separate and related utility for members of society. Artifacts help us navigate the abstractions of the social world—through their ability to signify—and manage the possibilities of the physical world—through their ability to extend human limitations. The sneakers we wear, the computers we use, and even the cutlery we buy are all artifacts that serve a dual purpose of both function and meaning. Consequently, the products that best satisfy these purposes for a particular community are those that are more likely to be consumed and adopted into the community's cultural practices as a shared behavior.

Behaviors are the set of actions, manners, rituals, traditions, and ceremonies in which members of a community engage. Birthday observations, bar/bat mitzvahs, Thanksgiving dinners, graduations, baptisms, weddings, funerals, proposals, baby showers, the singing of the national anthem before a game, and an endless list of other social performances make up the rituals that constitute the expected cultural behaviors of a community. Like rites of passage, rituals and everyday performative ceremonies (like reciprocal "hello" waves), these behaviors are intentionally embedded with symbolic meaning to exercise the underlying beliefs and ideologies of the culture.

Christians baptize their parishioners as a symbolic outward gesture (submerging oneself in water) of an inward belief (accepting Jesus Christ as their lord and savior). Jews commemorate the coming of age of younger community members through a rite of passage known as bar mitzvah (for boys) and bat mitzvah (for girls), which denotes a moment of spiritual adulthood. The rituals in which we engage are all impregnated with meaning, and over time, they become expected behaviors of community members. In other words, these rituals become socially normative—the performative rules and standards that are understood and expected by members of the community. These norms exist in many, many forms. Some are folkways (customs or behaviors like shaking hands or chewing with your mouth closed) or mores (norms of morality that are perceived as "right" or "wrong," like marital affairs), and others are laws (the societal norms, such as monogamy, that have moved from implicit rules to formal rules with specified consequences, for example, in cases of polygamy). These norms emerge when people expect that others will approve or disapprove of a particular set of behaviors, the result of which can lead to social cohesion or social punishment, respectively.

One of the best parts about being a marketing professor is that I get to travel the world, meet lots of people, and experience many different cultures. I get to partake in their way of life, if only for a moment, and sense what it might be like to be a member of their society. Over the years, I have become particularly fascinated by the traditions and social norms surrounding dating and courtship in different cultures because it reveals so much about people's beliefs. Do men make the first move? Do people date strangers? Do they kiss on the first date? All of these soft rules are culturally mediated and anchored by people's identity and the subsequent beliefs to which they have been indoctrinated. So after I touch down in a foreign country, gather my belongings, proceed through customs, and hop into a car to make my way to the hotel, I chitchat a bit with the cab driver and begin my investigation. "What's dating like here?" It's almost always met with a nervous chuckle. Maybe it's the wedding ring on my finger that gives them the idea that I'm looking for some debauchery during my travels. Or maybe it's an embarrassing question to ask because of how personal the inquiry might be. In any case, they are usually willing to talk about it after a few "ums" and awkward silences. Of all the places I've traveled and all the cab drivers I've interrogated, the most fascinating dating culture I've heard about is that of Sweden. Dating in Sweden is quite the choreographed dance, I've come to find. Apparently, you never directly ask someone out on a date. In Sweden, you ask someone out for "fika."

There is no direct translation for the Swedish word "fika," but the closest one might be the phrase "coffee break." In 1746, King Gustav III imposed a heavy tax on coffee and tea in hopes of reducing their consumption because of the fear that excessive drinking of these beverages could lead to health problems. Once this decree was lifted, coffee drinking became a cultural staple in the Swedish way of life. So much so that Swedes carved out a tradition, called "fika," where they would meet with friends, family, or colleagues to drink coffee and tea with an accompanying sweet on the side. In Sweden, fika is much more than just drinking coffee. It is an exercise of social bonding that Swedes take seriously, whether it is done with people they know or someone they are trying to get to know. So in the case of dating, you don't ask to "go on a date." You invite someone for "fika," and your first fika becomes your first date. In the States, getting coffee is almost seen as transactional, so a date over coffee in the United States doesn't feel as meaningful as a date over dinner, presumably because of the time commitment involved in having dinner with someone. However, in Sweden, coffee is meaningful, and therefore, dating life revolves around it. Behaving in a manner that is out of step with these societal expectations for dating in Sweden is tantamount to breaking the social rules that society has implicitly agreed to regarding the "normal way we do things around here." Violation of these rules can lead to social punishment and sometimes alienation—more on this in Chapter 4.

Social norms are so pervasive and so deeply embedded in our performative muscle memory that we typically engage in them without even thinking. When someone greets us and asks, "How are you?," we tend to respond automatically and oftentimes in the affirmative, with something along the lines of "I'm OK," or "Doing well," or "Not bad." The response is hardly ever "You know, I'm having a pretty awful day, and I'm really worried because there is talk of layoffs happening at my job," even though that may be the case. This degree of transparency upon greeting someone is typically perceived as socially awkward. The list of social norms within a given community or society is ever growing and ever changing as community members negotiate what is acceptable behavior based on the standing beliefs and ideologies of the collective. During this process, new rules are constructed and enforced to establish expectations for community members. Social norms could easily be reduced to practicing "good behavior," but it's much more than that. Social norms are the means by which social cohesion is achieved. Orderly living depends on them. And we navigate these rules, and thousands more like them, every single day that we engage in the world around us.

July 5, 1989, marked the debut of one of the most beloved and influential sitcoms to ever appear on television. The show was *Seinfeld*, the brainchild of comedic writer Larry David and stand-up comedian Jerry Seinfeld. *Seinfeld* was famously labeled "the show about nothing," which couldn't have been further from the truth. It was a show about social norms and the societal consequences that result when these norms are violated. Each week chronicled the lives of four friends—Jerry, Elaine, George, and Kramer—along with the many norms and rituals that govern our lives and the social rejection that comes from subverting cultural expectations. Don't double-dip your chip. Don't urinate in the shower. Don't stand too close when you talk. What we consider good manners are actually social norms that dictate what is culturally acceptable behavior for members of a community. Over the course of the 180 episodes that ran during its nine years on air, *Seinfeld* gave us an in-depth look at the dominant American culture and the rituals that exercise its underlying beliefs and ideologies. As members of the community, we perform these cultural rituals to promote social solidarity within the collective. Even when we visit new places with cultures foreign to us, we adopt their rituals with some fidelity so as not to offend or incur any unwanted social consequences. As the saying goes, "When in Rome, do as the Romans do," which evidences the influence of culture on groups of people through a given set of rituals.

Jimmy Faruggia was a World War II veteran who drove trucks for a living as a way to save money for his entrepreneurial pursuits. In 1954,

Jimmy achieved that goal when he opened Jimmy's Red Hots, a hot-dog stand located on the west side of Chicago, Illinois. However, Jimmy's contribution to the city would be more than processed meat on a bun. As the lore goes, Jimmy was an adamant opponent of ketchup. It's a puzzling position considering how ubiquitous the pairing of ketchup and mustard is as condiments on hot dogs. But Jimmy held the belief that ketchup was used to cover up the rotten taste of spoiled meat. To evidence the freshness of his hot dogs, Jimmy never offered ketchup as a condiment—ever. On the wall of the restaurant hung a sign that said, "Don't even ask!" Couple this with the idea that ketchup duplicated the taste that was already present on a Chicago-style hot dog—mustard, sweet relish, onion, tomato, a pickle spear, sport peppers, and a dash of salt—and the identity ownership associated with that hot dog, and you have what would soon become a long-standing norm among Chicagoans: nobody puts ketchup on a hot dog.

For Heinz Ketchup, a client of Wieden+Kennedy, this standing norm was not so good for business. To combat this resistance to its famed condiment, Heinz decided to conduct a social experiment. If you removed the social taboo from putting ketchup on your hot dog, would Chicagoans enjoy it? On National Hot Dog Day in 2017 (before Wieden+Kennedy's relationship with the company), Heinz introduced its new "Chicago Dog Sauce," which was merely ketchup by another name disguised in different packaging. Local patrons of a Chicago hot-dog stand were encouraged to try the new sauce while hidden cameras filmed their reaction. The patrons gave the mysterious condiment a shot upon the recommendation of the shop workers, though admittedly with reservations. As the sauce came out of the pump, one patron said, "I don't think I've ever seen anything this red on my hot dog before." Upon consumption, the praises for the "Chicago Dog Sauce" increased with every bite. However, when it was revealed that the new sauce was really ketchup, the patrons' praise immediately became contempt. One patron said, "I don't know if I can finish this [hot dog] now," while others responded with much more colorful language. While this campaign likely did not lead to more ketchup consumption in the market, it revealed a very powerful truth: rituals are hard to break, even if the alternative is better. As another patron from the experiment said, "You're challenging people's identity here, man. This is dangerous." Indeed, our identity, through which we subscribe to a culture, establishes a set of beliefs and ideologies that are exercised through the behaviors that are expected of us as community members. Leveraging a current ritual—or perhaps even catalyzing the adoption of a new one—can be very influential if you're trying to get people to move.

So far, we have examined two of the elements of the second system of culture—artifacts and behavior—in depth. Now, let's unpack the third element that makes up our shared way of life: language. The Bible tells a story of a time when the world had one language and one common way of speaking after the great flood in the days of Noah. The people settled on a plot of land and decided to build a tower so high that it reached the heavens to prepare for the possibility of another flood. According to the story, God saw this as blasphemy in that the people would forgo faith for a human-made structure. And the Lord said, "Behold, the people is one, and they have all one language; and this they begin to do: and now nothing will be restrained from them, which they have imagined to do." Language enables cooperation among individuals. So God confused their language, giving them different tongues so that they could not understand each other and therefore could not finish the tower. The book of Genesis refers to this place as Babel, which today means confused noise, like that of a baby's speech. The story of the Tower of Babel, as it is commonly known, illustrates the role that the lexicon of a community plays with regard to how it enables cooperation among its members.

The lexicon is the vocabulary, language, or dialect that is used among a group of people. Linguists refer to the lexicon as the set of words that are used to carry meaning—be it technical jargon or colloquialisms. For instance, growing up in Detroit, we would often use the phrase "you straight," which had many different meanings. "You straight" could mean, "Are you OK?" It could also mean, "You are OK," as in "No problem, I got it." "You straight" could mean "How have you been?" but also "Did you get enough [to eat]?" "You straight" could be a way to end a conversation contentiously, as in "You straight, stop talking to me," or a way to say, "You're welcome." "You straight" could also be a way to ask people if they needed something or a way to end a dispute, as in "No need to say 'sorry.'" It's the same phrase, but it has different coded meanings. It's no different than the word "bad" meaning something both negative (as in "that's not good" bad) and something positive (as in Michael Jackson's "Bad"). However, within a more specific cultural context, the shades of meaning associated with the lexicon of a group of people can be extremely nuanced, as in the case of "you straight" or even "wassup." On the surface, these words seem to carry one universal translation, but what lies beneath the surface is a rich tapestry of cultural meaning that is exchanged through the discourse of community members.

Community members use their lexicon, much like artifacts and behaviors, to signify their cultural subscriptions and exercise the beliefs and ideologies associated with it. It is expected that community members will not only use this language but also understand the nuanced meaning framed by the context in which it is used. Families, religions, fraternities, clubs, schools, and companies all have coded language that signal membership through the use and understanding of their lexicon. In the culture of cosplay, community members use the word "canon" to describe a costume that precisely recreates an outfit worn by a character at a specific point of time within a story. In the culture of gamers, community members use the term "FPS," an acronym for "first-person shooter" that describes the kind of game that is being played. They also use the term "KD," which is a shorthand for a user's "kill-death" ratio, a unit of measurement to evaluate the skill of a player. In the culture of electronic music, community members use the term "PLUR," an acronym for "peace, love, unity, respect," to communicate the shared beliefs that unite them. If you are not part of these communities, these terms might feel like a different language because, well, they are.

It's easy to write off the language of another community as "strange" until we stop and consider the peculiar nature of our own. Take all the business jargon used in corporate America, for example. For someone who is not of the business world, this lexicon might seem completely foreign. "Let's circle back on that. I'll flip that over to you ASAP, but it likely won't be until EOD. I'm curious to hear your POV, so ping me when you get a chance. I also want to double-click on that topic regarding the low-hanging fruit of thinking out of the box. Assuming, of course, that you have the bandwidth for it. Net-net, I think the synergies that might come from thinking glocal will be a win-win for the firm. Looking forward to giving you the download." What? To someone outside this community, you might as well be speaking Klingon. The same can be said of technical jargon, slang, religious phraseologies, and other casual language shorthands.

The culture writer and linguist Amanda Montell refers to language as the way we get people on the same ideological page and make them feel that they belong to the group. To know the hidden meanings within a coded language is to evince a level of intimacy within a community, a way of proving you're "one of us." The use and understanding of the lexicon within a community not only signals membership and intimacy but also provides a currency that community members can exchange as an act of social cohesion. Much like apes physically groom the hairs of other apes to foster community, we use the exchange of language to promote social bonding through the act of mimicry. When we engage in conversations with others, we begin to coordinate breaking patterns, use the same words and similar grammatical structures. These are all means of community building, and the lexicon of the group plays a large role in this performative act.

## CULTURAL PRODUCTION

The third and final system of culture is cultural production. This is the shared creative output of a community that reflects its perspective on the world. This could be art, architecture, movies, television, comic books, podcasts, stories, music, instruments, dance, literature, fashion, hairstyles, food, poetry, toys, or branded products. Community members use these productions as outward expressions or justifications of their beliefs and ideologies that are subsequently integrated (and sometimes mandated) into their way of life.

Cultural production also provides an avenue for us to learn about the expectations of what it means to be a member of the community as well as a way to engage in meaning making within the community. Artists, journalists, writers, and other cultural producers create text and materials to contribute a point of view about a topic or societal condition that either reflects or challenges the standing shared beliefs of a community. Be it a song like "This Is America," by the artist Childish Gambino that critiques our consumption of gun violence or a movie like *Do The Right Thing*, by Spike Lee, that tackles America's racial tensions, these productions offer a perspective on the world that is informed by the way a community sees the world. The creations of producers, like Gambino and Lee, act as a vessel of cultural information that is discussed and negotiated by the community to decide whether it reflects "people like us." When it does, we include these products in our cultural practices. We'll discuss this further throughout the book, but for the time being, let's explore cultural production through the lens of hip-hop.

Though commonly thought of as a style of music, hip-hop is much more. It is an entire culture with beliefs and ideologies, a way of life, and cultural production. Rap music is the cultural product of hip-hop culture. Hip-hop began in the late 1970s in the housing projects of the South Bronx, New York, where residents faced poverty, crime, and racial injustice. These challenges led to an infestation of drugs, a proliferation of street crime, and the adverse effects of a crumbling city infrastructure and the deindustrialization of American cities. These conditions produced an aspiration for something greater than what the South Bronx offered its residents. Hip-hop emerged as a response to these conditions and became a cultural force of creativity that provided an avenue for self-expression and a political voice for the disenfranchised youths of the Bronx. By the 1980s, most people who subscribed to hip-hop culture were producing or participating in the hip-hop cultural product, whether that was emceeing (spoken word over music), deejaying (sampling and scratching records), breaking (break dancing), or tagging (graffiti). It was not long before hip-hop reverberated across state lines and found a home in cities that mirrored the social tensions of the South Bronx. Young Black and Hispanic Americans across the country clung to hip-hop as a way to escape, rebel, and elevate their social status. Emcees—the storytellers of hip-hop—used their art form to narrate the realities of their environments as social currency in the form of stories that were relatable to audiences, many of which also came from similar environments.

The gravitational pull of hip-hop culture in the United States had a similar effect across the world. Although the environments outside the South Bronx were manifested differently, the same disenfranchisement that was felt in the streets of the South Bronx—poverty, crime, and racial injustice—could also be felt in the streets of South Africa, for example. The stories narrated in the music of hip-hop—rap music— tell a story of universal experiences, and the Internet both exposed international audiences to hip-hop culture and allowed hip-hop consumers to connect. These universal experiences—what the hip-hop scholar Halifu Osumare refers to as "connective marginalities"—are part of what made hip-hop so attractive: they reveal a shared sense of marginalization, frustration, and rebellion against oppression around the world.

Over time, hip-hop culture diffused beyond the inner cities and moved out into the suburbs, impregnating the popular culture and influencing peripheral markets. As the hip-hop journalist Jeff Chang described in his book *Can't Stop Won't Stop*, "The ubiquity of an art form developed by Black and Latino youths well exemplifies the theoretical observation that what is socially marginalized often becomes culturally centered." The runaway success of the Broadway musical *Hamilton*—which tells the life story of the American founding father Alexander Hamilton—is an example of hip-hop's permeation of the dominant culture. The entire two-hour-forty-five-minute show is performed in a rap-styled cadence, and *Hamilton* has performed to sold-out audiences, coast to coast, night after night, since its debut in 2015. More recently, break dancing has been provisionally approved as an Olympic sport for the 2024 games in Paris, France.

Hip-hop as cultural production is relatable and accessible. Its primary musical instrumentation is through sampling, where musical elements are borrowed from other artists' compositions, looped, and spoken over. Most forms of music require instruments, which can be expensive and unaffordable for marginalized or impoverished groups. In contrast, hip-hop is completely democratized, in some cases requiring nothing more than the human voice, which lowers the barrier to entry. With no instruments or equipment necessary to participate in the musical art form, literally anyone can contribute to the culture, and the same can be said of breaking and tagging. Such an easy on-ramp creates a wide door to membership in the hip-hop collective. The result of this ease of entry simultaneously drives creation and consumption, enabling anyone who subscribes to the ethos of hip-hop to contribute artifacts to the community and influence its cultural characteristics.

Today, rap music—a cultural product of hip-hop culture—is the most consumed music genre in the United States, and hip-hop fashion, vernacular, attitudes, and body language have been adopted throughout the country and beyond. The art form often takes preexisting material and reworks it through a new meaning frame or remixes it. The spread of rap music has led to the adoption of hip-hop culture the world over—spanning ethnic, linguistic, and geographic boundaries. People experience the cultural product and find alignment with the meanings embedded in it because they, too, subscribe to the ideologies that inform the output.

## THREE SYSTEMS OF CULTURE

These are the three systems that make up culture. Our beliefs and ideologies are the closest sphere to us. This sphere serves to help us make meaning of the world and frame our reality. The shared beliefs of our communities are realized and exercised by our way of life, which demarcates what's acceptable based upon the negotiated and constructed social facts of our community. Not only is this realization exercised in our way of life, but it is also expressed and reworked through cultural production. This operating system—culture—and its social facts provide both the unwritten rules of the community and the societal expectations of what it means to be a member in good standing of it.

These elemental codes of culture create a shared way of understanding the world and establish an orderly way of behaving in it—an operating system that governs everyday life. Durkheim argued that members who subscribe to a particular culture tend to act in concert to promote social solidarity among its members. He referred to this phenomenon as "collective effervescence." This concept is superpowerful because it suggests that what we believe, what we do, how we make meaning of the world, and how we communicate are all by-products of the cultural operating system to which we subscribe. This system drives our collective behavior. What we buy, what we drive, how we style ourselves, how we conduct business, what we eat, what we say, where we work, where we vacation, how we worship, how we marry, whom we decide to marry, how we celebrate birth, how we bury the dead, where we go to school, how we vote, what we watch, whom we support, and just about every other aspect of social life are all cultural acts.

This makes culture a pretty compelling vehicle for catalyzing collective behavior, not just for marketers but for anyone interested in getting people to move—politicians, managers, content creators, activists, clergy, and so on. The sway of culture has a way of subconsciously influencing our lives, and against its forces, we are relatively defenseless. Yes, you, too! Why? Because we—the human race—are wired that way.

This is why Budweiser's "Wassup" campaign had the effect that it did. The depiction of Stone and his buddies reflected the ceremony that was common among the culture of "bros" in the late 1990s. You've likely used the term "bro-ey" to describe the behavior associated with this group of people in a modern-day sense. The ad perfectly encapsulated the ease of quick verbal exchanges among friends during their day-to-day interactions as well as the comedy that ensues when more "bros" participate in these exchanges. Stone nailed this in his short film *True*, which made it perfect for Budweiser because it captured the essence of friendship and positioned the beer as the ideal complement to what friends do when they get together.

However, Stone's coup went beyond his pinpoint accuracy in depicting an aspect of culture. It was his contribution of language—"wassup"—that made the ad so unbelievably tangible for the culture of "bros" to use as social currency among its members, fortifying the relational bonds that connect them. "Wassup" was more than just a catchy phrase; it was a shorthand code that signaled "we are friends."

For a good three months, every time my dear friend Steven Snead called me, I was greeted with "Wassup!" in a spot-on imitation of Stone and his friends. What's more, Steven would call me from his dorm room, which would not register on the caller ID of my apartment landline, so I would answer the phone not knowing who was on the line. As soon as I heard "wassup" and recognized his voice, I immediately felt at ease.

Importantly, the adoption of "wassup" did not require a meeting or parliamentary procedure. It happened subconsciously, primarily because the ad evidenced the cultural system right before viewers' eyes—with every viewing—which created legitimacy. They saw the ad and saw themselves. The more people started using "wassup" in conversations among friends, the more other people started using it as well. The brand found itself steeped in the cultural zeitgeist, and its legitimacy within the culture led to increased beer sales. But as they say, all good things must come to an end.

## MADE IN AMERICA

By 2011, over ten years after the debut of "Wassup," Budweiser had lost favor among the bros. The brand that had once reflected their cultural system no longer seemed relevant to them or reflective of them. Not only was the brand facing its own challenges, but the entire premium beer category was under attack by IPAs and craft beers that had come into vogue at the time. Budweiser was in trouble, so it reached out to the New York–based advertising agency where I worked at the time, Translation, to help correct its course.

Translation started as a brand consultancy that helped ambitious brands thrive in contemporary culture. It was founded by music mogul–turned–advertiser Steve Stoute along with his silent partners: the legendary music executive Jimmy Iovine and the hip-hop superstar Jay-Z. Translation had a reputation as a cool agency with a special knack for recruiting celebrities and musicians as media vehicles for some of the biggest brands in the world. I met Stoute in 2010 when he asked me to join the agency and build its social media marketing practice. After a nine-month courtship, I decided to join Translation as the director of social engagement, developing and leading a team of social strategists, distribution and partnership managers, data analysts, and content creators. And the first assignment I was given? Help Budweiser's brand regain its cultural relevance.

The Budweiser brand is an American icon. The problem was that Budweiser represented yesterday's Americana. This wasn't the prior decade's flag-waving, salute the troops, belt out "I'm Proud to Be an American" Americana that resulted from increased patriotism as a response to the 9/11 terrorist attacks on the country. This was the "new Americana and we smoke marijuana" type of patriotism. This Americana didn't wave flags but wore them ironically on T-shirts. These Americans didn't believe in "the land of the free, home of the brave," but they did believe in the American dream—here, you can make something of yourself no matter where you come from. It was this cultural truth that would lead to Budweiser's way back. But getting there wasn't going to be easy.

Stoute had an early read on the solution. As a music executive at some of the most prominent record labels in the world and a trusted voice to the biggest names in entertainment, he had a keen sense for identifying cultural opportunities that involved music. Stoute knew that Budweiser had historically invested in music as a vehicle to connect with consumers through an endeavor called the Budweiser Superfest, an annual blockbuster summer concert. The first Superfest took place on July 19, 1980, and featured larger-than-life acts of the time such as Rick James, Ashford & Simpson, and Teddy Pendergrass. In later years, Stevie Wonder, Aretha Franklin, and Whitney Houston all graced the Superfest stage, playing to sold-out audiences that filled football stadiums in multiple cities each summer. By the time

Budweiser approached us in 2011, however, the Superfest had lost its luster, and crowd sizes had significantly dwindled. Knowing this, Stoute recommended that we reimagine the Superfest, considering the impact that music has on forging consumer connections, by approaching it with the contemporary music fan in mind. So on a July evening in 2011, thirty-one years almost to the day after the launch of the first Superfest, three of my Translation colleagues and I were camped out in a St. Louis Westin Hotel room in the wee hours of the night, preparing for our big pitch to Budweiser the next morning. It was the start of a chain of events that would lead to a partnership with Jay-Z, a documentary with the legendary filmmaker Ron Howard, and a shout-out by the then president of the United States, Barack Obama.

The original Superfest was a multicity concert that was headlined by megastars within the world of R&B music. But times had changed. Not only had R&B been usurped by hip-hop as one of the more dominant music genres, but the music industry had begun to turn away from the traditional concert format with a growing affinity for music festivals like Coachella, Bonnaroo, and Lollapalooza. Fresh off the heels of a recession, music fans wanted a way to see all their favorite artists across genres instead of seeing a handful of acts from the same genre at a comparable ticket price. This desire was also influenced by the way people listened to music. Long gone were the days of buying an album and listening to the full body of work from beginning to end. Instead, people listened to their music on shuffle thanks to the advent of digital music platforms and devices, like Apple's iTunes and iPods, that made it commonplace for users to mash up their music libraries and listen to songs from different artists and different genres in one continuous listening session. Music festivals were essentially the physical manifestation of listening to music on shuffle—fans could see a set from Radiohead, Kanye West, Jack Johnson, Coldplay, and Rage Against the Machine under one ticket price. Changing the Superfest from a multicity concert to a multiday festival seemed to be the logical choice. The next step was identifying a positioning of the festival that made sense for Budweiser.

Drawing on the brand's Americana association, we decided to look at the festival through the lens of the "New Americana." This Americana rested on the belief that in this country, people who create things and put ideas into the world can achieve the American dream. That no matter who you are or where you come from, if you have an idea, you can make something of yourself. Or, as we pitched it, the culture of the New Americana was driven by a new tribe—a neotribe—that we dubbed "Makers." "Makers" believe that self-expression is a way of life and that what you wear can be (and, arguably, should be) an expression of you, made by you. This is a collective of people who believe that creating isn't what you do but who you are.

This would be the angle that Budweiser would lean into, reimagining Superfest as a Maker music festival. This would be not just a music event but a celebration of the Makers—those who created the music, art, and fashion that fueled the New Americana, populated popular culture, and represented what makes this country so great. Those who were living out their pursuit of the American dream. And no one represented this ideology more than Shawn "Jay-Z" Carter.

Jay-Z was raised in the Marcy Projects of Brooklyn against the backdrop of crime, drugs, and street life. Once a drug dealer himself, Jay-Z traded a life of crime for a life as a rapper and ascended to meteoric heights as a musician, music executive, and businessman. He was the personification of the American dream, the modern-day rags-to-riches story, and the perfect face for our new music festival idea. It also didn't hurt that he had been a partner at Translation and was a close friend of Stoute's. But that aside, his congruence with the cultural characteristics of the Maker community was perfect.

Stoute pitched the idea to Jay-Z, and he was into it right away. With Jay on board, we took Budweiser's American iconicity and updated the brand to represent the more modern cultural system of the country by creating the Budweiser Made in America Festival—a two-day music festival that took place on Labor Day weekend at the heart of Benjamin Franklin Parkway in Philadelphia. Does it get more American than that?

As our partner, Jay-Z curated the festival's talent lineup, picking an eclectic range of artists whose diversity mirrored that of the American tapestry. From D'Angelo to Run DMC, the Hives to Pearl Jam, Made in America reached across generations, racial boundaries, and genres. On Labor Day weekend 2012, we kicked off the festival, welcoming ninety thousand attendees to a two-day Budweiser sampling event (the brand was the only beer on pour at the festival) with some of the biggest acts in music as the atmospheric backdrop. Through the legitimation of the festival, the Budweiser brand became a symbolic artifact that represented this New Americana and the system of beliefs and behaviors that governed its cultural members. At the time of this writing, Made in America is in its tenth year of existence and is counted among the top five music festivals in the country, providing new footing for Budweiser within the cultural system of the Maker community. Like its success with "Wassup" over a decade earlier, Budweiser (with our help) catalyzed collective behavior by leveraging the sway of culture—in particular, the shared beliefs, way of life, and cultural production of the Maker community.

Budweiser is only one example, but there are many more that span a wide diversity of industries, contexts, and targets. As different as the examples may be, the through line in each of these instances is consistent: the influence of culture holds a powerful sway over our day-to-day lives. It affects how we consume, how we interact, how we work, how we vote, how we present ourselves, and just about every other facet of humanity that you can think of. There is no vehicle more influential over human behavior than culture. And now that we've taken the guesswork out of what culture is, let's dig into why it has such a commanding and predictable effect on getting people to move.

## FROM KNOW-WHY TO KNOW-HOW

The abstract nature of culture makes it difficult to describe and even harder to leverage as a way to get people to adopt behavior. Therefore, it's critical that we have the vocabulary to talk about what culture is and a tangible perspective to describe how it works so that we can move beyond the nebulous and on to the operational and applicable. When someone says, "We want to get our idea into culture," what do they really mean? Into what culture? And to what extent? These delineations require an understanding that you now have.

Culture is a realized meaning-making system, a system of conventions and expectations that demarcate who we are and govern what people like us do. It is anchored in our identity (who we are) and made up of three elements: how we see the world, our shared way of life, and the creation of shared expression. The relationship between identity and the three elements is illustrated below in Figure 1. This is the system of systems that constitutes culture. Together, these elements—a community's social facts—inform how members of that community see the world and how they show up in the world. And if we can understand these social facts, then we can leverage their influence to excite people to move.

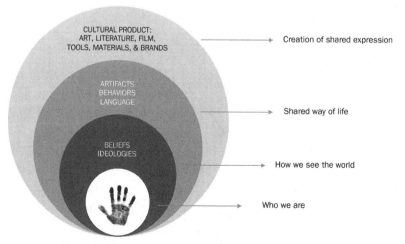

Figure 1. The systems that constitute culture

## CHAPTER 2

# FINDING A CONGREGATION

From adolescence, Yvon Chouinard had always been enthusiastic about the outdoors. He hiked, surfed, and fly-fished religiously, but his greatest love was mountain climbing. Yvon was one of the most prominent climbers of the 1960s. During his climbs up and down a mountain, he would come back with ideas on how to improve his climb. He would rethink the hardware that was used for climbing, which in those days was "crude," in his opinion. Climbers would drive metal objects into the rock to aid their ascent. With more climbers, over time, this would have a significant impact on the face of the rock and its natural state. That did not sit well with Yvon.

He held strong beliefs about the environment. In his mind, nature should be enjoyed but left alone, and humans should leave nothing behind. As Yvon put it, "There is a word for it, and the word is 'clean.' Climbing with only nuts and runners for protection is clean climbing. Clean because the rock is left unaltered by the passing climber. Clean because nothing is hammered into the rock and then hammered back out, leaving the rock scarred and the next climber's experience less natural. Clean because the climber's protection leaves little trace of his ascension. Clean is climbing the rock without changing it; a step closer to organic climbing for the natural man." With this anchoring belief, Yvon took up blacksmithing, manipulating hot pieces of metal into gear for clean climbing. With each new idea that came to mind to improve his climb, he would create it and sell it to other climbers. He had no intention of building a company. He wasn't driven by business; he was driven by his affinity for climbing clean and his conviction about preserving the environment. What started as a DIY hobby became a billion-dollar business known today as Patagonia—an outdoor retailer that sells clothing, athletic equipment, backpacks, and camping gear.

To say that Patagonia is a business would be an understatement. The company is more of an activist entity than a commercial entity. Yes, it sells its wares for commercial gain, but it engages in business to protect the environment. Patagonia holds this conviction so truly that the company has turned away lucrative opportunities that do not align with its beliefs. For instance, one of Patagonia's lines of business is outfitting high-end corporate clients with company apparel. Corporate vests and fleece jackets with the Patagonia logo etched on the chest became a sort of unofficial uniform for Wall Street bankers and Silicon Valley techies. Patagonia's premium-priced clothing made the brand a worthy nameplate to sit on vests beside the logos of Morgan Stanley, Facebook, and other corporate giants. This was a significant revenue driver for the company, but Patagonia had realized that some of its corporate clients dealt in business ventures that did not prioritize the planet. Once aware of this fact, Patagonia decided to end its business dealings with any companies that were incongruent with its beliefs. The loss of revenue was not worth betraying its convictions.

Patagonia's commitment to its beliefs runs deep. In 2011, the company ran a full-page advertisement in the *New York Times* telling readers not to buy its jackets. Why would a company spend advertising dollars to sell less product? Because Patagonia believed that excess consumption was bad for the environment, so it encouraged people to get their old jackets repaired instead of buying a new one. The company not only promised to repair every single piece of Patagonia product indefinitely but it also created a service that repairs non-Patagonia products. Even if you grow tired of a color or maybe gain a little weight, the company will help you sell the product to someone else. Or if the product is completely unusable, Patagonia will take it and recycle it in exchange for a store credit. It's a lifetime guarantee, and the aim of this initiative is to teach people that they don't have to throw things away; they can repair them, which is better for the environment.

Interestingly, the more Patagonia made decisions that would theoretically harm its business (like telling people not to buy more of its products), the bigger its business became. People just kept buying. But it wasn't because Patagonia products used the best materials or that its designs were uniquely better than those of its competitors. In fact, if you put a Patagonia coat next to a North Face or Columbia coat (all of which are outdoor clothing companies) and removed the logos, you likely wouldn't be able to tell one from another. It wasn't the products that set Patagonia apart from its peers in the category; it was the beliefs of the brand—its conviction about climbing clean—that drew people to consume. Patagonia didn't go out to find an audience to sell to. Instead, it found a congregation who shared its beliefs, and those people took action.

The word "congregation" usually refers to a group of people who come together for religious worship. However, congregations are also social vehicles whereby people find community, exercise their civic duties (like community service, for instance), and establish both collective and individual identity. The word "congregation" appears in the Bible over 350 times as a reference to a group of people, later described as "the church" in the New Testament, in which Apostle Paul wrote letters to many congregations about what it meant to be a part of the community. These letters, which expressed the teachings of Jesus Christ, established an understanding of the shared beliefs of the collective, the meaning of particular artifacts, the expected behaviors of congregation members, and the acceptable use of language in their daily lives. Congregations are cultural practitioners and producers that share ideologies that inform how people show up in the world and how they project their identity.

The context in which members of a congregation interact extends beyond a religious capacity. Like any social groups, congregations have deep and meaningful social connections built into them. Like business ventures, congregations often engage in commercial activities, like real estate purchases and construction projects. Although congregations are not artistic institutions, music and theatrical performances are created and shared among their members. Congregations are not schools, yet they conduct educational programs like Sunday school. Removed from its faith affiliation, a congregation is essentially a group of people who share the same worldview, which influences their shared way of life, outward expression, commerce, and collective consumption—dare I say—in a religious fashion. I've found this way of thinking about congregations particularly useful for companies and leaders who seek to influence behavior because congregations represent the perfect groups of potential customers, voters, or subscribers whom we seek to move.

Most companies focus their efforts on appealing to a target audience, a select group of people who are deemed most likely to buy because of the features and benefits of the product. Consider the people whom you direct your messaging toward and the products you create. This is your target audience. These audiences are inclined to buy because of what the product is. Congregations, on the other hand, are inclined to buy because of who they are, and this difference is significant. While outdoor apparel brands aim to compel audiences to consume based on the warmth of their coats, Patagonia inspires a congregation to move based on the beliefs that the members share. Consumption, in this way, becomes a cultural act for congregants (the people who believe in climbing clean), not merely a motivation for product utility. Audiences buy products because of their function. Congregations buy products as evidence of their beliefs.

By and large, congregations consist of an aggregation of smaller groups, what social scientists call tribes—social groups within society that consist of individuals who are bound by geography, familial relations, and ideological similarities. For instance, there are a host of tribes, such as conservationists, environmentalists, and recyclers, that share the worldview of the Patagonia congregation. They all believe in "climbing clean." However, they exercise themselves in their own unique and nuanced ways. This is seen in almost everything from politics—the "liberals," "progressives," and "moderates" who make up the congregation that is the Democratic Party—to media consumption—the "gijinka," "crossplayers," and "kigurumi" who make up the cosplay congregation. Members of these groups share common beliefs, adorn themselves with certain artifacts, adhere to a set of norms, and commune through cocreated dialect. Tribal groups are organized around, and governed by, a system of cultural characteristics that establishes social cohesion among their members and enables the social cooperation necessary for the collective to thrive. Members of the tribe construct designated roles—labor roles, gender roles, and social roles—that inform how individuals within the group are to behave. Subsequently, members of the tribe play their roles and adhere to the cultural characteristics of the group to stay in good standing within the community.

Tribes have existed as far back as the beginning of humankind, across the globe, and throughout societies. The impact of industrialism, however, shifted our traditional understanding of tribes. What was once demarcated by geography became uprooted thanks to the rise of the Industrial Revolution, which compelled people to leave their small towns for economic opportunity in densely populated metropolises. Cities like London, Paris, Berlin, and, soon after, New York and Philadelphia saw an influx of people looking for work during the boom of manufacturing in the Western world.

Individuals from all walks of life descended on these cities and brought with them a diversity of ideologies, norms, and other cultural characteristics that created a haven of discovery for these new city dwellers. People were introduced to new ideas and perspectives through the process of cultural exchange, which led to a breakdown of traditional tribes and the construction of new cultural characteristics that led to new beliefs and new practices. It was the equivalent of sending a newly minted eighteen-year-old high school graduate off to college to experience life on their own for the first time without the social pressures of interpellation and familial conformity. As soon as college freshmen descend on campus, they are introduced to a population of differentness—new people who come from different places, subscribe to different beliefs, practice different norms, use different languages, wear new kinds of clothes, listen to different kinds of music, watch different kinds of movies, and buy different kinds of products. It's all different. And it's here, in college, that young adults learn about themselves through their social interactions, just as they learn about the world through their academic studies. So it was for tribes during the Industrial Revolution. People left their small-town pounds and came to the big city to find work—and simultaneously found their new selves in a sea-sized society.

However, as most anthropologists will attest, humans are wired to live in curated collectives, as opposed to mass societies. So people formed new tribes within a larger society in order to find a "place" where they belonged. The French sociologist Michel Maffesoli referred to these new tribes as "neotribes." The behavioral patterns within these neotribes act similarly to Durkheim's notion of collective effervescence, discussed in the previous chapter, where a community comes together to participate collectively in the same action. Within a neotribe, the legitimation—what is deemed acceptable and valid—of new beliefs, rituals, artifacts, and language is negotiated and constructed (both implicitly and explicitly) by its members, resulting in new political dogma, consumption habits, technology adoption, and colloquialisms among members of the social group.

Much like the biblical congregations of the New Testament, our modern-day tribes are social collectives that are bound by the shared beliefs and ideologies that govern daily living. They are cultural collectives, like clubs, teams, and organizations, that help us navigate the world. We are all members of someone's tribe—every one of us. And we adhere to the cultural characteristics of the tribe in a religious fashion. The question is not whether we're in a tribe but to which tribe do we belong, and how do we self-identify?

## IDENTITY AND WORLDVIEW

Tribal membership is an exercise of choice. Outside our families, our original tribe, we join tribes of our own volition. We choose a group of people with whom we share a worldview, and they choose us. Every fall, a legion of young college women present themselves as candidates for the sorority of their choosing, hoping that the sorority will see them as a good fit among their current roster of "sisters." The sisters evaluate potential recruits to join their organization based on the extent to which these individuals embody the characteristics that reflect the organization's values. If she's someone "like us," then she's someone with whom we want to be associated. Likewise, an organization is evaluated by potential members based on whether it is an appropriate extension of their own identity. There is congruence seeking on both sides—from individuals looking for like-minded groups and groups looking for like-minded members.

This is worth keeping in mind as you seek to recruit new members for your organization or new consumers for your brand. People are looking to be a part of something just as much as you are looking for people to join you. You just have to find the right congregational fit. Sometimes you will find those people, as in the case of Patagonia and the congregation of "clean climbers." And sometimes they will find you, as we saw with hipsters and PBR, because of your expressed beliefs—more on this in Chapter 4.

We are all in search of community—at our schools, at our jobs, in our cities, and online. As Aristotle once postulated, "Man is by nature a social animal." We traverse the social world asking ourselves, "Are these my people?" "Do we see the world similarly?" "Do I want my identity associated with them?" These are the questions we ponder, subconsciously or otherwise, when membership is evaluated within a particular tribe that is representative of a larger congregation. When there is alignment, we are inclined to seek membership. When there is misalignment, we look elsewhere. The process is the same with brands. When the brand belief is aligned with our belief, we not only gravitate toward it but also find community among people who behave similarly. When the brand's beliefs are at odds with our beliefs, however, we tend to reject it.

Identity and worldview require alignment. This relationship is the cornerstone of social life and tribal membership. It applies to joining a new group or deciding to stay in one. As the saying goes, "You don't talk about money, religion, and politics at the dinner table." Why? Because these topics reveal people's beliefs and ideologies, and when we find that "our people" don't see the world the way we do, we tend to ask ourselves, "Are these people really *my* people?" We may suffer the performance of avoiding these topics at Thanksgiving dinner to keep the peace, because we are aware of Aunt Karen's social views, but we are less likely to do so in groups that we join of our own free will.

If we question the beliefs and ideologies of a religion because it is no longer aligned with the way we see the world, we might leave the church, or the religion altogether. When the tribe's worldview is no longer aligned with our worldview, we leave the group. We've seen this play out in the Republican Party over the last few election cycles. As the ideologies of the GOP grew more radical with the rise of the Tea Party in late 2000s, and more recently with the election of Donald Trump in 2016, many self-identifying Republicans withdrew their subscription to the Republican tribe because their beliefs were no longer aligned with those of the group. The lack of belief and ideological congruence created a subsequent identity incongruence. Since their worldview was no longer aligned, people didn't want their identity associated with the party, so they went off to establish new tribes that were a better fit with their identity. Likewise, Republican Party members whose worldview no longer aligns with the new worldview of the party—for example, Liz Cheney—might find themselves excluded from the collective. This evaluation process happens simultaneously between the collective and the individual based on the similarities and differences in how we live our lives as a manifestation of our worldview.

Identity, beliefs, and ideologies are inextricably linked. Beliefs are the truths we hold about the world. They help us explain why things are the way they are. Ideologies are the narratives we tell ourselves about the world based on these truths. Our identity is the character we assign ourselves in the story that demarcates how we fit in the world. Together, they frame the randomness of the world and give meaning to what we observe and experience. We hold specific beliefs that are aligned with our identity and, since we self-identify by certain monikers (family name, title, organization, religion), we are inclined to adopt the worldview that is associated with these categorical labels. This relationship is foundational to how we navigate the social world, and it directly influences the collective behavior of the congregation and the many tribes that constitute it. The congruence between our identity and worldview acts as a union card for the tribes to which we subscribe, and membership in the union is governed by the cultural characteristics of the collective—artifacts, behaviors, and language.

You could argue that football—American football, that is—has overtaken baseball as America's favorite pastime. Towns assemble to watch their local high school teams play under the Friday night lights, so much so that a movie and television show (with the same title) were made to chronicle the hyperbolic experience of football in these towns. Saturday afternoons, however, are reserved for another beast entirely: NCAA football. Legions of fans and spectators congregate in stadiums, living rooms, man caves, bars, and backyards across the country to pledge allegiance to their school affiliation. It's a spectacle. Students swarm the stands decked out in body paint and over-the-top school paraphernalia. Alumni come from all over the country to relive old memories and participate in the time-honored tradition of football tailgating. Towns practically shut down to accommodate the influx of people. For many local shops, these Saturdays are the lifeblood of their business, and they prepare accordingly. I live in Ann Arbor, Michigan, where over 107,000 people gather in the Big House on Saturdays to watch the University of Michigan Wolverines play (Go, Blue!). It's the largest assembled crowd in the country on any given Saturday.

This rabid fandom then reaches its zenith on Sundays, when the National Football League's (NFL) teams hit the field. It's so pervasive that I've even seen Sunday-morning church services end early so that parishioners can get home in time for the game. It's a real thing. And it has become a new ceremonial ritual in American culture, upstaging the original sentimentality of "Take me out to the ball game." However, one fateful Sunday potentially threatened all of it.

During a 2016 preseason game for the San Francisco 49ers, starting quarterback Colin Kaepernick decided to sit during the playing of the national anthem before the start of the game. His actions were a protest against the racial injustices that many people of color face due to systemic issues in our political and judicial systems. Kaepernick wanted to demonstrate that we can't honor the country's ideals, as expressed in the anthem and the raising of the flag, until we decide to live by them. His actions did not go unnoticed. Not only did Kaepernick sit during this preseason game, but he would also go on to kneel during the playing of the national anthem throughout the entire season. This caused tremendous controversy in the country. Opinions on the matter were discussed and debated in print, online, and on seemingly every news station, radio show, and sports media outlet. Everyone had an opinion. Even former president Donald Trump weighed in on the topic. (Not exactly a high bar, I know.) Kaepernick would later be cut from the team—only to further fan the flames of controversy and conspiracy—and file a high-profile lawsuit against the NFL. People boycotted the NFL. Celebrities voiced their abstention from watching the games. Musical artists declined invitations to perform at the NFL Super Bowl, the largest media moment in the country, all in solidarity to "stand with Kap."

Two years after Kaepernick's first demonstration, Nike—our founding client at Wieden+Kennedy—debuted a print advertisement that featured a black-and-white photo of the shunned football player with a simple but provocative statement superimposed on Kaepernick's face: "Believe in something, even if it means sacrificing everything." Nike, the beloved athletic brand that has been telling the world to "Just Do It" (another campaign created by Wieden+Kennedy) for decades, just did it. The brand's statement signified on what side of the debate it stood and, as a result, kicked the hornet's nest of public opinion across the social web. Legions of people expressed their anger at Nike for its actions and vowed to never buy the brand again. Some people even went so far as to publicly burn their Nike apparel to underscore their disapproval. Hundreds of videos graced the Internet with documentation of such demonstrations.

Why would people do this? Why would they destroy their own property after spending their hard-earned money because of a Nike ad? I'll tell you why. Because Nike's ad wasn't just an ad, it was the brand communicating its point of view—expressing its beliefs and ideologies. The people who had purchased Nike products but didn't share Nike's view of the Kaepernick situation saw this as a betrayal—or, at the very least, an ideological misalignment. If Nike believes Kaepernick's protest is just, then do I implicitly support its belief by wearing its products? In sociology, this is referred to as self-congruence, and it happens when an individual's concept of self—how they see themselves and how they want to be seen by other people—is evaluated based on its alignment with the brands and products they buy. If the brand's belief and projections are out of sync with the individual's, then there is incongruence and a subsequent cognitive penalty. Therefore, we, as consumers, aim to reach self-congruence, or alignment, with the products and brands we purchase. Does this brand align with my worldview? If yes, we move forward. If no, we abandon the brand right away.

This is what was happening in the case of Nike consumers who were not "standing with Kap." Their worldview was seemingly misaligned with Nike's, and, therefore, they didn't want to buy from Nike again. Moreover, being seen wearing Nike apparel could erroneously signal to others that they, too, were "standing with Kap"—and that just would not do. So they decided to burn their Nike shoes and throw away their Nike clothing as an act of ideological dissent. They didn't agree with Nike, and they wanted to let the world know even if it meant destroying products that they had already purchased.

Meanwhile, Nike's Kaepernick ad had the opposite effect on a large congregation of tribes who believed in Kaepernick's protest.

In fact, these people not only shared the same view of the matter as Nike and Kap but were also compelled to buy more Nike products as a demonstration of their ideological congruence, which resulted in a 31 percent increase in Nike's sales. That's the power of a shared worldview; it provokes us to move because of who we are. This is referred to as identity-driven effects, where people have the tendency to pay more attention to stimuli that relate to who they are. When a stimulus is aligned with who we are and how we see the world, we are more inclined to notice it, prefer it, select the media source that projects it, and adopt the behaviors associated with it. This effect moved consumers to wear their Nike products proudly and generated a $6 billion market increase for the Nike brand.

People who share the same worldview are more inclined to act in concert with other members, not because they "love" the brand or politician but because the brand or politician is an extension of themselves. These brands, leaders, and organizations serve as a receipt of who we are, a badge of identity. We transfer meaning from the cultural world, fashion it into products and political affiliations, and ritualize them into our identity. Brands like Nike act as a totem—a consecrated artifact— among a congregation of people, and the companies, organizations, and leaders that achieve totem status among members of the congregation are the ones that are adopted into their cultural practices. Far too often, we tend to think of branding as an executional activity—logos, colors, monikers—as opposed to an ideological exploration. That's because our view of branding is far too narrow. Brands are signifiers that conjure up thoughts and feelings about a company, product, or entity, and they can unlock opportunities for leaders to catalyze collective behavior when they are ideologically aligned with the collective.

The original meaning of "brand" was to burn or permanently mark, as with a branding iron that farmers would use to identify and distinguish their livestock as a mark of ownership. One of the earlier established brands on record was a pottery company called

Wedgwood that was incorporated in the late 1770s. When merchants would bring their goods to the marketplace for exchange, the founder, Josiah Wedgwood, needed a way to distinguish his wares from those of others with similar offerings. So Wedgwood affixed the name of the company to the products to make them identifiable and, thus, distinguishable from other merchants' goods. Brand, in this case, was used as a "legal mark" so that people would know what goods legally belonged to what company.

As people continued to buy from companies that bore a particular legal mark, over time, trust began to develop. Consequently, brand evolved from being a "legal mark" to a being a "trust mark." It's like that saying, "No one ever got fired for buying IBM." Why is that? Because IBM can be trusted—at least that's how the saying goes—which has certainly benefited its business over the years. Trust is key. And where there is trust, love is right around the corner. This was the next evolution of brand, from "trust mark" to "love mark," where people developed deep feelings and relationships with brands, which often led to the irrational consumption of branded products. People continued to buy from these companies because they loved them, which was the apex for marketers who brought their branded products to market.

While love can certainly compel people to act, identity has a far greater draw, and today's most powerful and sought-after brands benefit from identity-driven effects. These brands have evolved from "love marks" to "identity marks" that people use to communicate to the world who they are and to what congregation they subscribe. As we saw with Colin Kaepernick and Nike, even when a beloved brand finds itself out of sync with people's identity (due to belief and ideological incongruence), people won't consume. But when their identities are aligned and their worldview is congruent with the brand, people are much more likely to move. This is not because of the functionality of the branded product per se. Rather, it's because of what the brand says about us.

This phenomenon is described in sociology as role theory, a concept that argues that our everyday activities are merely roles that we act out as characters in the social world. As William Shakespeare penned in his play *As You Like It*, "All the world's a stage, and all the men and women merely players; they have their exits and their entrances." Indeed, we are all social actors who have selected characters to play based on the identity projects we've chosen to present. If you self-identify as a skater, then you likely behave in a certain manner, dress the part in the appropriate costumery, and speak from the script that is expected of skaters—by skaters—to signal that you're "one of us." These are, after all, the social facts that constitute what it means to be a member of the collectives to which we subscribe.

As social actors within these collectives, we curate our presentation of self to control and manage our public image, and we act based on how we see ourselves and how we want to be seen by others. Suffice it to say, we adopt the costumes that go with the role we choose to play in the same way that doctors wear white coats and construction workers wear Carhartt. The brands with which we adorn ourselves, the universities we attend, the companies where we seek employment, and the organizations we join all act as badges of identity to outfit our social character. Consequently, identity influences what we buy, where we go, how we show up in the world, and with whom we choose to congregate. Take a moment to consider what the brands you own say about you. Perhaps they are subtle signals of association that use coded language to communicate identity, like my sweatshirt that simply says "1914," the founding date of the fraternity of which I am a member, Phi Beta Sigma. This relationship is likely unknown to most people I pass on the street, but there are those who do know—particularly other members. Or maybe it's more overt, like my wife's "I'm with her" T-shirt that unambiguously signals her support of Hillary Clinton's 2016 presidential run. Regardless of how unassuming the signal may be, these brands communicate who we are based on the characters we choose to play as actors in society.

## CONGRUENCE AND INFLUENCE

Our beliefs and ideologies demarcate who we are, and we choose our tribes accordingly. What makes tribes so special is not merely the fact that, as social animals, people have a proclivity to be connected but also that the connections that bring us together have an influence on how we collectively behave. We act one way with our friends from work and another way with our friends from back home. With our buddies from college, we might curse like a sailor, but in front of our parents, we're more inclined to abstain from profanity. Why? Because we adapt to what is deemed acceptable behavior for "people like us." Therefore, we act according to what is "normal" for the tribe based upon the social facts that we have collectively established. This influence isn't always overt, but its impact is substantial. We talk a certain way because of our tribal affiliation. We act a certain way. We dress a certain way. And our opinions and beliefs are shaped to reflect what is aligned with the ideology and cultural operating system of the network.

This dynamic is present in every tribe to which we belong. Take my family, for instance. I am Marcus Collins, and I belong to the *Collins family* tribe. We believe that family and church come first, so every Sunday morning, I can be found in the church sanctuary. If I wasn't, I could expect a passive-aggressive call from my mother on Sunday afternoon asking, "How was your morning, Marcus?" This is a social consequence of behaving in a manner that is out of step with the cultural norms of the tribe. I must note that I signed no contract or stone tablet to commit to going to church on Sundays. That would be ridiculous considering our societal standards in the United States of America— the ideological construct that makes up the cultural characteristics of the country. However, I attend church every Sunday morning, not because I have to but rather because I believe that this is what people like me do. This is what Collinses do, and since I self-identify as such, this is what I do.

That said, I have cousins who are Collinses, but they don't go to church religiously like the rest of us. While they are still a part of the family, they don't entirely feel like "one of us." Likewise, I'm sure they probably feel like an appendage to the tribe as opposed to a greater part of its body. They come to special events, like graduations, and visit over the holidays. But the familial bonds that bind us are relegated to ceremony and nostalgia. I don't think we love each other any less, but we certainly don't see the world similarly, and therefore, we don't behave similarly.

As a professor and two-time graduate of the University of Michigan, I also self-identify as a member of the Michigan Wolverine congregation—particularly of the engineering and business school tribes, seeing as those were the programs in which I earned my bachelor's and master's degrees, respectively. As a congregation, we tend to believe that Michigan is the best school ever. I suppose that's debatable, but this is a long-held belief. Indeed, we are a proud bunch. Whether this belief is objectively true is one thing, but there is a truth that remains unarguable, and that is the deep-seated loathing for Ohio State University among the Michigan Wolverine congregation. It's more than just a rivalry. The Michigan Wolverine congregation carries bad blood for the entire state of Ohio simply because it houses OSU in its capital, Columbus. However, the origins of this feud, which dates back almost two hundred years, were inverse. When the state of Michigan was preparing to enter the union of the United States of America in 1835, it campaigned for the inclusion of the Toledo strip, a land mass that bordered it and its neighbor, Ohio. As history tells the story, this move was fought by the state of Ohio, and a deal was made in which Ohio would get Toledo and Michigan would get the Upper Peninsula of the state (affectionately known as the "U.P."), which was at that time largely unsettled. Once the University of Michigan football team faced off against Ohio State University in 1897, the inherent tension in the states' histories played out on the field. And to this day, Michigan Wolverines can't stand OSU Buckeyes, and as I understand it, the feeling is mutual.

This is not hyperbole, by the way. Before I entered college at the University of Michigan, I was completely indifferent about Ohio State. But once I was admitted, I, too, adopted disdain for the school. There was no box for me to check to agree that I would hate Ohio State when I signed my acceptance letter from Michigan. I didn't pledge my allegiance to the feud between these two rival schools when I matriculated, but I most certainly did—figuratively, that is—once I adopted the identity of a Michigan student. It felt both cognitively easy and fitting. I was a Michigan Wolverine, and this was what people like me did. It was the implied expectation, and, as such, I accepted it. Oddly enough, those feelings of contempt for Ohio State changed when my identity changed from "Michigan student" to "Michigan professor."

To illustrate this association, I do an exercise with my students (both those in degree programs and executives) in which I introduce the tribes of which I am a member and then ask the students to describe their own tribes by identifying (1) the name of a tribe, (2) a shared belief, (3) an unwritten rule of the group, and (4) a common phrase that might be unique to the group. After laying out these instructions, I describe one of my tribes through the same rubric: (1) Collins family, (2) family and church come first, (3) church on Sundays, (4) "Amen!" In my family, we say "amen" as a sign of agreement, as in "Let's get cheeseburgers for dinner tonight!" "Amen." "What do you think about blowing off our plans and just making it a movie night at home?" "Amen." The situation may not be in a religious context at all; it's just how we speak—although the vernacular is cultural and reflective of our religious beliefs.

There's also (1) the tribe of Michigan Wolverines, who (2) think we're the best school ever. Though that may be debatable, we all agree to (3) dislike Ohio State and to say to anyone wearing Michigan apparel outside campus, (4) "Go, Blue!" In fact, I purposefully wear a University of Michigan baseball cap when I travel, whether internationally or domestically, because without fail, someone will see it and say, "Go, Blue!" And in that instance, I immediately feel that I am not alone, as if my tribe is with me even when I'm away. We are social animals, after all, and our tribal affiliations help us connect to people who previously were complete strangers.

After describing my people, I give students some time to identify and describe as many of their tribes as possible using the four-question rubric. Once they've had some time to think this through and commit their people to paper, I then have them partner with each other and share their groups with the objective of pinpointing similarities and differences. After a few minutes of dialogue, I bring the class back together to discuss what they discovered. Every time I do this exercise, no matter where I am in the world, the results are always the same. Some people name their family, their peeps from college, a close group of friends, maybe their coworkers, a sports club they are a part of, a band, or some other special-interest social group. I've heard many of them over the years. No matter what the groups are, they all find that the characteristics are both universal—where many people share similar traits as other people's tribes—and nuanced—where the way things play out within the tribe is very specific. Overwhelmingly, I've found that there is a broad doorway to enter but a narrow path to belong. Belonging requires intimacy and knowing the codes of how broad beliefs are exercised within a particular group. We can all agree that freedom is important, but the meaning of freedom and how it is manifested depends on the social facts of the tribe.

I continue the exercise by asking, "What happens when you break the unwritten rules of the tribe?" The response is always the same: "You get kicked out." Deviance from the social standards of the tribe leads to excommunication from the group. For a group of girlfriends in São Paolo, Brazil, who call themselves "the Wine Club," an unwritten rule was that members did not date each other's ex-boyfriends. For a group of Republicans in South Bend, Indiana, an unwritten rule was that members did not disagree with another Republican in public. For a group of buddies who played intramural soccer in college and played recreationally as adults, an unwritten rule was that members didn't miss a game without forty-eight hours' notice and a good excuse. (By the way, the first intramural sports department in the United States was established on the campuses of the University of Michigan and Ohio State University in 1913. Indeed, the rivalry runs deep.) Failure to abide by these unwritten rules would lead to dismissal from the group, so we abide by the rules. This is the influence of our people. No matter the group (be it the sneakerhead tribe or the tribe of skateboarders), there is a set of cultural characteristics that govern what it means to be a member of the community—a set of shared beliefs, designated artifacts that are full of meaning, behaviors that are normative, and coded language that we use. Therefore, to remain members in good standing of the community, we adhere to these cultural characteristics. These characteristics govern our daily lives as community members of the tribe and help fortify the bonds that connect us to other members. Try this exercise yourself and see what you find when you consider your own tribal affiliations.

I always conclude the in-class exercise by asking a seemingly simple question to which I already know the answer: "Why does it matter if you're kicked out of the group?" You don't need a PhD to figure this one out. The people in our tribes are the most important people in our lives. They help us frame the world we experience, and through these groups, we define who we are in the world. This isn't a matter of social cohesion alone; this is about our identity. To be cut off from these people would equate to social alienation and identity abandonment. So we hold on tightly to these tribes, abiding by the cultural characteristics that govern them. In some cases, we even defend these cultural characteristics when their merit is called into question because to question the legitimacy of the tribe's way of life would be to question our own identity. Therefore, tribes practice and protect their cultural characteristics like religious congregants practice and protect their spiritual affiliation. I am my tribe, and the tribe is me.

Does everyone in the tribe act exactly alike? Of course not. There is always variability when it comes to people. Some people break the rules, while others are stringently committed to them. However, on average, people tend to stay in line with what the tribe deems legitimate because of the social pressures that are put on them to be "normal." These pressures are the cultural expectations of the tribe that ensure that people behave and present themselves in a way that the group deems acceptable.

These cultural expectations are the measure of centrality within a group of people. The more aligned with the cultural characteristics of the tribe we are, the more "normal" we are. As members of the tribe, our aim is to stay in good standing with the tribe, so we fall in line and follow the rules. We act in lockstep with the culture of the tribe. Of course, there are always social actors who exist in the tribe but do their own thing. They are a part of the population but deviate from the cultural characteristics of the collective. This is where subculture happens—a culture within a culture. People on the fringes of society, who subscribe to some cultural characteristics of the group but not all, like most "normal" folks, tend to create their own subculture that best identifies who they are and how they see the world. This has often been referred to as counterculture, like beatniks, hippies, and hipsters. These social groups live inside the greater population until the subculture becomes the new norm, the dominant culture of the greater tribe, and influences new beliefs, artifacts, behaviors, and the language of the group.

This identity congruence between our tribes and ourselves runs so deep that it subconsciously informs our day-to-day behavior without our knowledge. Each day, we make a host of decisions in the misconception that they are of our own volition when, in reality, they are largely by-products of a mental framework that is reflective of our tribe's cultural characteristics. The framework is simple: I am a member of [name of tribe]; we believe [shared belief of the tribe]; therefore, I [behavioral norm]. I am a Collins; we believe family and church come first; therefore, every Sunday morning, I'm in the church sanctuary. We all go through this framework hundreds of times a day to decide how to show up in the social world. Tribal members act in concert on the strength of one simple question: "Do people like me do something like this?" If the answer is yes, they do it. And if the answer is no, then they don't. It's as simple as that. We may not even be aware that we're working through this framework, but make no mistake, it is indeed at work within the mind of every single one of us—for all our many tribal affiliations. In philosophy, there is the famous statement "I think, therefore I am"—translated from the original Latin text, "Cogito, ergo sum." However, with regard to tribes and congregations, it's more like "I am, therefore I do." I am a Collins; therefore, I go to church on Sunday mornings. And so is the case for all of us, and all of the tribes with which our beliefs and ideologies are aligned and on which our identities are projected.

This creates a massive opportunity for marketers, entrepreneurs, leaders, or managers who seek to catalyze collective behavior among a population. People move in concert with their tribes, and their tribes adopt cultural characteristics that are aligned with the worldview of the collective. Therefore, when the beliefs and ideologies of a brand, institution, or movement are congruent with those of a tribe (or an aggregate of tribes—a congregation), members of the tribe are more inclined to adopt them. They are more likely to move than anyone else. So take a moment and ask yourself what your organization believes. What are the ideologies that frame the way your brand sees the world, and what are the cultural characteristics associated with that perspective? When the beliefs of the brand align with the beliefs of the tribe, members of the tribe will use the brand to communicate their identity to the world, where the brand is no longer merely a mark of ownership but a mark of identity.

## DO YOU BELIEVE?

I graduated from business school at the height of the 2008 financial collapse. It was tragic. I was $116,000 in student loan debt, with no job and no leads. This is the worst nightmare for an MBA student. I worked at Apple during my last year of the MBA program, but organizational shifts within the department where I sat ended my tenure by the end of the school year. So after graduation, I packed two suitcases and moved to New York to try my luck on the East Coast. Fortunately, I'd saved quite a bit of my Apple salary, which helped cushion the blow of the NYC cost of living. But, as anyone who has ever lived in New York can attest, money doesn't last long in the city.

After three months in NYC and countless disappointments, I was still jobless and at the end of my rope until an email introduction from my wife's cousin Lauren landed my résumé in the inbox of Mathew Knowles, the father of Beyoncé Knowles. Mathew was the business mastermind beyond the meteoric rise of Destiny's Child and CEO of the group's management company and record label, Music World Entertainment. Mathew and I met twice in Houston, where the company was based, before he offered me the job of running digital strategy for the company and all its artists—including its breakout megasuperstar, Beyoncé. I was over the moon.

Beyoncé had just released her third studio album, *I Am . . . Sasha Fierce*, the year prior to my starting in 2009. Her single "Halo" was just catching fire while she was still riding the success of her runaway hit "Single Ladies (Put a Ring on It)." Not only did "Single Ladies" win three Grammy awards, including Song of the Year, but it was also accompanied by a critically acclaimed music video that was just as attention grabbing as the song itself. The song featured a catchphrase, "put a ring on it," that became the mantra for unmarried women in long-term relationships. The video included a hand gesture that went with the catchphrase and made the song a global cultural phenomenon. Beyoncé was unquestionably one of the biggest artists in music at the time, even without the knowledge that she would soon become one of the biggest global figures on the planet. It was the perfect time to be in the Beyoncé business—not that there's ever a bad time to be in the business of Queen Bey—and I had a front-row ticket to the show and the opportunity to contribute to her queendom.

During my tenure with Music World Entertainment, running digital strategy for Beyoncé, I helped launch her first perfume, Heat, which sold out at Macy's on the first day it was made available; promoted her directorial debut music video for her single "Why Don't You Love Me"; and supported the release of her live concert films, among other projects and product offerings. But the most rewarding experience for me working with Beyoncé had little to do with these successes and everything to do with a failure that would become one of the greatest lessons of my career at the time: the Beyontourage.

"The Beyontourage" was a term we used to identify Beyoncé's most dedicated fans. It combined her nickname, "Bey" (pronounced "bee") with the word "entourage," which was used in reference to a celebrity's team of assistants, bodyguards, friends, and the like. This was at the height of HBO's show *Entourage*, so at the time, the Beyontourage seemed rather clever. Naming conventions aside, our error wasn't what we called these fans so much as the perspective from which we saw them. The Beyontourage, in our minds at least, was our take on the digital fan club. If you're reading this, I imagine that at one time, you were likely a part of a fan club—if not officially, then certainly in your heart. (Mine was Boyz II Men. I was obsessed.) Fan clubs were the primary way by which fans and artists interacted beyond the music itself. Fans would write letters to their favorite artists (most of which would go unanswered) and profess their undying love for the artists and appreciation of their work. These fans would bare their souls in prose, describing how they saw themselves in the artist's music or how a particular song helped them get over a rough patch in their lives. Before the Internet, these exchanges were mostly handwritten and terribly one-sided. (I'm still waiting on my reply from Boyz II Men some twenty-seven years later. I'm just saying.)

The Internet created more opportunity for fans to hear from artists directly and interact with each other—conversing about their shared love for their favorite artist and their experiences with the artist's music, concerts, and the like. The digital world made fan clubs less transactional and more meaningful for fans as well as artists. The conversations that took place within these online fan clubs provided rich information about what fans liked and disliked about the artist and, in many ways, acted as a street team that would help promote new music and appearances. The Beyontourage was our attempt to codify Beyoncé's online fan club, which would center around the awesomeness that was (and is) Beyoncé. But what we got was so much more.

While we were busy trying to build an online fan club, Beyoncé's fans were building a tribal network all on their own. We called her fans the Beyontourage. They called their community "the Beyhive." We created an online group around Beyoncé. They created a community around each other. While we focused on the fandom that centered on Beyoncé's music and celebrity, they constructed a culture that was aligned with Beyoncé's beliefs and ideologies because they—her fans—subscribed to the same beliefs as Beyoncé: women's empowerment.

They had their own norms: one "bey" should never turn on another, beys should defend each other, and beys should always be good to each other. They established their own language, like "pollen," which referred to any news about Beyoncé. They behaved in concert, and they didn't tolerate any disrespect of their queen. If ever a celebrity or public figure uttered any unsavory words about Beyoncé, the Beyhive would swarm, i.e., attack. Once the country/rock singer Kid Rock said in a *Rolling Stone* interview that Beyoncé "doesn't really f%&king do much for me," and the Beyhive unleashed its wrath. Thousands of beys left a litany of negative comments about Kid Rock across the Internet and populated his social networking channels with their signature bee emoji. Overwhelmed, Kid Rock responded on Instagram with an image of a Raid can, acknowledging who was responsible for the attack. Unsurprisingly, the Beyhive did not take kindly to this gesture and, therefore, continued its swarm. Its attack continued for three years after the initial interview.

Once the team took notice of the Beyhive, the strategy for Beyoncé's fan club completely changed. It was no longer about sustaining fandom around Beyoncé, the artist; it was now about facilitating a community of people around a shared worldview—the beliefs and ideologies that had always been present in her music, from "Independent Ladies" to "Survivor" and from "Single Ladies (Put a Ring on It)" to "Who Runs The World (Girls!)." This was what people gravitated to and shared on a cultural level, beyond the music. Beyoncé's music was simply the cultural product that people used to communicate their shared worldview and engage in social discourse. Doing so helped them project their identity and demarcate where they fit in the world. It is through this lens of cultural identity that we establish connections within the tribal networks that we choose to join and, subsequently, act in concert with.

The Beyhive was much more than we could ever have conceived of in a fan club because we had the wrong perspective. We were looking for fans when we should have been looking for believers. Watching this all go down completely challenged the way I thought about getting people to move. Instead of trying to convince the nonbelievers, what if we activated the collective of the willing—those who already believed?

Marketers go after potential customers. Politicians go after potential voters. Fundraisers go after potential donors. But the rise of the Beyhive (and the subsequent failure of the Beyontourage) taught me that there are people out there who see the world the way you do. They hold a similar set of beliefs and ideologies in their minds that inform how they behave. Therefore, based on what we now know about tribal identity and worldview congruence, instead of trying to create a community around you, perhaps you'd be better off trying to find the people who already believe what you believe and facilitating the network that connects them.

In 2018, the Grace Cathedral in San Francisco, California, welcomed parishioners to worship in what they called the Beyoncé Mass, a service that explored issues of race and gender through a religious frame. The service didn't position Beyoncé as the deity to be worshiped. No, this was still very much an Episcopal church. However, it was the beliefs and ideologies shared between the church, Beyoncé, and the service attendees around women's empowerment that inspired over nine hundred people to attend service on a day when normally fifty people would have shown up for church. If you want to inspire people to move, your best chance is to find your congregation—the aggregate tribes of people who see the world the way you do. These people are more inclined to act in concert and to do so in a religious fashion because of who they are. They move as an expression of their identity and cultural subscriptions, not because of the value propositions of your offering, like the music is better, the car goes faster, or the battery lasts longer. They are believers, and they will do as other believers do. As social animals, this is how we're wired, and this is the power of culture within a tribe. It influences us to move in lockstep with other members of the tribe as an act of social solidarity and belonging. To achieve this level of influence, we must first decide what we believe and then identify the tribe(s) of people who see the world similarly.

You know what you believe. You know the set of ideologies and beliefs that you hold. Who else out there holds the same beliefs and shares the same ideological worldview? In marketing, we call this segmentation and targeting. Segmentation is the act of taking a heterogeneous group of people, where everyone is different, and putting them in homogeneous-like clusters, where everyone is more alike than they are different. When we segment a population of people, we divide them into groups based on different preferences and attributes so that we can serve them with the best products and marketing messages that will influence them to adopt certain behaviors. That is, after all, the core function of marketing: influencing behavioral adoption. Once the population has been divided into these segments, marketers then select the segments to which they will offer their products. This is the act of targeting. We target (select) a segment (or a number of segments) to pursue that we believe will mostly likely adopt a desired behavior—buy, vote, watch, subscribe, attend, etc. Although our product may potentially be useful to "everyone," we focus our efforts on the people with the highest propensity to move. Considering the influence that culture has on our behavior, due to the social pressures of our tribes and our pursuit of identity congruence, tribes present themselves as the most compelling segment to target.

This perspective calls for a strong consideration if for no other reason than the fact that tribes are real. They're made up of real people, and people use them to communicate who they are and demarcate how they fit in the world. Segments, on the other hand, are not real. They are a construct that marketers create where people are placed into homogeneous-like groups based on a loose proxy that helps us identify who they are and predict what they are likely to do. Segments are clean and neat. But real people are complex and messy. As the astrophysicist Neil deGrasse Tyson once tweeted, "In science, when human behavior enters the equation, things go nonlinear. That's why Physics is easy and Sociology is hard." Real people don't fit into neat little boxes, though we try our best to put them there.

Marketers aren't the only ones guilty of this; we all do it. We put people in boxes to simplify the complexity of the world so that it's easier to make sense of it—not for accuracy but for efficiency. Here's an example. Meet my friend Deborah. Deborah drives a minivan. Does Deborah have kids? Do her kids play a sport? What sport do they play? And where does Deborah live? As you read those questions, you likely drew your answers fairly quickly. You probably thought, Deborah drives a minivan, so she must have kids, who play soccer, and they all live in a cul-de-sac. Sounds about right, right? Well, here's the thing. I gave you one data point about Deborah (she drives a minivan), and you mapped out her entire life. This is what we do—with great cognitive fluidity, I might add. We put people in boxes based on the shortcut characteristics that we assign to people's identity. Meet Mike. Mike has a mohawk. What kind of music does Mike listen to? What kind of clothes does he wear? What kind of vehicle does he drive? What color is Mike's skin? I do this exercise across the globe, and the responses are almost always the same and typically done in unison. Why? Because these are the boxes that we have established for minivan drivers and mohawk wearers. Not because it's accurate but because it's easy.

These boxes are typically formed based on stereotypes that have been constructed and socialized over the years—all women love to shop or all men are dogs. It's easy to see where this goes. These stereotypes are deeply flawed because there is nothing that "all women" do beyond the biological constitution of being a woman. That said, gender is so fluid that even biology has its shortcomings in describing what "all women" do. Nevertheless, there is nothing inherent to being a woman that makes a person predisposed to like shopping. While there are social forces that impose certain gender norms on women, these norms are cultural in nature. That is to say, our behavior isn't dictated by our hardware; it is governed by our software—our cultural characteristics.

Unfortunately, this delineation is often lost on marketers, who rely on demographics to describe people based on their age, race, gender, household income, geography, and education. Demographics provide discrete boxes to put people into and help us make the world neat. But here's the thing: demographics, while factual, don't accurately describe who people are. Take my demographics, for example. I am African American. At the time of writing this book, I'm forty-three years old. I'm from Detroit, Michigan—born and raised—and I went to public schools my entire life. If a marketer saw this description of me—my age, race, and geography—as their target of interest, they would likely put me in a box based on the stereotypes they have constructed in their minds about what forty-something-year-old Black men who live in Detroit do. It's the same as we do for Deborah, who drives a mini-van, and Mike with the mohawk. Deborah must have kids. She must live in a suburb. Her kids must play soccer. All women love to shop. And all Black people do [fill in the blank: something racist].

As flawed as this may be, these are the cognitive shortcuts that marketers and nonmarketers alike fall victim to on a daily basis. While, yes, I am forty-three years old, I am Black, I am from Detroit, and I did attend public schools my entire life, none of this gets at the fact that I grew up playing jazz as a kid or that I swam competitively from age six through high school (my brother, Eugene, swam through college). I wrote love songs for a living in my twenties and grew up loving the Monkees just as much as I loved A Tribe Called Quest. These experiences help shape how I see the world, which ultimately informs how I behave in the world. Demographics never get close enough to capture the nuances that make me who I truly am. However, my tribes do, which makes tribes a better means of segmenting the market than demographics. Plus, people self-identify by their tribes and adhere to the cultural characteristics of the tribes, and of the congregation more broadly. Therefore, our behaviors are much more likely to be predictive of the behaviors of people like us than the fictional boxes that marketers construct.

Through this lens, segmentation and targeting become very clear. We divide the market into two segments: those who believe and those who do not. We then target the believers, who are more inclined to move, and move on past the nonbelievers. And, oh, by the way, there are probably more believers out there than you are aware of. Remember, multiple tribes combine to create congregations. As we saw earlier with Patagonia and the congregation of people who believe in climbing clean, there are people in the going-green tribe, a collective of individuals who try to live a more environmentally friendly and ecological lifestyle, who also likely believe in the notion of climbing clean. Likewise, there are people who self-identify as members of the tribe that is committed to reversing climate change who are also believers. These are two different tribes that share the same worldview as the brand. Together with other similarly minded tribes, they make up a congregation—a collection of individuals with shared beliefs and ideologies that inform how they show up in the world and how they project their identity.

Even religious congregations are made up of many tribes, typically familial tribes. There are the Collinses, the Hentons, the Davises, the Sims, the Finleys, the Thomases, the Ewings, and others who, together, make up the congregation, just as the Romans, Corinthians, Ephesians, and Philippians were all individual tribes that made up the congregation of Christianity. These tribes make up a congregation because they share the same worldview. The House of Israel was made up of twelve tribes, each with its own nuanced program for living—for instance, members of the Tribe of Levi were priests, and members of the Tribe of Judah were kings—but they all shared common beliefs and ideologies. There are a number of tribes that believe what Beyoncé believes and a number of tribes that believe what Patagonia believes, just as there are tribes that share the same worldview as Nike and Kaepernick. The collections of these tribes make up the respective congregations for these brands. They are the tribes of people who see the world the way we do and act in concert religiously, which makes them, hands down, the most likely to move when activated. So if you want to get people to move, you should start by finding your congregation.

## NETWORKED TRIBES

The NFL's Super Bowl is one of the biggest media moments in the country. Roughly one-third of the US population tunes in to see the best two teams of the two conferences that make up the NFL (the American Football Conference and the National Football Conference) battle it out for the championship title. More than just a football game, the Super Bowl has become one of the nation's cultural moments and brings with it a host of rituals and ceremony that its viewers religiously undergo year after year—from the assembly of people to the consumption of chicken wings and, of course, the viewing of commercials. Advertising has become such an important part of the Super Bowl experience that news coverage of the game following the championship is often overshadowed by which brand had the best commercial. As such, advertisers invest a small fortune to reach this captivated audience during the big game. In 2022, the average cost to air a thirty-second commercial during the broadcast of the Super Bowl was $5.6 million. That's often more than many companies' entire marketing communications budget for the year, yet the who's who of brands shows up to the game with their biggest, most star-studded ads because we (the people) tune in—sometimes not even to watch the game (like my wife) but to watch (and talk about) the ads.

Though Facebook (now called Meta), the social networking platform juggernaut with over 2.5 billion users, spent $382 million on ads in 2018, the company was absent from the Super Bowl advertising spectacle until the 2020 game, when Facebook aired its very first Super Bowl ad. The sixty-second ($11.2 million!) advertisement spotlighted its Facebook Groups feature, which allows people to connect with other people who share common interests. Unlike the traditional Facebook functionality, Groups allows users to build communities with people they likely do not know or have never met. The commercial opens to the screeching tires of a green van, reminiscent of the '80s. Twisted Sister's "I Want to Rock" is playing in the background at the onset of the ad, so when the back door of the van opens, and out steps a lanky, long-haired young man with a few of his pals, it's easy to assume that they are a rock band. However, we soon find that that is a red herring. The camera then cuts to the same guy and his pals lined up along the shore of a lake, skipping rocks across the water. We then see the group posed with the words "Table Rock Lake Facebook Group" on the screen. The camera then cuts to a new group of people mixing cocktails (on the rocks) with the words "Craft Cocktail Club Facebook Group" across the screen. Again, the camera cuts to a new group of people rock climbing and reveals that this group is the "Moab Rock Climbers Facebook Group." The commercial continues with the "Starting Strongman Facebook Group," who are seen lifting boulders as a workout, the "From the Front Porch Facebook Group," who are sitting together in rocking chairs, the "Rock Buggies Facebook Group," the "Amateur Experimental Rocketry Facebook Group," the "Alcatraz Triathletes Facebook Group," and quick shots of many other "rock"-related Facebook Groups. The ad ends on the steps of the Philadelphia Art Museum—made famous by the iconic scene from the movie *Rocky*—with, fittingly, the "Rocky Balboa Going the Distance Facebook Group" and a misdirect between Chris Rock and the star of the *Rocky* films, Sylvester Stallone.

The commercial, which was created by Wieden+Kennedy, does more than merely communicate the Facebook Groups feature. It also serves to remind us that we're all connected to other people through our interests and affiliations. These interests are in no way generic. They are highly nuanced and meaningful. They are constituted by a set of beliefs and ideologies that we hold dear, and they are governed by cultural characteristics that inform how we show up in the world. Though Facebook calls them Groups, we can refer to them by a more fitting name: *tribes*. And, of course, these tribes are made available to us on a social networking platform like Facebook because the individuals in our tribes are all connected through network structures.

If you were to put our tribes under a hypothetical microscope, you would see a series of ties, invisible to the naked eye, that connect us to our people like the inner workings of a spiderweb. Each tie connects one person to another, and collectively, the series of ties connects us all to each other. Though we tend to refer to these ties through the nature of our relationships ("boyfriend/girlfriend," "best friend," "teammate," "coworker," or "mentor"), they are—in essence—the covalent bonds that make up the network that connects the tribe.

Together, these ties constitute the network connections of the tribe—a tribal network, as it were—with each connection linking one person to another, enabling the exchange of information, experiences, and resources from person to person throughout the entire tribe. These exchanges are the way in which beliefs and ideologies are socialized, artifacts are co-opted, behaviors are normalized, and new language is created to make up the cultural characteristics of the tribe. This doesn't happen serendipitously. Rather, it occurs structurally through the networked social ties that bind members of the tribe together. So if we want to catalyze collective behavior, our consideration must extend from "tribes" as we know them to "tribal networks."

Our tribes are networked, which enables the exchanges that inform social intelligence and foster community. Networks provide a useful handle to view our social groups because, like the people in our lives, networks are all around us. Our waterways are networked, with streams and rivers feeding into oceans, connecting one body of water to another within the larger ecosystem. Our brains are networked to maximize neural communications and resource exchanges. This is likely why our power grids are designed as networks to maximize the greater system. Our highways are networked. Our airports are networked. Our cell-phone towers are networked. Likewise, so are our social groups: our tribes.

The study of social networks dates back to the late 1800s with precursor ideas around social groups and their dynamics. One of the early pioneers of social network exploration was a German sociologist named Georg Simmel who explored the relationship between the dynamics of social groups and their network structures. With increasing research through the turn of the century, more was revealed about the relationship between network structures and how objects (information, experiences, and cultural characteristics) flow across the ties that connect members of the tribe. One idea that was brought forward came from a legendary leader in broadcast radio and television, David Sarnoff. Sarnoff led the Radio Corporation of America (RCA) for over fifty years, starting shortly after its founding in 1919. RCA would later diversify into music, movies, and hardware, but during Sarnoff's tenure, it grew to be one of the largest broadcast networks in the world. (In the decades to follow, RCA would go on to create NBC at 30 Rockefeller Plaza, which created such programming as *Saturday Night Live, Seinfeld, The Office, Friends, The Fresh Prince of Bel-Air, The Golden Girls, Cheers, Law & Order, 30 Rock*, and countless others.) As Sarnoff assessed the growth of RCA, he surmised that the value of the network was directly proportional to the size of the network. That is to say, the more people who tuned in to his shows, the more valuable RCA would become. What Sarnoff described was the structure of a broadcast network, where many nodes connect to one node. In this case, the many nodes were viewers and the singular node was RCA. The more people connected to RCA via its programming across the radio waves and televisions airwaves, the more valuable RCA's network would be. This would go on to be referred to as Sarnoff's law—the value of a network is directly proportional to the number of nodes connected to a central node.

Just as Sarnoff's tenure at RCA was winding down, a Harvard PhD student in computer science was working on hardware that would link minicomputers together to form a local network. With his partner, David Boggs, he invented the Ethernet, the local area network structure that we currently use to connect our offices, college campuses, and even homes through hardwired ports. That gentleman's name is Robert Metcalfe, the engineer and entrepreneur who helped lay the groundwork for the Internet as we know it today. Metcalfe's work on local area networks revealed that the value of a network increases when the network is decentralized from a focal node. Unlike Sarnoff's broadcast network, where many nodes are connected to one, in a Metcalfe configuration where many nodes can connect to each other, the value of the network is greater because of the increased utility that is created with each exchange. This would go on to be referred to as Metcalfe's law, where the value of a decentralized network is a by-product of the number of nodes and their connections within the network.

Metcalfe's law was a significant step forward in our understanding of network structures and their value. However, another computer scientist, this time from MIT, offered a new perspective that made a profound contribution to computer networks and communications networks. His name is David Reed, and he argued that in Sarnoff's broadcast network, content was the exchange for which audiences gave their attention and were thereby connected. RCA produced and aired television programs in direct competition with other broadcasters for the eyes and ears of the viewing public—the nodes of the network. The more people viewed, the more valuable the network became, which made content (in this case, television programs) the most important object to flow across the network ties that connected viewers to RCA. In a decentralized Metcalfe network, Reed explained, transaction took center stage. The ability to exchange with other people through the Internet enabled the flow of content (YouTube), information (blogs), communications (Twitter), money (PayPal), and services (Fiverr). However, in a decentralized network, where people can connect with other people who share the same beliefs and see the world similarly, the central role of the network is the construction and exchange of cultural characteristics that flow across the network ties that bind the nodes. Consequently, a Reed network is quantitatively and qualitatively more valuable.

The Harvard marketing professor Jill Avery attested that our identities, the narratives we construct and negotiate with each other that describe who we are in the world and how we show up in the world, are created and confirmed through our social interactions. And these interactions are governed by the cultural characteristics of the collective. This phenomenon is quite valuable for those who aim to get people to take action—not "marketing segments" but real people who subscribe to a particular set of beliefs and ideologies. We are looking for congregations of people, not a collection of labels.

When I teach this idea of congregations and networked tribes to senior leaders, I am often met with the argument "But wait, we use a lot of data to describe people—who they are and how they behave." In marketing, we refer to these descriptions as personas. They run the gamut from thorough and detailed to general and trite. For instance, a persona might read like so: "Tiffany is a twenty-five-year-old single woman living in Chicago, Illinois. She works at a start-up and binge watches *Married at First Sight* on Netflix while scrolling through TikTok and Instagram after a run and a shower once work is over. On the weekends, she hangs out with friends and checks out the newest restaurants in the city." Sounds awesome, right? Sure! It's descriptive, and you likely have a mental picture of who Tiffany is and a box in which she belongs. However, the challenge in using personas is that they typically describe one prototypical individual in hopes that you can envision who she is and how she sees the world. But we are neither typical nor individual agents in this world. Instead, we live in a complex social system—which I call the network—that is governed by cultural characteristics that influence our day-to-day behavior.

In other cases, when marketers construct personas as a group of people instead of an individual who represents a group, these groups are often referenced by made-up names like Aspirers, Cautious Traditionals, Comfortable Progressives, and Discriminating Pragmatics. (For the record, these are all real naming conventions that a previous client of mine once used to identify segments.) Imagine that for a moment: a room full of marketers saying, "We're targeting Cautious Traditionals." Huh? I don't even know what a "Discriminating Pragmatic" is. But one thing is for sure—no one looks in the mirror and says to him- or herself, "I'm a Comfortable Progressive." Because it's not a real thing. No one self-identifies by these naming conventions. And since we don't identify as such, there are no beliefs, artifacts, behaviors, or language that are normative for these people. Instead, we look in the mirror and say, "I'm a Collins, and this is what I believe and how I behave." Some people are sneakerheads, some are vegans, some are hackers, some are designers, and some are marathon runners. These groups, and many more like them, are all based on identity congruence, and the people who self-identify with them adhere to the social facts that govern what it means to be a member of the tribe.

Our social groups are extremely important to us for this very reason. They help us self-identify, make meaning of the world, and decide how to behave in the world. The more we value the group, the more likely we are to be influenced by it, even if other members don't share the same demographic makeup. There are plenty of people who support the Black Lives Matter movement who aren't Black; thus, they are a networked tribe because of their ideological congruence.

Just because we put a title on things, it doesn't make them real. We put titles on people and apply characteristics to them based on our biases, not their identity. Take generationalism, for instance—millennials, gen Z, etc. These, too, are constructs that don't actually describe real people. These generational titles are arbitrarily assigned to a group of people based on their date of birth—a demographic. And we have a mental picture of who these people are. Millennials are said to be self-entitled and lazy. They don't want to "put in the work," but they want everything on demand. Sounds about right, right? Countless articles, blog posts, and think pieces have accused millennials of killing everything that's good in the world. According to the headlines, millennials are responsible for ruining brunch. They have killed hotel loyalty programs and somehow single-handedly destroyed wine corks—whatever that means. But there are eighty million millennials in the United States. How can we say that they are all the same just because they were born in a certain time span? People aren't governed by their demography; they are governed by their cultural subscriptions, which are reflected in their tribal memberships. This is about disposition, not demography. No wonder so many people don't take action when marketers try to get them to move. The marketers are targeting labels, not real people.

But tribes are real, and their members act together to promote social solidarity among themselves, which is superpowerful for anyone who aims to excite people to take action. For managers, leaders, and activists who aspire to do so, finding your congregation—the different tribes of people who see the world the way you do—creates the perfect target for your pursuits.

## FROM KNOW-WHY TO KNOW-HOW

Culture is a realized meaning-making system. It is anchored in our identity and shaped by our worldview, which subsequently influences what we do and how we consume. To leverage the power of culture in an effort to sell a brand, promote a candidate, or inspire people to join a cause, you must first look inward and ask yourself, "What does my brand believe?" "How does my candidate see the world?" "What's the ideology of our cause?" This is where we want to start—identifying the brand's beliefs.

The brand belief should be the articulation of something substantive as opposed to vain platitudes and empty statements like, "We believe in integrity." While that may indeed be true, what you want to unearth is "why does integrity matter to the brand?" What is the conviction that drives you and your company to have integrity? As we saw earlier in the chapter, Patagonia believes in "climbing clean" and that informs everything the brand does—from the products it makes to how it communicates its products. Patagonia's conviction to "climbing clean" is so strong that instead of taking the $3 billion company public or selling it off to the highest bidder, Yvon Chouinard and his family recently decided to give it away. In a September 2022 statement, Chouinard announced that he and his family were transferring ownership of the company to a trust and a nonprofit organization that will fund people who are actively working to save the planet. Now, that's conviction!

Identifying the belief system in this way is critical because it's your belief system that will inform whom you'll target—the people who are most likely to move because they share the same worldview. If your brand believes that life is an adventure and should be lived as such, then you can imagine the kinds of people you'd target: adventure seekers, X-Gamers, or adrenaline junkies. These are the people who see the world similarly to the brand, and they'll be more inclined to consume than most people would be, not (just) because of *what* the product is but also because of *who* these people are. As you identify your brand's belief, make a list of all the different communities that probably share the same belief system. Resist the urge to rely on demographics. Instead, think about real collectives that already exist. Together, these networked tribes will make up your congregation. And once you've found your congregation, it's time to preach the gospel.

## CHAPTER 3

# PREACHING THE GOSPEL

B LACK FRIDAY IS THE SINGLE MOST IMPORTANT DAY OF the year for retailers in the United States. In fact, the name itself is attributed to the mass consumption that takes place the day after Thanksgiving, when many retailers either make or break their revenue goals for the entire year. And Black Friday has become a cultural event. In twenty-one states across the country, the day after Thanksgiving is even observed as a holiday, where government employees are given the day off. If Thanksgiving is the day that we reflect on all that we have, then Black Friday is the day that we realize we don't have enough. And who can blame us? The sales that go on during Black Friday are unbelievable. Who could say no to a twenty-dollar forty-inch flat-screen television? Or half off everything in the store? I certainly couldn't. I don't have that kind of willpower. And the big-box retailers, like Walmart and Target, know this all too well. It has become a dance between retailers and consumers. People line up at the door, and the retailers deliver the show—slashed prices on the year's most coveted items that are just too good to pass up.

This ritual has become so pervasive that some Black Friday sales have crept into Thanksgiving Day, with stores opening as early as 6 p.m. with "door-buster" sales. You'd better carve up that turkey early and get these deals before they're gone!

This has become an arms race that retailers can't help but play, each outdoing and one-upping the other, because to not participate would mean risking potential purgatory "in the red." So the sales among retailers become more and more outrageous just to compete. That was the case for the Washington-state-based outdoor retailer REI until the company had a gut-check moment during a leadership retreat in 2015 that compelled it to reexamine itself.

REI (Recreational Equipment Inc.) sells precisely what you would expect from an outdoor recreation shop: water-resistant windbreakers, bikes, hiking shoes, tents, and the like. There's nothing unique about the products that the retailer offers. However, the brand is an entirely different story. Structured as a co-op, where consumers pay a lifetime membership and purchase threshold to own a piece of the company, REI believes that "a life outdoors is a life well spent." But if this is what the brand truly believes, the leadership had to question its participation in the Black Friday ritual. If REI believes that "a life outdoors is a life well spent," then why would its stores be open when so many people in the country have the day off? Of course, conventional wisdom would say, "Well, this is the day that we go from 'red' to 'black.' That's why!" And this is when a cultural thriller would retort, "A true act of conviction is when one stands on their beliefs despite the repercussions." And that was exactly what REI did. On Black Friday in 2015, REI closed the doors to all 142 of its stores, suspended online sales, and paid its employees to go out and play because these actions directly aligned with its brand beliefs—even though they meant sacrificing financial gain.

With this bold move, REI invited everyone else who shared its belief to join the brand in "opting outside" instead of crowding into the aisles of retail stores. What happened next was unbelievable. After REI announced its plans to #OptOutside, 170 other businesses and organizations joined the cause and followed suit by also closing their doors. Hundreds of state parks, which are typically closed on Black Friday, opened their gates for free in response to the campaign so people could go out and play. Most impressive of all, 1.4 million people who had previously been indoctrinated in the mass consumption ritual opted outside as well. What's more, REI experienced its highest Black Friday sales ever that weekend thanks to the people who shared the same conviction as the brand—subscribing to its cultural characteristics—and said to themselves, "That's my kind of brand."

What's happening here? Instead of communicating its inventory selection and great customer service, REI decided to communicate its belief to the people who shared its worldview, and this activated people to move—to go outdoors *and* consume. Simply put, REI found its congregation—the collection of networked tribes who subscribe to the same beliefs and ideology as the brand—and preached the gospel to them, which inspired collective behavior.

I've spent my whole life listening to preachers as a member of the Israel of God's Church. I grew up singing in the choir, spending summers at church camp, and going to church conferences across the country throughout the year with my family. I am a "church boy," as they say, and I come from a long line of preachers. My grandfather Bishop Joseph Thomas was a preacher. My uncle Rev. Hurley Collins was a preacher. My cousin Rev. Terrance Collins is a preacher (and my current pastor). So I think it's safe to say that I know a thing or two about preachers. In the religious sense, preachers are proclaimers who are appointed—or ordained—to speak publicly about theological matters and lead discourse regarding social expectations through a spiritual lens. The primary job of a preacher is to serve as a vessel to deliver the word of God and proclaim the gospel—the teachings and life of Jesus Christ—to their congregation as a set of principles and beliefs by which congregants should live. Then, those who subscribe to said beliefs know how to behave as members in good standing of the congregation.

In the colloquial sense, the word "preach" bears a similar connotation; it, too, means to proclaim. While the subject matter may not be spiritual in nature, the proclamation is typically rooted in a set of principles and beliefs that is shared with others. When someone expresses their opinion about a matter, it is not uncommon to hear someone say "preach" in response to signal their ideological agreement. We even use the idiom "preaching to the choir" as a way of denoting agreement with someone's beliefs or ideological stance. This, of course, comes from the religious association of "preach," where the preacher—the deliverer of the proclamation—and the choir—the leaders of collective praise—work in tandem during worship to facilitate spiritual solidarity among the congregation.

Likewise, the word "gospel" is often used in the colloquial sense as a reference to "truth," much like Christians consider the teachings and life of Christ to be "true." Therefore, to preach the gospel is to speak the truth in hopes of inspiring people to move. It's the same in the colloquial sense. Marketers, activists, politicians, and the like who preach their gospel—their ideological truth—can catalyze groups of people to take action when they preach the gospel to the people who see the world similarly: their congregation. Curious to know why preaching the gospel has this effect on us? Well, look no further than the brain and the biology of behavioral adoption.

## THE BIOLOGY OF BEHAVIORAL ADOPTION

If you remember anything from high school biology, it's that the brain is responsible for everything we do. It takes in tons of information from our five senses—seeing, feeling, smelling, hearing, tasting—and synthesizes these data points into "if-then" statements that result in the behavior we perform. Our brains are prediction machines that help us stay alive based on the experiences of our past that stand at the ready in both our long-term and short-term memories. These experiences are retrieved much like a hard drive on a computer recovers a file from its digital storage system for our use. Our brains access experiences from the recesses of our memory so we know what to do and how to respond in a given situation to increase our chances of surviving it. That's the job of the brain—keeping us alive—and it relies on a complex system of circuitry to do just that. However, at a macrolevel, the brain can be compartmentalized into three major systems. The first is the reptilian brain.

According to evolutionary anthropologists, who argue that it took millions of years for "man" to develop into what we know as mankind today, the reptilian brain is the oldest part of the brain. It is associated with primitive bodily functions that we take for granted, like controlling our heart rate, breathing, and blinking. This brain system is also associated with the "fight or flight" response, which is involuntary because we're wired for it.

The second system of the brain is the limbic system. This part of the brain is associated with emotions like love, trust, and connection. Within the limbic system live complex structures like the hippocampus—a structure that plays a major role in learning and the formation of memories—and the amygdala—a structure responsible for the emotional salience of our memories. These two structures work together in the limbic system to associate memories with emotions so that we know how to respond to stimuli in the world. It's no surprise that the amygdala is also connected to our "fight or flight" response based on the emotional experiences that have been logged into our long-term memory. As Jon T. Willie, a neurosurgeon and director of the laboratory for behavioral neuromodulation at Emory University in Atlanta, put it, "If you have an emotional experience, the amygdala seems to tag that memory in such a way so that it is better remembered." This is likely why emotions flood our brains with rich memories when we hear a song that takes us back to a certain place and time when that song was prevalent in our lives. We become overwhelmed with the feelings associated with that emotional tag, which compels us to relive that experience or repel it. That's the limbic system at work.

Not only is the limbic system associated with emotions, but it is also a part of how we make decisions. That is to say, the part of the brain responsible for our feelings is also associated with how we decide what to do. We know this intuitively, but we call it "gut instinct." We feel it in our gut, and then we act accordingly. However, that association has nothing to do with our stomachs and everything to do with the activity that goes on in our limbic system. When it comes to "gut instinct," it's often difficult to put a finger on why we feel the way we do. It just feels like the right thing to do, so we do it; or it feels wrong, and we don't. What's worse is that we typically can't explain it, either. The rationale for these "gut instinct" decisions is hard to put into words. If someone asked me how I knew my wife was the woman I wanted to marry, I wouldn't have a clear answer. I just knew it. I can't put into words why, nor can I identify the exact moment that I knew. I felt it in my gut—the limbic system—and I went for it. This separation between articulation and "gut instinct" is also a factor of biology because language is not associated with the limbic system but rather it is a function of the third system of the brain, the neocortex.

The neocortex is the part of the brain where higher-order cognitive functions, like abstract thought, language, and rationality, are performed. Between the limbic system and the neocortex, we have one system that is associated with emotions and behavior—the limbic system—and another associated with language and rationality. Think of it as Captain Kirk and Mr. Spock from *Star Trek*. The passionate, emotion-led Kirk would say, "Just go for it," while the rational, data-driven Spock would say, "Wait a minute, let's think this through a bit more." While we love to think of ourselves as Spocks (especially in business settings), we are often far from it. We're not rational human beings; we're *rationalizing* human beings. We make most of our decisions based on shortcut heuristics that are informed by the emotional tags we place on our memory associations, which informs how we feel—and, ultimately, what we do.

The truth of the matter is that we know what decisions we're going to make before we make them based on how we feel. After that, we cherry-pick the data to support our feelings. In psychology, this is called the Texas sharpshooter fallacy, a cognitive bias in which we ignore the information that differs from our perspective and choose the data that supports it. This bias is based on the metaphor of a gunman who shoots at a wall and then draws the target around the bullet holes afterward—as is the case of our "rationality," or lack thereof. Our behaviors are biologically connected to our feelings—our limbic system. So if we want to get people to move, our best chance to do so is to appeal to the limbic system by activating the emotional side of the brain that informs behavior.

But how do we appeal to the limbic system? How do leaders pull at the emotional cords of the brain that catalyze behavior? How do marketers make connections that get people to move? We do so by speaking directly to the thing that makes us who we are: our identity—the anchor of culture—and our subsequent beliefs—the first system of our cultural subscriptions. When we communicate our beliefs to the people who hold the same ideological points of view, it resonates on a deeply emotional level that transcends rationality and inspires people to take action. Why? Because "people like me do something like this." That's the key. Preach the gospel to your congregation and they will move because of who they are and how they see the world. And they'll do so in an effort to achieve identity congruence and promote social solidary. That may seem a bit abstract, so let's explore this with more pragmatic precision.

The author and educator C. C. Chapman put it simply: when we're trying to make emotional connections, our communications should "start with the soul and end with the sale." We begin with the emotional appeal, which is informed by how we see the world (appealing to the limbic system), and end with the rational argument that appeals to the neocortex. This approach can be applied to just about any context—marketing, leadership, politics, you name it—because it is based on our biology, not our circumstances. Take Max Lanman, for example. Max is an advertising copywriter whose girlfriend was interested in selling her used 1996 Honda Accord. At the time, 2018, the car was twenty-two years old with 140,000 driven miles on the odometer. Without question, this was not a very compelling offering, but like any ambitious advertiser, Max was up for the challenge.

Ultimately, Max decided to make a film that communicated the value of the vehicle. It featured his girlfriend driving the car with a makeshift radio, a coffee pot in the passenger seat (because the cup holder was broken), and an unkempt interior. Over these visuals was the following narration:

> You? You're different. You do things your way. That's what makes you one of a kind. You don't need things. You're happy with who you are. You don't care about money. You have everything you've ever wanted. You don't do it for appearances. You do it because it works. This? This is not a car. This is you. It's a lifestyle. A choice. Your choice. Introducing a used 1996 Honda Accord. A car for people who have life figured out and just need a way to get somewhere. Luxury is a state of mind.

Once the video was completed, Max posted it on eBay with an asking price of $500, and the car sold for $150,000. Not because of the car's features but because of its ideological congruence. The car was an extension of the buyer's identity project, and the purchase of this car was to say, "I believe that luxury is a lifestyle, so much so that I drive this car." The car became a receipt of identity, a way for the buyer to communicate who they are and what they believe. The sociologist Ivan Ross referred to this phenomenon as the concept of self and asserted that our purchases and brand preferences are influenced by our conception of ourselves—our identity. More specifically, he said that "people purchase a product [or brand] only if these are consistent with, enhance, or in some way fit well with the conception they have of themselves." It's our identity, and the beliefs associated with our identity, that appeals most to our emotional limbic system and excites us to move. When there is ideological congruence between us and the brand, the company, the organization, or the cause, rational propositions don't matter nearly as much as cultural associations do. As the biology of decision making and behavior adoption reveals, people aren't driven by rationality; they are driven by their emotions—and nothing is more emotional to us than "us." That's why Max Lanman was able to drive the selling price of a rundown Honda Accord three hundred times higher than the original ask: he started with the soul and ended with the sale.

The products we buy, the organizations we join, and the things we use to adorn ourselves have very little to do with their functionality. That's a rational outcome. Instead, they are more associated with our identity, which is an emotional outcome. The author and motivational speaker Simon Sinek put it this way: "People don't buy what you do, they buy why you do it." I'm a big fan of this provocation because it speaks directly to what culture has been telling us for centuries: people move to stay aligned with their identity, beliefs, and ideologies. Therefore, we are inclined to act—buy, watch, share, sample, recycle, attend, etc.—when these behaviors are a part of our cultural subscriptions.

After his popular TED talk about "starting with why," Sinek faced a healthy amount of skepticism with regard to his idea of first focusing on "why" the company or organization exists and then narrowing in on the product benefits—first the soul and then the sale. Business leaders would say, "Look, man, I'm here to make money. What are you talking about? This isn't a philanthropy." It's hard to blame them for having such a point of view, as most business schools teach their students to prioritize profits and increase shareholder value above all else. But making money is a by-product of what you do, not why you do it. Similarly, although the body must make white blood cells to live, making white blood cells isn't the meaning of life. We exist for something greater. This is our "why."

The same thing goes for businesses, organizations, institutions, people, and politicians. Why do we exist? What's our conviction? How do we see the world? It's this belief system that drives what we do—the rational stuff. Steve Jobs put it this way: "What do we [Apple, the company he cofounded] stand for beyond the bits and bytes? Where do we fit in this world? What we're about isn't making boxes for people to get their jobs done, though we do that well." What we do is a by-product of why we do it, and everything is informed by our conviction.

Furthermore, we talk about rational things like features, benefits, and specs, but when we talk about our beliefs and convictions, we tend to do it with much more fervor. We speak the "what" but preach the "why," the gospel. As Sinek mentioned, there is no better example of this than the Reverend Dr. Martin Luther King Jr. When Dr. King was on the stage of action in the 1960s, he wasn't the only civil rights leader fighting for the people. There were many others, like Malcolm X, Marcus Garvey, and Medgar Evers, who were all powerful figures and great orators. They all sacrificed their lives, and the lives of their families, for the betterment of the people. They were beloved and revered. Yet Martin Luther King remains the face of civil rights some sixty years later. Why is that? Because Martin had a dream, a belief to which people subscribed. They followed him and established him as the face of civil rights because of his dream—his belief—that this nation would be unified, that every boy and every girl, every man and every woman would be granted the same liberties promised by this nation's creed. They, too, believed in his dream.

We have all heard the refrain of Dr. King's "I Have a Dream" speech. It has been cited as one of the best speeches ever delivered. But an interesting fact about the "I Have a Dream" speech is that Dr. King had delivered it several times before the famous rendition that we all know of from the March for Civil Rights and Equal Pay on the steps of the Lincoln Memorial in Washington, DC, on August 28, 1963. His first delivery was nine months earlier in North Carolina in November 1962. He had many drafts and iterations of the speech—retooling it, extending it here and shortening it there.

When he took the stage on August 28, 1963, he intended to give a different speech. It was at the behest of the legendary gospel singer Mahalia Jackson that Dr. King decided to change course. She said, "Tell them about the dream, Martin," after having heard the speech in Detroit months prior, and he went on to give one of the most famous speeches of all time. What made that speech so powerful in that moment was not merely the mechanics of the speech but the conviction that was carried in his words. He preached the gospel to the congregation of believers who saw the world similarly, and they collectively took action because of it. For entrepreneurs, leaders, and activists, this makes for a powerful vehicle to get people to move—not just any people, of course, but your congregation.

## AS JOBS ONCE SAID . . .

The best marketers on the planet understand this better than most. They all have very clear and salient convictions. They preach the gospel—starting with the soul and ending with the sale—and it inspires congregations to move. Take Coca-Cola, for instance. Coca-Cola believes in spreading optimism and happiness. We've known that ever since it told us, "I want to teach the world to sing in perfect harmony."

So when Coke says, "Open happiness," which was its tagline for quite some time, it makes a lot of sense. Of course, Coke would say that because it makes sure everything about the brand is steeped in happiness. One of my favorite examples of this is the 2010 "Coke Happiness Machine" campaign. The premise was simple: Coke installed special Coke-branded vending machines in the campus cafeteria of St. John's University that would surprise unexpecting users with more than just a single can of Coca-Cola. Some patrons received multiple cans to share with others, while others got high fives, flowers, and even a box of pizza. The delight on the faces of the purchasers, and the onlookers in the cafeteria, was contagious. You can't watch the film that captured the stunt without smiling. As Wendy Clark, the senior vice president of integrated marketing communications and capabilities at the Coca-Cola Company at the time, explained, "It is such a simple yet compelling concept, and one that so accurately portrays Coca-Cola for what it ultimately is; one of life's simple pleasures." The "why" is demonstrated by the "what." Coca-Cola found the delta between average and happy and closed the gap. Coke just happens to sell bubbly sugar water, but it does it to spread happiness, and that's the gospel it preaches.

Likewise, Nike is a brand that believes that every human body is an athlete. Big, small, short, tall, able-bodied, or disabled, we are all athletes, and we are all able to achieve our inner athlete. All of us. So what does Nike tell us? "Just do it." This has been the brand's mantra (a tagline created by the late great Dan Wieden, the cofounder of Wieden+Kennedy) for over forty years now. It's the gospel that Nike preaches, and as a brand, Nike exists to help people realize their best athletic self. Nike just happens to sell sneakers, athletic apparel, accessories, and technology. You'd be hard-pressed to find a Nike ad that expounds on the features and benefits of the product, like the quality of the leather or the comfort of the fit. This is not how Nike advertises because Phil Knight, the founder of Nike, hates advertising in its conventional sense.

Advertising is the way in which marketers publicly communicate to make people aware of the products and offerings of a company, institution, organization, or person. Historically, advertising has been product focused and led by value propositions (the sale) rather than being ideologically driven (the soul). That was not compelling to Phil. It wasn't supercompelling to Dan Wieden and David Kennedy, either, which is why one of our isms in the agency today is "Start realizing that what you're supposed to be doing is not advertising; it's evangelizing the faith." We don't make ads for Nike; we preach the gospel that every human body is an athlete. Nike's approach to preaching the gospel to its congregation inspired other companies to adopt this means of communication, perhaps none more famously than Apple.

When Steve Jobs rejoined Apple in 1997, he introduced a new marketing campaign that would signal the return of the company, which had slipped in stature—and market share—since his ousting (from the company that he had started, no less) a few years prior. Before revealing the new campaign, Jobs expressed his admiration for Nike's marketing, saying, "The best example of marketing the universe has ever seen is Nike." He reminded the audience that Nike sells a commodity—shoes—but the thought of Nike evokes more than just a shoe company. In fact, Nike hardly ever mentions its shoes when it communicates with consumers. One campaign from the late '80s featured Michael Jordan and Spike Lee declaring that the shoes had nothing to do with Jordan's greatness. Lee professed, "It's got to be the shoes," to which Jordan simply replied, "No." Instead, Nike honors athletes, the people who set out to realize their best athletic selves. The company started by paying homage to the best athletes in the world and, years later, began to honor everyday athletes—like you and me—because greatness is not a rare DNA strain, nor is it a gift given to the chosen few. "Greatness is no more unique to us than breathing," one Nike ad declares as we see an overweight teenage boy running on an open road in what appears to be the flatlands of America. And just before the ad ends, the boy continues to run—slow but determined—and the narrator says, "We're all capable of it [greatness]. All of us." Nothing about the shoe. Nothing about where the company sources its leather or how shock absorbent the soles of the sneakers are. Nothing about the rational arguments. Just pure conviction. Pure ideology. It's from this playbook that Apple created the campaign that helped the company preach its gospel—"Think Different":

> Here's to the crazy ones,
> the misfits, the rebels,
> the troublemakers,
> the round pegs in the square holes.
> The ones who see things differently.
> They are not fond of rules.
> You can quote them,
> disagree with them,
> glorify or vilify them,
> but the only thing you can't do is ignore them
> because they change things.
> They push the human race forward,
> and while some may see them as the crazy ones,
> we see genius,
> because the ones who are crazy enough to think that they
>     can change the world,
> are the ones who do.

As a brand, Apple believed in challenging the status quo, and just as Nike honored the greatest athletes, Apple used this campaign to honor the greatest status quo challengers across a myriad of genres, from sports (Muhammad Ali) to aviation (Amelia Earhart) to art (Pablo Picasso) and entertainment (Jim Henson, the legendary puppeteer). Apple just happens to sell computers, phones, tablets, watches, music, movies, and the like. But its conviction is to challenge the status quo, and this is the gospel that Apple preaches to people who see the world similarly. And who were the early adopters of Apple devices? In those early years, you typically saw artists and creators using Apple products. The ones who saw the world differently and believed that they could make an impact on the world. They bought Apple products as a badge of identity, affixing Apple stickers to the bumpers of their cars and any other surface available to publicly display their ideological congruence. This is the power of preaching the gospel to your congregation: it activates the limbic system and excites people to take action.

I remember being on the subway in New York City in the early 2000s, listening to my second-generation Apple iPod, wearing the white earbuds that accompanied the device on a train filled with black wires. This was the early years of iPod, and only the most devoted Apple fans owned these new music players. And there I was, an early adopter, a budding songwriter trying to make my way in New York City amidst a sea of black-corded earphone users. However, out of the corner of my eye, I saw another person wearing white earbuds. He noticed me, too. And just like that, we gave each other a look as if to say, "We get it." We were a part of the congregation, and the white earbuds were the artifacts that signaled our affiliation.

This is exactly how REI inspired people to move, and so did Dr. King, Coca-Cola, Nike, and many others. They preached the gospel to their congregation—by starting with the soul and ending with the sale—and got them to move. We see this in politics as well, most notably (and recently) with the rise of Donald Trump. Trump didn't necessarily run on any particular legislative ideas or political policies. He ran on ideology, a set of beliefs that also happened to be held by the racial underbelly of fringe society. Trump brought these beliefs to the forefront and awakened a population of Americans that had otherwise been ignored and undervalued. The radical racism introduced into politics by the Tea Party in the late 2000s was merely an amuse-bouche to the brand of politics Trump would offer some ten years later. The gospel he preached was just as a simple as King's "I have a dream," but Trump's conviction was completely antithetical: "Make America great again."

While he never specified to what period he was referring when he said, "again," we know for sure it was not the eight years prior, when President Barack Obama was in office, because of the outlandish attacks Trump made on Obama during his presidential campaign in 2007. Trump questioned Obama's American citizenship, claiming that he was born in Kenya, which resulted in what we now know as "birthergate." Whatever that moment in time might have been to which Trump wanted America to return, it likely was not a time that was relished by people of color, immigrants, women, or marginalized communities because these people were constantly under attack by Donald Trump—before, during, and after his presidency.

While his political daggers and venomous remarks seemed vile to many of us, to others, they were a megaphone for the voiceless in politics. Those words, "Make America great again," would signal like a dog whistle to all those who saw the world the way he did. While the Republican Party at first denounced him and declared his 2016 candidacy a national joke, the congregation of people who subscribed to his ideology began to mobilize. He preached the gospel to his congregation, and they moved, exciting millions of them to vote him into office in 2016 and instigating hundreds to storm the Capitol on January 6, 2021, in a deadly insurrection. This is the power of identity and beliefs, the foundation of culture. When the gospel is preached, it provokes people of like minds to move.

## THE GOOD, THE BAD, AND THE UGLY

Whether it's activism, consumer packaged goods, sneakers, or politics, the effect that preaching the gospel has on people is not only context agnostic but also independent of the brand's validity. Take WeWork, for example. At its core, WeWork is a modern real estate company that purchases long-term leases and rents out shared workspace for organizations, start-ups, and entrepreneurs as short-term leases. However, WeWork presented itself as a contemporary tech company despite having no semblance of technology in its business offerings—and people bought into it. Why? Because the company's founder, Adam Neumann, preached a gospel that "started with the soul and ended with the sale," which transformed WeWork from a run-of-the-mill landlord business to something far greater.

WeWork believes in the power of "we," that the possibilities are endless when people come together. The company grew quickly because of its ability to aggregate a congregation of believers—including SoftBank's founder, Masayoshi Son, who invested $9 billion in WeWork. It was not the value proposition of the company that made it so attractive to the thousands of employees who joined the ranks or the product differentiators that compelled Son to invest so aggressively. It was the ideology of the company, the gospel that Neumann preached, that inspired people to move. That ethos hid a host of deficiencies that caused the company to crash and burn just a year later when its shortcomings could no longer be concealed—like its labor issues, egregious executive spending, and, of course, the fact that it is not indeed a tech company—once it tried to go public. WeWork was a classic example of a bad product that benefited from good preaching, and it was working well for the company until the truth was exposed.

Similarly, Elizabeth Holmes became the darling of tech and the beneficiary of nearly $1 billion in venture capital thanks to the company she founded, Theranos. The company promised a blood technology that could extract a large amount of data from a few drops of blood taken from a person's fingertip, a feat that had previously seemed scientifically impossible. Holmes, a distant admirer of Steve Jobs, did not talk about the specs of Theranos's technology. Instead, she preached the gospel about a transparent world where lives could be saved through the availability of information and democratized access to health care. The nineteen-year-old Stanford dropout was able to convince executives at Walgreens (who agreed to partner with Theranos to distribute its products), former US secretary of state Henry Kissinger, former defense secretary Jim "Maddog" Mattis, media tycoon Rupert Murdock, the Walton family (of Walmart fame), and the senior associate dean of engineering at Stanford, Channing Robertson, to invest with very little data or proof of the company's technology. Instead, she sold them the gospel, and they bought it—quite literally—before the company was dismantled and riddled with legal actions.

It's easy to point at this situation and say, "How could anyone fall for that?" But we all fall for something and behave accordingly, not because it's "true" per se but because it aligns with the story we tell ourselves about the world (ideology) and how we fit into the world (identity); therefore, we act in accordance with it (culture). All we need is for someone to preach the gospel so that we know what to do and how to act. Think of all the amazing things your organization sets out to do to make people's lives better and all the many ways your product might enrich people's day-to-day comings and goings. If preaching the gospel can influence people to buy into a shady product or a questionable company, imagine what it can do for a good product and an upright company.

This seems easy enough, right? Identify what you believe, find your congregation, and preach the gospel to catalyze collective behavior among them. However, when I teach executives about using culture in this way to get people to move, they all nod vigorously, responding with a resolute "of course," "absolutely," or "100 percent." But as soon as they go back to their offices, it's business as usual, focusing on product features and benefits. Now, don't get me wrong. Features and benefits are important. They are a part of the "sale," but we must first start with the "soul" if we are to get people to move. As Bill Bernback, cofounder of the advertising agency DDB, put it, "You don't persuade people through intellect. You do it through their passions." I've always loved that quote because most people see "passion" and think "interests," as in I have a passion for music or a passion for reading. But the etymology of the word "passion" comes from Christian theology, and it means "suffer." What Bernback is ultimately saying is that we don't persuade people through intellect—i.e., rational arguments, value propositions, and benefits. No, we persuade people through the gospel that we preach, the beliefs and ideologies that we hold for which we are even willing to suffer. This is the definition of conviction. We're willing to stand firm on a belief even if we are the only ones standing.

Here is the hard part. While we know this intuitively, it is quite difficult to abandon our muscle memory for the way we have traditionally communicated about our products (goods or services), organization, or initiatives. I call this the razor-blade conundrum, and I ask these executives the following: Say Caleb sells a man's shaver with three blades, and his competitor Andrew sells a shaver with four blades. What will happen next? To which one exec will respond, "People will likely wander over to Andrew's product because four blades will probably provide a closer shave than three, so Caleb will have to make a four-blade razor soon to compete with Andrew." Correct. And that's exactly what happens. Caleb makes a four-blade razor, and he adds a gel strip on the head of the shaver to provide a smoother shave.

I then ask, what happens next? Another executive responds, "Now Andrew needs to add more innovation to his shaver." Correct again. Andrew adds another blade (five blades in total) and a gel strip and makes the shaver head vibrate to wake up the hairs on your face. You can imagine where this goes, right? Caleb then adds six blades to his shaver with a gel strip, a vibrating head, and a pump that excretes aloe vera lotion to soothe razor irritation. Before long, the back-and-forth between Caleb's and Andrew's shavers has led to a shaver with thirty-five razor blades and a voice-activated artificial intelligence–based technology that speaks to you and reads your tweets as you shave. It's insanity. And this is precisely when I ask the executives: When there is nothing left that could be added to the shaver and no more (physical) room for "innovation," what dimensions are left on which Caleb and Andrew can compete? After a few moments of silence and blank stares, someone raises their hand and answers, "I suppose all that's left is to drop the price," which (again) is correct and is exactly how we turn our product offerings into a commodity.

This is what happens when we prioritize the value propositions: the rational offerings like my razor's sharper, my battery lasts longer, or my car goes faster. It leads to transaction-based relationships. Sure, if your product is the fastest, people will be inclined to consume it. If your product is cheaper, then people will be more inclined to choose it over your competitor's product. And if you have eight blades when all the others have seven, people will probably choose you. But as soon as someone else is faster, cheaper, or has nine blades to your eight, you're done. Welcome to commodity land. This is the case for the entire pizza category. When I was growing up, a large pizza with one topping cost around $17, which sounds ridiculous today after Little Caesar's introduced its hot-n-ready pizzas (a large one-topping pizza ready to eat for $5) to the market. The entire category is now primarily based on value propositions.

However, when we focus on the convictions of the organization or brand, we build identity-based relationships that are predicated on how we self-identify. The brand isn't just a brand. The T-shirt isn't just a T-shirt. The school isn't just a school. The institution isn't just an institution. It is an extension of who we are.

At the start of the COVID-19 pandemic, the future seemed uncertain, and financial stability for many companies and employees alike was unknown. This backdrop inspired the CEO of Columbia

Sportswear, Tim Boyle, to reduce his salary from $3.3 million a year to $10,000 a year to help ensure that the company's other employees could receive their regular pay. Even the 3,500 retail workers were still compensated despite the temporary store closures due to the shutdown. It was important to Boyle that his employees had security and the ability to pursue the things that mattered to them. This aligned with Columbia Sportswear's conviction to connect with active people and their passions. Boyle's pay cut essentially ensured that his employees would be able to do just that, even in the face of uncertainty. As a brand whose products literally help people weather storms, the company demonstrated its beliefs in its behavior as well. When this news broke, my friend Helen posted the article with the caption "Adore! I love my Columbia jackets even more now!" Her Columbia jacket didn't get any warmer than it was before she read the article. The jacket didn't fit her frame any better than it did before this announcement, yet the brand became a better identity fit because its beliefs and ideologies—as demonstrated through its actions—were congruent with her worldview, so she felt more emotionally connected to it.

Evidence from a study published in *Harvard Business Review* suggests that emotional connections matter more than functional benefits. It's the activation of the limbic system that gets people going, not the value propositions. And when the brand's belief is aligned with our belief, we feel connected. Subsequently, the brand becomes a receipt of our identity that helps communicate who we are and how we want to be seen in the social world. Our identity and the corresponding cultural characteristics to which we subscribe are the biggest drivers of our behavior. We make sure that our actions and our belief systems are aligned. Otherwise, we find ourselves wrestling with the discomfort of cognitive dissonance.

There is no question that the idea of preaching the gospel to your congregation flies in the face of long-standing marketing communication practices that tell brands to communicate their product features to a specific target audience—a specific group of people. I've never been a fan of the term "target audience" because audiences are passive. They are groups of people who wait for messages to be waved over them, a captive assembly that is just waiting to see what you will do next. But people—real people—are not passive at all. They have a million and one things to do each day, and the last thing they are thinking about is how much fluoride your company has added to its newest line of toothpaste. Instead, they're thinking about whether they fit in, whether they're doing it right, whether their kids are safe, and just about every single thing possible before they think about you and your cause—unless, of course, unbeknownst to them, your cause is actually also their cause. But this would require us to see people as real human beings, not machines that eat messages and crap cash.

When brands connect with people who subscribe to the same belief, the congregation of people who subscribe to the same ideology, not only do those people buy from said brand, but they also use the brand to communicate their identity and share it with people who are just like them. And those people share it with other people who are just like them, and so on, and so on, and so on. The idea of preaching the gospel isn't about blasting the message to everybody who might be compelled by your value propositions. It's about activating the network effects within the congregation of people who subscribe to the same belief system, which will inspire them to preach the gospel to other people on your behalf.

## CONVERTING NONBELIEVERS

It is quite likely that the last new show you watched, the last new restaurant you visited, or the last new product you purchased was not directly due to an ad you saw. In some cases, you may not have even seen an ad for the show. Instead, you heard about it from someone you know, someone you trust. They recommended a show about an eclectic group of people who capture and care for big cats, and before long you found yourself watching ten episodes of *Tiger King* on Netflix. Why? Because someone told you to, just as someone told them, and so on, and so on, and so on. This is the network effect at its finest, propagating shared beliefs and cultural characteristics to keep the network bonds of the congregation tight.

While on the surface, *Tiger King* may not seem like a cultural product for any particular congregation beyond that of the wildlife realm, the show acted as a vehicle for people within communities to rehearse their shared beliefs and ideologies with each other. The comments and discourse about the show that were exchanged between tribal members—and their aggregate congregations—helped them negotiate and construct what people like them should feel and how they should react. These exchanges are all mediated by our cultural subscriptions, and they influence us to act accordingly.

The US presidential election of 2008 was a hotly contested battle. On one side was a war veteran, Republican senator from Arizona John McCain, and on the other a former community leader, Democratic senator from Illinois Barack Obama. The old guard and new blood. The race was further exacerbated by the fact that Obama, an African American born in Hawaii, was being pegged as a Muslim, which he is not, during the post-9/11 time when Islamophobia was running rampant in the country. Beyond the standard brand of racism that has always plagued the United States, the attacks on Obama had reached a fever pitch, particularly in Florida—a critical swing state for the election.

Throughout the state, McCain supporters ran ads that assigned a host of unsavory labels to Obama—anti-American, pro-Iraq, and, perhaps most troubling for a state with a high population of aging Jewish Americans, anti-Israel. The strategy for the ads was to position Obama as someone "unlike me" or, in this case, "anti-me." But, of course, that was not the case. To combat these political ads, the Jewish Center for Education and Research (JCER) felt compelled to respond. Realizing that shouting the truth louder than the opposing voice would not produce the results it desired, it decided to leverage the most influential voice for older Jewish Americans: their grandchildren.

The JCER enlisted the help of Sarah Silverman, a brilliant Jewish American comedian, to make a video urging young Jewish Americans to travel to Florida and convince their grandparents to vote for Barack Obama. The video was a part of a campaign called *The Great Schlep.* Sarah opens the video by posing a simple question: "If you knew that visiting your grandparents could change the world, would you do it? Of course you would. You would have to be a douchenozzle not to." She then goes on to declare, "If Barack Obama doesn't become the next president of the United States, I'm going to blame the Jews." While Jewish Americans are historically known to be liberal and progressive in their politics, there is a population of Jews who, as Sarah puts it, "are not that way, and they go by several aliases: Nana, Papa, Zaide, Bubbe, and plain old Grandma and Grandpa." The video continues with all the talking points as to why Obama would make a better candidate and how his policy ideas are actually more favorable for Israel than McCain's. She ends with a call to action to young Jewish Americans: register on the Great Schlep website, get on a plane to Florida, and convert your grandparent.

Sarah preached the gospel to the congregation of the willing—by starting with the soul and ending with the sale—which inspired over twenty-four thousand Jewish Americans to register on the site and schlep to Florida. Though it targeted a specific network of people, young Jewish Americans, the campaign was covered by just about every major news outlet from the *New York Times* to the BBC. What's more, Obama ended up winning Florida with a higher percentage of votes from Jewish voters in three of the most populated counties in the state. Frank Rich of the *New York Times* wrote, "Obama drew a larger percentage of Jews nationally and—Mazel Tov, Sarah Silverman!—

won Florida." She activated the network within her congregation, and they convinced others to move.

Again, this is a complete departure from the traditional means of marketing communication. Marketers have long approached communications and persuasion through the marketing funnel, where you reach as many people as possible at the top of the funnel (awareness) and the population narrows as you get closer to the bottom (conversion). Through this lens, marketers invest vast resources in getting their message in front of as many people in the total market as possible in hopes of acquiring a portion of this population (what marketers call the serviceable available market). Whatever the total market size may be, marketers aim to reach as many of these people as possible, using a suite of different media vehicles. However, only a percentage is ever really reached (let's say, arbitrarily, 70 percent), and maybe 20 percent of these people respond to a call to action (*click here for more information*, *learn more here*, or *sign up here*), leaving only 0.02 percent of that population who eventually buy something. That's a pretty wasteful system, even if it has been the status quo for the marketing industry for decades. Perhaps it's time for all of us to "think different."

When we target a congregation of networked tribes, something magical happens. As in the case of *The Great Schlep*, focusing our efforts on the people who are the most demonstrative representation of the congregation—the people who most closely adhere to the cultural characteristics of their tribe—can catalyze a propagation cascade where the product, idea, belief, behavior, language, or artifact diffuses from person to person within the population. The result of this phenomenon increases the reach within the congregation—see Figure 2, below. This is a provocation brought forward by the brilliance of the late Griffin Farley, who called this idea "propagation planning," where you plan not for the people you might reach but for the people whom those people will reach through social pass-along.

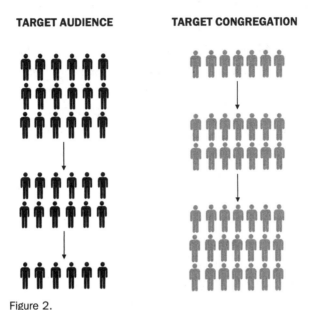

Figure 2.

Unlike traditional marketing communications, the reach that is achieved here is more than just people hearing a message from a company or brand. They hear about it from someone whom they trust, someone like them, which increases the likelihood of adoption for the next person. As the network scientists Nicholas Christakis and James Fowler posited, "When a small group of people begin acting in concert—displaying similar visible symptoms—the epidemic can spread along social network ties via emotion contagion and large groups can become quickly emotionally synchronized." This is the network effect that is activated when you preach the gospel to the congregation of people who see the world the way that you do.

People, not marketing communications, convert people. Marketing communications create an exogenous shock to the system of the networked tribes—within a congregation—and, collectively, the members of the tribe decide whether it aligns with the cultural characteristics of the tribe (more on this in Chapter 5). This realization altered my practice and inspired my research on cultural contagion and meaning making. I have since been applying this philosophy to brands, NGOs, institutions, and personalities. Furthermore, I see these parallels in religion as well. It's rare for people to show up to a new church for the first time because they saw a flyer or because the church was just there. Instead, guests typically visit a church for the first time because they were invited by someone who is already a member of the church. People talk about how much they've received from attending the church or temple and, subsequently, encourage their friends and colleagues to attend.

Both religious texts and marketing jargon refer to these people as evangelists, bringers of good news. In the religious sense, the term "evangelist" is used to describe someone who tries to persuade people to become Christians. In the marketing sense, "evangelists" are people who try to persuade others to try a product that they swear by. We also evangelize for our respective cultural characteristics—telling people to try this, look at something a particular way, or refrain from doing a certain thing based on what "people like us" do. When you preach the gospel to your congregation, you empower evangelists to convert the nonbelievers—the apathetic, the naysayers, and the incredulous. As the gospel hymnal proclaims, "I once was blind, but now I see," and thus, these newly sighted people feel compelled to tell the good news wherever they go. They, too, preach the gospel on your behalf because they believe. This is the network effect of evangelism.

This phenomenon happens the same way that SoulCycle—often referred to as a cult—recruits new members, through referrals. In fact, before the COVID-19 shutdown, 80 percent of new SoulCycle members came from personal referrals alone. When we preach the gospel to the congregation and activate the network effect, they segment and target the people that they believe will likely convert because they identify people who are most like themselves.

Let's look at the NBA team the Nets. The franchise was established in 1977 as the New Jersey Nets. Throughout its thirty-five-year history, the team had made only two NBA finals appearances and was generally regarded as a noncontender in the league. In September 2009, it was acquired by Mikhail Prokhorov as a principal owner. Among other minority-stake owners was the hip-hop mogul Jay-Z, who had a 0.67 percent ownership stake in the team. Prokhorov's bid to purchase the Nets also included initial funds to build an arena for the team in Brooklyn, New York, which would later be known as the Barclays Center. The arena was located in the heart of Brooklyn's Atlantic Terminal, an iconic area of the borough. This, of course, meant that the New Jersey Nets were leaving New Jersey and moving to Brooklyn to become the Brooklyn Nets. The team's first season in its new Brooklyn arena was set for November 2012. The charge from the Nets' new CEO, Brett Yormark, to us—the team's then creative agency, Translation—was that "the Nets should be to Brooklyn what the Knicks are to Manhattan." Easy enough, right? Wrong!

There were many controversies that plagued the development of the Barclays Center, including the potential environmental impact on the area and the lack of continued public financing to cover the construction. The most wide-reaching issue was the outcry from local Brooklyn residents. For this cohort, building the Barclays Center in Brooklyn meant the displacement of long-standing businesses and homeowners in the area due to upheaval and the effects of gentrification. Activists held protests and demonstrations in front of the construction site and fought borough officials to challenge the development of the arena. Their contention was frequently covered in the local media and spawned a well-received documentary called *The Battle for Brooklyn*. With such resistance against the arena, there was naturally plenty of disinterest in the basketball team as well—a losing basketball team at that.

With a November 2012 opener, achieving Yormark's charge to make the Nets "Brooklyn's team" seemed increasingly difficult—if not impossible. At least, that was my thinking as I stared at the assignment brief, wondering how we might attack this problem. While I had dealt with products that were not well regarded before and helped brands that faced public ridicule, I had never faced a problem of a questionable product from a brand that was encountering public disdain. Instead of focusing on the brand or the product, we decided to start with the people, the Brooklynites.

The people of Brooklyn are a proud bunch. Of all the residents of the five boroughs in New York City, those who live in Brooklyn are by far the most vocal about their devotion to their home turf. It is no wonder that hip-hop artists often ask, "Where Brooklyn at?," to hype up the crowd. Brooklyn pride is a formidable thing. So we decided to use that pride to get Brooklynites to act by taking a page from Edward Bernays's propaganda theory, uniting a group of people by declaring an enemy of the state. Fortunately for us, there was a natural enemy of Brooklyn: Manhattan.

We built an entire campaign on the back of an inherent rivalry, Brooklyn vs. Manhattan. If you live in Brooklyn, then you know the struggle of commuting back and forth, in and out of the city, every weekday for work. In many ways, there is built-up tension between the two boroughs. As a former Brooklyn resident, I can testify that when you get home from a full day in Manhattan, it's a challenge to go back into the city—so much so that after the start of the weekend, many Brooklyn residents won't return to Manhattan until Monday morning. Don't believe me? Try making plans with a Brooklynite for brunch in the city on a Sunday morning. It will be a challenge.

With this in mind, we kicked off our efforts by first stoking Brooklyn pride. We borrowed language that was once used by Brooklyn royalty, the Beastie Boys, and later sampled by another Brooklyn native, Jay-Z. That phrase, of course, was "Hello Brooklyn." With this language identified, we asked other notable Brooklynites—like the legendary radio personality Angie Martinez and the front man of Gym Class Heroes, Travis McCoy, to tweet about their beloved borough using the "Hello Brooklyn" phrase without mentioning the team. The hope here was merely to plant the seed and recontextualize the language for what was to come next.

We then took out billboards in the highest-traffic areas of Brooklyn with headlines such as "If you're not with us, the bridge is right there. #HelloBrooklyn." Another billboard said, "Brooklyn's always had balls, now it's just official. #HelloBrooklyn." Each billboard was meant to catalyze the deep-seated pride that exists within Brooklynites. Accompanying the copy on the billboards was an empty shield that later would be revealed as the silhouette of the new Brooklyn Nets logo. We redesigned the New Jersey Nets logo to something more akin to the personality of Brooklyn, with a new font and a stripped-down color-way (black and white) that felt more raw than the colorful and inviting original. But we maintained the shield. And since the launch was about the people of Brooklyn and not the team, we decided to remove everything from the logo but the shield to act as a watermark. That way, when we were ready to reveal the logo, people would know that it had been us all the while.

After a few weeks of running the stealth billboards in Brooklyn, we set our sights on our rivals across the bridge. We identified the most highly trafficked train stops from Brooklyn to Manhattan and put up billboards that read, "Bridges will be crossed. #HelloBrooklyn." Other billboards read, "Of course it's personal. #HelloBrooklyn," so that Brooklynites would carry their Brooklyn pride with them to their rival's stomping grounds. Before long, we put up new billboards with the populated shield and new copy that read, "Brooklyn now has a home team. #Hello Brooklyn" and "First home game since 1957. #HelloBrooklyn," referring to the time when the Brooklyn Dodgers left to become the LA Dodgers.

By this point, the Brooklyn Nets were trending nationally on Twitter despite the hyperlocal nature of the communication executions. Most importantly, though, Brooklyn took notice. Before the roster of the team was even announced, the total volume sales for Brooklyn Nets gear in the first two days of purchase was ten times the total sales of the New Jersey Nets in a typical year. In fact, the New Jersey Nets had been #30 in merch sales for the season prior to the move (2011–2012), but by the end of the Brooklyn Nets' first season (2012–2013), the team was #4 in merch sales.

What was happening here? Brooklynites adopted Brooklyn Nets fandom and bought Brooklyn Nets gear not because of the team but because of what the team represented. The team hadn't even played its first game, but merch was selling out of the stores. Why? Because the Brooklyn Nets became a badge of Brooklyn residence, and Brooklynites bought gear to communicate their identity. Even Buzzfeed noted in its "19 Signs You Are from Brooklyn" list that "When the Nets came to Brooklyn, you obviously showed them love." This had nothing to do with the team and everything to do with what the team meant to these Brooklyn residents. This is the power of the gospel when it aligns with people's identities, beliefs, and ideology. The product, organization, entity, or movement takes on new meaning for the congregation, and they adopt it as a cultural product and use it to signal their identity to the world.

## FROM KNOW-WHY TO KNOW-HOW

The influence of culture on what we buy and all that we do is unparalleled. We consume not so much for "what it is" and "what it does" as for "who we are" and "how we see the world." The impact of culture's influence enables marketers to sell products, organizations to recruit members, and leaders to motivate teams. This influence can help just about anyone excite a collective to adopt behavior. To do so, however, we must first identify the way we see the world and find the people who see the world similarly.

This is your congregation, the collection of networked tribes to which you will target your communications. Call them your tribe, your network, your community, or whatever works best for you. The nomenclature doesn't matter much. In fact, I often use these terms interchangeably because they all boil down to the same thing: these are *our* people. And when you communicate with your people, don't lead with the benefits and features of your offerings. Instead, preach the gospel about your beliefs and the way you see the world. This will connect with people by activating the part of the brain that stirs up emotion and, ultimately, catalyzes behavior.

We've seen examples of gospels preached throughout this chapter like "Opt Outside," "Just Do It," and "Think Different." These words should not be mistaken for mere taglines. Rather, they are articulations of belief. They are the expression of the way these brands see the world, and they have a strong gravitational pull on people who see the world similarly. This pull is so strong that it not only inspires these people to take action but also motivates them to encourage other people like them to take action also.

As you consider this, ask yourself, how would you communicate your company's or organization's worldview? How would you preach the gospel to your congregation? Don't focus on the words so much because that might seem like an intimidating creative exercise—you can save that for the speechwriters and advertisers. Instead, start with a statement of truth, as you did at the end of the previous chapter: "We believe [fill in the blank]." This is the soul.

Once you've communicated the soul, then end with the sale: "We believe [fill in the blank], so we created [fill in the blank: product or organization] to realize this belief." REI believes that a life outdoors is life well spent, so it closed on Black Friday to encourage people to opt for playing outside instead of shopping indoors. Nike believes that every human body is an athlete, so it creates products to help people realize their best athletic self—so people can just do it. Apple believes in challenging the status quo, so it challenged people to think different and consider going against the conventional norm. What do you believe? What is your company's worldview? This is the gospel you will preach. These are the words you will communicate to get people to move. But the words alone are not enough. Because what we say is not always what people hear. Therefore, we must also consider the way people interpret our words and how they make meaning, a topic we'll interrogate in the next chapter.

## CHAPTER 4

# MAKING MEANING

I MET MY WIFE, ALEX, WHILE PURSUING MY MBA AT THE ROSS School of Business, University of Michigan. There's an old saying about students in MBA programs: some come for an "MBA," some come for an "Mrs." Indeed, a lot of romantic relationships are kindled in business schools, and they often evolve into marriage. Neither Alex nor I was interested in the latter. She was very focused on her scholastic endeavors, and I was still mourning the loss of a five-and-a-half-year relationship that ended terribly.

Alex was unlike most people you'd meet in business school. She wore black most days, or some hue of dark blue, which I would later learn is sort of a New York thing. I don't think I ever saw her in school paraphernalia—for a school as spirited as Michigan, this was atypical. She wasn't particularly social, snubbing the implicit obligation in business school to befriend all your classmates and "grow your network." She mostly stuck to herself, maintained a small group of friends, and radiated a "leave me alone, I have stuff to do" kind of vibe. So naturally, like a premise straight from a '90s rom-com, I was attracted to her. Despite her initial unwelcoming demeanor, I found Alex to be quite lovely once I had a chance to interact with her. At that point, I made a conscious effort to connect with her whenever I could, and what started as purposeful flirting led to a full-out relationship. Years later, I decided that it was time to take the next step and ask her to marry me. Two big questions immediately came to mind: (1) How was I going to propose, and (2) where would I get the ring?

The proposal idea came pretty quickly. I had been working in social media marketing for a few years by that time, so I relied on an old trick of the trade: when in doubt, crowdsource it! With this in mind, I secretly reached out to mutual friends of ours who had been a part of our relationship from its early beginnings in Ann Arbor to our cross-country stage—when she lived in New York City and I in the Bay Area—to our then current state in Brooklyn, New York. I asked our friends to send me a quick video, unbeknownst to Alex, detailing their recommendation for the best way to propose to her. Some were fanciful—take her on a trip to Paris and propose on the Eiffel Tower. Some were predictable—take her to dinner and put a ring in a champagne glass. And some were over the top—take her to the fifty-yard line of the Big House and pop the question with the Michigan marching band in the background. A host of submissions from our friends came in, and I went to work stitching together a video that would serve as the appetizer to my entrée of a proposal. The plan was that her sister, Dori, would meet her for lunch at work and pull up the crowdsourced proposal video on YouTube under the guise of a hilarious video that Alex just had to see. Meanwhile, I'd be waiting just outside Alex's office to pop the question at the precise moment that the video ended. Pretty cool, right?

Although the proposal plan came to me fairly quickly, the ring required a little more thought. Unlike the proposal, which was an intimate event, the ring would be far more visible. This would be an artifact that she would wear for at least a year before the wedding and perhaps after the fact. It would be a symbol to tell the world that she was committed to someone and a measurement by which I would be judged when she announced our engagement to her friends and coworkers. I had to get this right. Thankfully, my soon-to-be mother-in-law relieved a lot of that anxiety by providing me with a diamond that she had been holding for Alex for years. I could now use that diamond (which was in great condition, by the way) to construct a new engagement ring for my soon-to-be fiancée without spending a boatload of money on a rock. Hallelujah!

When I tell this story to my guy friends, it's typically met with "Man, you're so lucky!" Why? Because, like me, they, too, stressed about buying the ring and all the considerations that come with it. What cut? What color? What size? Is the clarity what it should be? And, of course, how much will it cost? These questions are a major source of anxiety for folks who are looking to pop the big question. And we all have the De Beers corporation to thank for it.

In the late 1940s, De Beers, an international diamond company, released its "Diamonds Are Forever" campaign in the United States. It set off a cascade of events that still impacts the way we propose almost eighty years later. Before De Beers, people didn't propose with a diamond. It wasn't a thing. But De Beers changed all that. The campaign instructed young men, in the aftermath of the Great Depression, "If you want to show her you love her, say it with a diamond." A diamond—the rare, precious gem that symbolizes the unique bond that you and your love share—was to be kept forever, just as your love would last for an eternity. It's a lovely sentiment. One problem: diamonds aren't rare at all.

De Beers practically owned a monopoly on the diamond industry, so it suppressed the supply to make diamonds appear to be rare. Oh, and that "forever" bit? Yeah, De Beers wants you to keep your diamond forever because the resale value of diamonds is awful. In fact, the former chairman of De Beers, Nicky Oppenheimer, was once quoted as saying that "diamonds are intrinsically worthless, except for the deep psychological need they fill." This campaign has to be one of the most successful advertising efforts of all time. Since De Beers launched the campaign in 1948, the adoption of the "propose with a diamond" ritual has increased by record amounts. Fifty percent of wedding engagements in the US in the 1960s were initiated with a diamond-ring proposal, and that number shot up to 80 percent by the 1990s, according to a study by the Bain & Company consulting firm. The "Diamonds Are Forever" campaign had a similar effect in Japan, reaching an almost 60 percent adoption rate by 1981, up from 5 percent after its launch in the late 1960s.

What's going on here? If diamonds are so low in quality and high in supply, why do they command such a hefty price? And why in the world are we still proposing marriage with a diamond ring? I'll tell you why. Thanks to De Beers's marketing campaign, a diamond ring is no longer simply a (not so) rare gem. Instead, a diamond ring is now a symbol of long-lasting love and societal status because we, collectively, reworked the meaning associated with a diamond ring as such in response to a company's catalyst. As a result, we propose with a diamond ring to signify the cultural ritual in which we voluntarily decided to engage. This is the power of meaning, the translation of our experienced reality, and it's through these frames that we see the world and make sense of it. And, as we've discussed in previous chapters, the way we see the world informs the way we behave in the world. However, the challenge is that we all don't see things that same way, so meaning differs for different people.

Imagine you wanted to say "OK" to someone without saying it aloud. How would you communicate "OK" with your hand? It is likely that you would touch the tip of your index finger to the tip of your thumb to make a circle and extend the remaining three fingers out like a fan. This is commonly known as the "OK" symbol. However, this hand gesture is also known as the symbol for White supremacy. If you're on a college campus, you might see a group of young Black men use this symbol to signify their membership in a Black Greek Letter Organization called Kappa Alpha Psi. If you are in South Central Los Angeles and see a different group of young Black men use this hand gesture, it might signify an altogether different fraternal affiliation, the Bloods street gang. Or if you're in Brazil, this hand gesture is the equivalent of the middle finger here in the United States. Meaning—the interpretation of one's reality—is not objective. It is subjective, and its interpretation is determined by the worldview associated with our cultural subscriptions.

In 2011, the global bank HSBC launched an advertising campaign to emphasize the importance of understanding cultural nuances when doing business in different countries. The campaign depicted different people in foreign parts of the globe trying to navigate a world where meanings differ. One of the television ads showed a middle-aged Asian man falling asleep on a subway. He is modestly dressed in what appears to be a prototypical outfit of a normal day—a plaid, button-up collared shirt and a Members Only jacket. As he slowly drifts off into dreamland, he lays his head on the shoulder of a fellow subway rider, a burly White American, who is taken aback by what's happening. It becomes clear that this Asian man is not riding the subway in an Asian country. He is on a crowded subway in New York City. And just as the man is falling asleep, the commercial's narrator says, "In some Asian cites, it's considered acceptable for a commuter to fall asleep on a stranger. In New York, it's quite a different story. Of course, you can always adapt. We're the global bank that never underestimates the importance of local knowledge."

To accompany its campaign, HSBC created complementary print ads that displayed one object with three different cultural meanings across a series of situational vignettes. One poster showed a cow with the word "leather" superimposed on it. Next to this image was the same cow with the word "deity" superimposed on it. And just to the right of this second image was the same cow, but this time with the word "dinner" superimposed on it. Same cow, different meanings. Another poster had a rug, one with "decor" written over it, another with "souvenir," and a third with "place of prayer." Same rug, different meanings. HSBC's campaign underscored exactly what the differences in the "OK" symbol illustrate: the interpretation of meaning is not objective. It differs because we see the world differently. Meaning is not universally fixed. It is socially constructed and culturally mediated. What may be acceptable to some can be seen as an offense by others because things aren't the way they are; they are the way we are. To understand the way we are, we must understand the way in which we make meaning.

Researchers across an array of academic disciplines study meaning and its importance to social living. One field in particular, semiotics, examines signs and symbols and their interpreted meanings. Pioneering work from scholars like Ferdinand de Saussure and Charles Pierce has unearthed much of what we know about humans' ability to communicate and achieve collective outcomes because of our ability to express and understand shared meaning. The significance of this ability cannot be overstated. Without shared meaning, social living would be unnavigable. Is it a souvenir or a place of worship? Is it dinner or a deity? Is it a protest or insurrection? Is it good or bad? Orderly living—within our tribes—depends on our ability to see the world similarly, which requires collective meaning making. This is especially important considering the fact that everything around us is inherently meaningless. Look around you. Everything your eye can see at this very moment (even these words) has no intrinsic or built-in meaning. Instead, we collectively negotiate and decide meaning.

Take the color red, for instance. What does "red" mean? It's an odd question, I know. Red is a color, but what does it mean? It has no inherent meaning. However, if you're driving down the street and you approach a red light at an intersection, red means "stop." Why? Because we collectively agreed that red means "stop," just as green means "go" or yellow means "slow down"—unless you're like me and yellow really means "hurry up." But red also means "passion." It also means "danger." And it also means hot, angry, and sexy. "Red" has many different meanings, but none of them are inherent to the word. These are the meanings that we, as a society, have constructed to be signified by the color red, much as we have collectively agreed that a diamond ring means long-lasting love.

In the 1980s, the state of Texas was dealing with a littering problem. It was spending roughly $20 million annually to clear the empty beer cans and other trash that Texans threw out their car windows and onto their highways. State policymakers tried to curb this behavior with a campaign that consisted of signs that read, "Do Not Litter." For Texans, however, these signs read more like an obligation than a rallying call for state beautification. And if you know anything about Texans, you know that they do not like to be told what to do. The semiotics of the campaign were out of sync, and needless to say, the campaign did not work and the littering continued. So the Texas Department of Transportation partnered with a Texas-based advertising agency, GSD&M, to conceive of a different campaign—one whose semiotics signaled a desired meaning that would be congruent with the way Texans might interpret it.

Instead of creating a campaign that seemingly told Texans what to do, they decided to play into the great pride that Texans have in their state by creating language that Texans could use to project their identity. And with that identity came a set of implied behaviors that were expected of those who identified as Texans. The campaign messaging was simple but powerful: "Don't mess with Texas."

This campaign was not about obligatory action; it was about identity congruence. For Texans, the new campaign meant "You don't mess with us, and you don't mess with our state." This linguistic symbol signified a shift in meaning that led to a shift in subsequent behavior, which resulted in a 72 percent decrease in litter on Texas roadways between 1987 and 1990. Indeed, meaning matters, and the lenses through which we see the world—and make meaning of it—are framed by our cultural subscriptions.

Like the study of semiotics, "meaning" has deep roots within the field of anthropology. In a quest to understand what makes us human, anthropologists study the many aspects of the human experience, including the creation and transmission of how people interpret, make sense of, and navigate the world based on their cultural subscriptions. Many scholars have argued that semiotics and anthropology are inseparably linked for this very reason. While semiotics is the study of the interpretation and communication of meaning, anthropology is the exploration of the historical context that affects why and how we make meaning. Cultural anthropologists, in particular, investigate norms, values, and symbols to unearth how we as a species make meaning from both our present and past existence.

The breakthrough work of the cultural anthropologist and scholar Grant McCracken on the movement of meaning provides a window into how contemporary meaning is made and how it moves from cultural production to cultural consumption. Meaning, McCracken wrote, originates from the beliefs and ideologies that we use to frame our everyday experiences and make sense of the world. From this culturally constituted world, meaning is embedded in products by way of four unique fashioning systems—advertising, news outlets, highly esteemed individuals, and fringe societies—and reworked into our identities through four unique ritualized practices—possession, exchange, grooming, and divergence. This process is widely accepted in the world of marketing, and other tangential disciplines, as the de facto description of how meaning is made and how meaning moves from one entity to another.

The first fashioning system comes from creativity and advertising, where cultural characteristics are built into consumer products through messaging and decoration to give them meaning. You can see this in the case of De Beers and diamond rings as well as the "Don't Mess with Texas" antilittering campaign—which shows this fashioning system's power outside traditional commerce. Similarly, designers reflect cultural characteristics in their products to transfer meaning into what would otherwise be just a sweater, for instance. You see this in streetwear where designers use patterns, oversized logos, and slogans that are reflective of cultural ideals. For example, the streetwear brand OBEY, which was founded by the artist, designer, and activist Shepard Fairey, typically displays the word "obey" on the chest of its garments as a sarcastic critique of societal propaganda. The intended meaning of OBEY clothing is rooted in the countercultures of punk rock and skaters. OBEY channels the disregard for conventions, commercial marketing, and popular politics that is held within these cultural frames and instills them in a product to supplant what would normally be merely a T-shirt.

The second fashioning system involves news and magazine media, where publications, newspapers, blogs, and podcasts help frame how brands and organizations are seen. For instance, publications like *Vogue*, *Cosmopolitan*, and *Elle* frame traditional feminine beauty, while *GQ* and *Esquire* frame traditional masculinity. In November 2019, *New York Magazine*'s dedicated content for shopping intelligently, the *Strategist*, posted an article about a quilted puffer coat sold exclusively on Amazon. The Women's Thickened Down Jacket, by Orolay, was a standard oversized parka. Aside from the two big pockets and zipper tassels, the coat was unremarkable. However, the *New York Times* later wrote about the coat in a piece about stylish Brooklyn moms, which contextualized the coat—now commonly known as "the Amazon coat"—as more than just a coat. It was now an artifact that signified the hippest New York mothers.

The third system is the high-esteem fashioning system. This system consists of opinion leaders—or modern-day influencers—whose point of view of or reference to a particular product gives the product new meaning. Let's revisit Beyoncé. For the 2016 release of her sixth studio album, *Lemonade*, Beyoncé debuted the single "Formation," in which she said, "When he f**k me good, I take his a** to Red Lobster ('cause I slay)." In this case, what was once known as a seafood chain restaurant, famous for its wildly popular Cheddar Bay biscuits, now stood for a place where couples go after sexual intercourse. According to CNN Business, after the launch of "Formation," Red Lobster experienced a 33 percent increase in sales, an effect of cultural consumption due in large part to this new meaning.

The fourth and final system is the fringe society fashioning system, which consists of groups of people who exist on the margins of society and collectively rework products to give them new meanings based on the community's cultural characteristics. Take, for instance, the LGBTQ+ community—a group that was considered fringe in 1986 when McCracken wrote his seminal paper. The LGBTQ+ community collectively reframed the rainbow to mean gay pride. Commissioned by the first openly gay elected official in United States, Harvey Milk, the American artist and gay rights activist Gilbert Baker designed the rainbow flag in 1978. Prior to Baker's design, the community had historically used a pink triangle as a representative signifier. Though rainbows are typically a symbol of hope, a biblical promise that God will never destroy the earth with a flood again, as is detailed in the book of Genesis, the rainbow was assigned new meaning within the frame of the LGBTQ+ community. As Gilbert stated, "Our job as gay people was to come out, to be visible, to live in the truth, as I say, to get out of the lie. A flag really fit that mission, because that's a way of proclaiming your visibility or saying, 'This is who I am!'" Through Baker, and the broader gay community, the rainbow has now been assigned a new meaning: pride.

These are the four fashioning systems that marketers use to infuse products with meaning when communicating to the public. By the same token, these fashioning systems are the different ways by which you can preach the gospel to your congregation. Maybe you leverage the advertising fashioning system to preach the gospel through a post on Instagram. Or maybe you use the magazine and news fashioning system to preach your gospel through an article that a writer composes about your candidate on a blog. Or perhaps you tap into the high-esteem fashioning system to preach the gospel through a gamer who talks about your product on Twitch or tap into a community to preach your gospel through the fringe society fashioning system. Whichever you choose, these systems—both individually and collectively—are all levers that you can pull to communicate on behalf of your product, company, organization, or cause and imbue it with meaning.

These systems act as vehicles that transport meaning from the culturally constituted world in which we live to the brands that we consume and later adopt as part of our own cultural practices. Each one of these fashioning systems—advertising, news and magazines, high esteem, and fringe society—provides a way to communicate a message and preach the gospel about an organization, company, or initiative. These systems can work individually, but savvy communicators devise strategies that enable them to work in concert. For instance, a politician might place billboards around town about their candidacy (advertising fashioning system), solicit articles to be written about them in a regional publication through their PR agency (news and magazine fashioning system), and seek endorsements from notable members of society (high-esteem fashioning system). Together, these efforts help signal an alchemy of intended meaning that positions the product or brand to be consumed and potentially adopted into people's cultural facts. However, to achieve this coveted feat, there is one last hurdle to overcome: people must make meaning themselves.

## MAKING MEANING

As we've established, you can move meaning from culture into your brand by making use of the fashioning systems we just discussed. Once a brand has signaled meaning to a desired target, this meaning must be woven into that community's identity in order to truly take hold. This happens through a set of rituals that we undergo to work brands into our lives. The first is the possession ritual, in which we purchase items to outwardly express who we are—think about decorating a new office or putting bumper stickers on a car. The second is the exchange ritual, in which a product takes on new meaning because it has been given as a gift. Gifting transforms what was once merely a shirt into something that is imbued with all the emotional intent of the gift giver. I still have a T-shirt that was given to me by a dear friend almost twenty years ago. It's now tattered and out of style, and I hardly ever wear it. But I'll never get rid of it because it was a gift from someone I care about. The third is the grooming ritual, in which we invest time and effort in the presentation of self by cultivating the meaningful properties of an object through preparation. Consider the energy invested in the beautification of cars—the washing, polishing, and waxing—to recast something old into something new. These are grooming rituals by which individuals rework the potential meaning of the car—e.g., it looks good—into heightened properties of their own status-seeking identity projects. The last is the divestment ritual, which is actually a ritual of removal, in which we empty meaning out of a product to exorcise any relation to the previous owner or strip away any of the intended meaning originally signaled by marketers. It's why when you buy or rent a house, it is often painted all white—a blank canvas upon which the new owner can paint—or when a product is communicated for an intended use, people rework it for something altogether different. Through these different rituals, we ensure that the products that we buy, the organizations that we join, and the institutions that we frequent are all aligned with the identity that we have established for ourselves.

The goal for marketers and leaders, therefore, is to ensure that the intended meaning signaled through these fashioning systems is the same as the meaning that people ritualize into their identities. When this—meaning congruence—is achieved, something magical happens.

A shirt is no longer just a shirt. A sneaker is no longer merely a shoe. A car becomes something more than just a vehicle to get me from here to there. Instead, they become a symbol of something far greater

Once again, I think it's helpful to think of this in religious terms. In religious texts, this process would be called consecration, when something that was once common becomes sacred or set apart. It might seem odd to think of a mass-produced product as something people might consider sacred. But according to neuroscientists, it's not a far-fetched idea. In 2011, researchers conducted a magnetic resonance imagining (MRI) study on the brains of Apple fans after they were presented with messaging from the brand. The researchers found that the Apple fans experienced stimulation in the same region of the brain as religious people when exposed to their respective artifacts. The same feelings, reactions, and excitement that are activated in the minds of religious practitioners during worship are conjured in the minds of zealots who subscribe to the cult of Apple when engaging with the brand. Brands can indeed be consecrated and elevated to totem status when meaning congruence is achieved. Plenty of our favorite, most beloved brands, like Apple, are.

The act of consecration illustrates just how powerful meaning making can be for humans and how important meaningful brands are to who we are—both individually and collectively. When it is done well, the meanings and imagery that we associate with brands become shared and salient in the minds of a community, so much so that the process creates a shorthand that gives the brand permission to exist beyond the products it traditionally makes. Try this old adage as a comparison: imagine if Nike were to start a chain of hotels. Can you envision what that hotel might look like? Most likely, yes. But if I told you that the Westin Hotel had decided to make a sneaker, it would be much harder to picture because, in our minds, the Westin is a hotel and nothing else. Its collective meaning stops there. Nike, on the other hand, means so much more. When you think of Nike, you envision rich imagery and relevant associations that extend beyond its products. These memory structures are evoked because of the meaning congruence between the gospel Nike preaches and the meaning that people have ritualized into their own identity, which allows the brand to venture into any category it chooses so long as it is in line with how people perceive it. That's superpowerful.

But here's the trick, which you may have already noticed. Although brands and leaders have the ability to preach the gospel in hopes of infusing your product with meaning, they don't actually make meaning—people do. Marketing signals intended meaning through the fashioning systems available to us, but people do the meaning making. The philosopher Roland Barthes underscored this point by saying, "The author has no sovereignty over his own words. It belongs to the reader who interprets them." While marketers own the brand mark, control how the brand expresses itself, and decide which products the company might offer, it's the *people* who decide what the brand expression means and whether it fits with their cultural identity. People are the sole meaning makers, and meaning congruence is achieved when the intended meaning of what is signaled is aligned with the meaning that people assign to it. That is to say, meaning is socially constructed, and therefore, it belongs to the people.

As an academic, I became fascinated with the concept of meaning making and its impact on consumption. During my doctoral studies at Temple University, I explored how brands and branded products spread within a community through social contagion—the effects of peer influence—and collective meaning making. When social contagion occurs within a community, brands are not only adopted by the community but also normalized and elevated from utilitarian functions to identity markers. We've seen examples of this in previous chapters, like the adoption of PBR, Patagonia, and the Brooklyn Nets. These brands, and others like them, transcended their product features to become important components of cultural meaning. And much like brands spread from person to person to achieve cultural transcendence, meaning is passed from person to person to achieve collective congruence.

## EVALUATION AND LEGITIMATION

The spread of brands and branded products within a community requires coordination among its members. This coordination typically happens without the direction of an authoritative figure or a drum major who leads the group. Rather, it happens through collective judgment (people deciding whether something is "good" or "bad") and shared acceptability (people deciding whether something is "in" or "out"). In sociology, these processes are called evaluation and legitimation, respectively. Harvard sociologist Michèle Lamont asked, "How does an art object, a literary work, or a scientific theory gain value to the point at which it is consecrated and integrated into the canon?" How does a product gain value to the point that it becomes integrated into the cultural zeitgeist? To find out, we need to look at the relationship between evaluation and legitimation and how they, together, help us collectively give something meaning.

Evaluation is exactly what it sounds like—a judgment about the value of something. And every community does it. Whether it's a physical object, a behavior, an institution, or even other people, we are constantly assessing value to answer a simple question, albeit subconsciously: Does this fit within the cultural characteristics of people like me? Are these sneakers cool? Does this jacket look good? Is this an "old person's" car? Is this a good school? Does this dance look silly? The answers to these questions, and many more like them, are subjective in nature and based almost entirely on the meaning that the community attributes to them. Though individuals engage in the evaluation process, evaluating an object is a collaborative effort in which the whole community decides whether that product is cool based on the social facts of the community.

Like meaning making, evaluation is socially constructed, as my opinion of a company, product, or movement is biased by the opinions of others, especially other people like me. We all have a desire to fit in and a need to belong. The coordination of opinions helps us do just that. Therefore, my opinion of a brand is influenced by the accumulation of opinions from my tribe—even if someone offers a different opinion as an opportunity to distinguish themselves from others in the community, considering the human paradox of wanting to fit in but also stand out. This person's judgment is also informed and influenced by the judgment of others. Evaluation is a social process, as is legitimation.

Legitimation happens when we, as community members or members of society more broadly, decide what is okay. For instance, thirty years ago, the idea of having visible tattoos was reserved for the rebellious—rock musicians, biker gangs, and other fringe groups. It was deemed unacceptable by society, so much so that if you had tattoos, you'd likely try to cover them up for a job interview because of what they might mean in the mind of the interviewer. Today, however, people wear visible tattoos freely and are not seen as degenerates for doing so. Over the years, having tattoos went from meaning "outcast" to being "normal," generally speaking. This is a by-product of legitimation.

Athletic apparel was once suitable only for workouts and yoga classes, never to be worn in public or at social functions. But now we have athleisure, through which yoga pants and tapered joggers have become acceptable in many different settings. The legitimation of athleisure drove this industry to become a $411 billion market in 2021, and it's expected to grow to over $793 billion by 2028. The companies that were early to capitalize on this phenomenon—like the Canadian-based athletic apparel retailer Lululemon—experienced an economic windfall, while the athletic brands that did not move so quickly, like Under Armour, missed out. These late movers, unfortunately, placed their strategic bets elsewhere despite the shifts in cultural consumption, and these brands are still paying the price.

Online dating is another great example. The idea of meeting a potential romantic partner online was considered a sign of desperation twenty years ago. At the time, the conventional wisdom was that meeting someone online meant you were unable to meet someone in the "real world." But that perception has since changed. By 2020, prepandemic, 30 percent of all initial dating encounters happened through online dating, which was up from 3 percent in 2010. Over the course of ten years, we completely legitimated online dating. What once meant "loser" now means "normal."

"Do people like me do something like this?" This is the question we ask ourselves as we navigate our day-to-day lives. The theoretical framework for understanding how social structures—like norms and practices—are established as guidelines for social behavior is referred to as institutional theory. According to this theory, the process of legitimation is shaped by imitation. We observe others who we think are like us to decide what is acceptable behavior for us. The world-renowned scholar of social psychology and influence Robert Cialdini referred to this phenomenon as social proof, where we copy the actions of others to fit in. Social proof provides a signal of what is deemed acceptable behavior among our people, and, subsequently, we receive the behavior as acceptable and act in concert to promote social solidarity.

Legitimation is socially constructed and plays a critical role in the process of meaning making. Every time a community is introduced to something new (an exogenous shock to the system like a new product, new music, or any breaking news that comes through our news feeds and across our screens), members of the community collectively make sense of it (make meaning) and decide whether and how it will be integrated into their culture. Once your brand has been legitimated by the congregation, you're set!

There is undeniable evidence that smoking is not good for us. Smoking is terribly addictive. It alters our neurochemistry. And, worst of all, it can kill us. Yet for decades, smoking was considered "normal" among Americans. Doctors smoked in their exam rooms. Musicians smoked. Expecting mothers smoked while they were with child, and no one batted an eye. As of 1965, over 42 percent of Americans were considered "smokers," according to the CDC. It is likely that that percentage was even higher in the decades prior. Despite the adverse effects of cigarettes, smoking did not equate to something negative in the minds of Americans. It held a different meaning. Instead of meaning "eventual death," smoking was a symbol of masculinity that signaled rebelliousness. The cultural product of that day helped to influence these associations through the movement of meaning. For instance, the high-esteem fashioning system signaled that smoking was a sign of rebel cool, as portrayed in James Dean's character in 1955's *Rebel Without a Cause* or Sharon Stone's character in 1992's *Basic Instinct*. These films, and countless others, signaled an interpretation that led to the legitimation of smoking among Americans. But perhaps no fashioning system was more influential than the advertising fashioning system in moving the meaning of cigarettes. While the Lucky Strikes packaging that displayed doctors on the front with a label that read, "20,679 physicians say 'Luckies are less irritating'" was certainly influential in its ability to subvert any mortal consequence of smoking, it was the Marlboro Man that really made the difference.

Introduced in 1954, the Marlboro Man signified everything that masculinity aimed to be—adventurous, rugged, and pioneering. The Marlboro Man was a cowboy who rode a horse across open land, wore apparel straight from the pages of the Wild West, and always had a cigarette at the ready. At the time of his debut, American life was the antithesis of the Marlboro Man's universe. Instead of taming the Wild West, White Americans were moving to the suburbs, following the economic boom after World War II, to live a domesticated life with white picket fences. Smoking cigarettes gave men a sense of rebellion in an otherwise docile existence. Marlboro signaled this intended meaning through the mythology of the Marlboro Man, and Americans understood what the story was meant to signify. Americans connected with the story, and just like that, smoking was legitimated. The Marlboro Man campaign ran for forty-five years and has been deemed one of the most impactful advertising campaigns of all time because of its ability to influence behavior as an iconic cultural symbol.

The philosopher Marshall McLuhan once famously said, "All media work us over completely. They're so pervasive in their personal, political, economic, aesthetic, psychological, moral, ethical, social consequences, they leave no part of us unaffected, unaltered." And he was right. The media work us over completely. That is to say, the stories that cultural producers tell us—and the subsequent stories that we tell ourselves in many forms—largely determine what gets legitimated and what doesn't. Furthermore, when a brand or organization is legitimated within a community's shared cultural frame (its constructed social reality and collective meaning), the object is symbolically integrated into the community's cultural practices. When this happens, people within the community consume, vote, subscribe, and the like as a cultural act.

Evaluation and legitimation are constantly happening all around us—all the time, in real time. It's through these processes that people make meaning and behave—in concert—accordingly. Therefore, if you want to get people to move by leveraging the unparalleled influence of culture, it's not enough to just preach the gospel to the congregation; you must also understand how they make meaning. This provocation set the stage for my doctoral dissertation. With an understanding of social contagion and a curiosity about meaning making, I decided to study how brands and branded products are evaluated and how they become legitimated within a cultural context. More specifically, I set out to answer the following question: What are the mechanisms of evaluation and legitimation when a brand spreads within a particular community—in the case of my research, the hip-hop community? I analyzed forty months of historical data—amounting to over twelve million lines of text and 4.8 GB of data—as I watched members of the hip-hop community make meaning through their exchanges on Reddit.

Reddit is a community-based online platform that refers to itself as "the front page of the internet," suggesting that it is a gateway to the most interesting and relevant content on the Internet. The content on Reddit is submitted by users and voted on by the community—via up-votes and down-votes—based on its interest and relevance. Up-votes signal that user-submitted content is valued by the community and credentialed as having been vetted by the community and representative of its collective approval, while down-votes signal the opposite. The content on Reddit often becomes the catalyst for topics, discoveries, and memes that are later exchanged and discussed on other popular platforms like Facebook and Twitter. Reddit is home to over 430 million monthly active users who congregate in "subreddits" that are, in effect, communities of people who are dedicated to different topics of interest. These subreddits are managed and supervised by moderators who ensure that the conversations are on topic and aligned with the norms of the community. Moderators also post questions to the subreddit communities to inspire dialogue among their members. In this way, Reddit is a "community of communities" whose members construct and negotiate the cultural characteristics of the communities.

Over the course of my two years of research on the platform, I uncovered four mechanisms of evaluation and legitimation at work: responding, recontextualizing, reconciling, and reinforcing.

## MECHANISM #1—RESPONDING

The responding mechanism is the way by which members of a community participate in the processes of evaluation and legitimation. And the language choice of community members—explicit or implicit—informs how meaning is made and attitudes are shaped about a brand or entity. Of the Reddit conversations that I studied, 41.5 percent of the mentions were statements of *implicit* judgment, meaning people gave their opinion about the brand or branded product by mentioning it in the context of a lyric, person, event, or perhaps even another brand. Here's an example about the online video game Fortnite:

**Weezy f baby. The f is for fortnite (u/excrowned, 9/30/19, r/ Kanye)**

In this post, the user u/excrowned used a lyrical reference from the hip-hop artist Lil Wayne (aka Weezy F. Baby) in relation to Fortnite. In his 2003 song "Da Drought," Lil Wayne says, "My name happens to be Weezy F. Baby. The 'F' is for you to find out, man." In subsequent releases, Wayne added, "the 'F' is for fly," "the 'F' is for fresh," and "the 'F' is for fashion." Whatever the case, "F" is an implied signifier of something good or desirable. So saying "The f is for fortnite" is an implicit way of saying Fortnite is considered desirable or good.

On the other hand, I found that roughly 44 percent of brand mentions from the community were statements of explicit judgment, where people clearly and obviously stated their opinion about the brand or branded product. Here's another example about Fortnite:

**Fortnite = un-wavey (u/Jacksokool, 02/18/2019, r/Kanye)**

The community member u/Jacksokool used a colloquialism, but his opinion is explicit in its meaning. The term "wavey" is slang for cool or looking good, as in "When I go out, I have to keep it wavey," so by saying "Fortnite = un-wavey," this community member is saying that Fortnite is unequivocally not cool.

Here's the takeaway: when a person uses an implicit statement of judgment when talking about a brand or branded product, it allows them to critique the brand while also mitigating potential risk. They can enter the conversation by communicating an opinion about the brand, but the implicit nature of their statement gives them flexibility to change their stance during the social exchange if they find themselves out of sync with the rest of the community. So marketers and leaders must pay attention to the coded language that people use when they talk about their brand or organization because their language is full of meaning—even more so when the topics of conversation are more personal. As my research revealed, if the topic of discussion was seemingly benign, like the value propositions of a product, people were more likely to use explicit statements because the probability of inciting conflict with other members of the community was fairly low. However, more controversial topics, like whether they agreed with Nike's support of Kaepernick, had a greater risk of social incongruence, so people tended to use implicit statements in their conversations.

This mechanism reminds me of growing up in Detroit, watching the neighborhood kids play Double Dutch jump rope. Double Dutch is a game where two long jump ropes are rotated in opposite directions and children masterfully jump in sync within the turning ropes so as not to stop the ropes' motion. It requires a lot of skill and is made more intense by the social pressure of onlookers. Before you jump into the game, you carefully study the cadence of the rotating ropes so as to perfectly time your entrance. The way community members engage in evaluation and legitimation is similar. They are purposeful about their use of language when participating in the conversation. They respond to the exchanges that are currently in motion—much like the rotating ropes—in a way that mitigates the risk of any social consequences if the entrance isn't successful.

## MECHANISM #2—RECONTEXTUALIZING

The recontextualizing mechanism refers to the way tribal members evaluate and legitimate by taking a product from one context and placing it in another context that is more relevant to them. A great example of this is the use of memes and their cultural replication through the imitation of ideas, fashions, and beliefs. Considering its frequent use, there's a good chance that you've seen the meme known as "Distracted Boyfriend," which captures a man checking out another woman while walking down the street with what appears to be his girlfriend. The image was uploaded to a stock photo site under the literal description "disloyal man with his girlfriend looking at another woman," but Internet users took the photo and began to recontextualize it with their own meaning. One recontextualization had the text "the youth" superimposed over the boyfriend, "capitalism" superimposed over the girlfriend, and "socialism" superimposed over the other woman to communicate the notion that today's youth prefer socialism over capitalism. Another recontextualization featured the word "me" over the boyfriend, "multiple pressing matters and responsibilities" over the girlfriend, and "a nap" over the other woman to communicate the propensity to prioritize napping over anything else. Internet users rework memes as a cultural product that communicates the nuanced characteristics of people like them, and people share them as a way to project their identity. The act of recontextualizing seems to happen repeatedly in communities through implicit statements of judgment that use referential coded language to make meaning.

For the hip-hop community, members often use rap lyrics as references to move the expressed meaning of a product from one context to another. Consider a lyric from Kanye West's "No More Parties in LA" : "Some days I'm in my Yeezys, some days I'm in my Vans. If I knew y'all made plans, I wouldn't have popped the Xans." In this lyric,

Kanye declares that sometimes he chooses to wear the sneaker brand that he cofounded with Adidas (Yeezys), and other times he chooses to wear a sneaker of a different brand. The recontextualization is typically made in reference to the second line, where he admits that if he was aware that plans for the evening had been made, then he would not have taken the branded sedative known as Xanax, an anxiety-reducing prescription drug. In an exchange between members of the hip-hop community on Reddit, someone asked, "Anyone ever watch this movie high?" To which another community member responded, "If I knew y'all had watch plans I wouldn't have popped xans." Here, the lyrical reference was recontextualized as a response to a situation that seemingly had nothing to do with the song or with the branded product. Additionally, the repeated use of the Xanax brand in such a cavalier manner implies a positive evaluation of it—or at the very least a neutral assessment—which can potentially erode the taboo against what can only be perceived as the recreational use of a prescription drug. The use of reference as a recontextualizing mechanism allows members of the community to cast their votes as the community collectively engages in the process of evaluation and legitimation. Likewise, the use of referential code, like memes and lyrics, enables members of a community to make meaning of the world and express their opinion about the world through their shared cultural frames.

## MECHANISM #3—RECONCILING

The reconciling mechanism is how members of a community engage in the evaluation and legitimation process by pursuing cognitive consonance when their behavior is out of sync with the cultural norms of their community. The act of reconciling helps relieve any discrepancy between the beliefs and behaviors of the individual and those of the community in the mind of the individual. In some cases, when a cultural event happens and causes conflict between a community member's actions or beliefs and those of their tribe, members can shift the focus of the evaluation to reconcile the dissonance and return to equilibrium. This is similar to the frequent use of "whataboutery" in contemporary politics, where individuals discredit criticism by shifting the focus of the argument instead of directly refuting or resolving the critique. In these instances, reconciling often allows community members to misdirect the locus of evaluation in order to maintain cognitive consonance while continuing their current consumption behavior.

On the other hand, some community members wrestle with the incongruence of their actions and their preestablished cultural meaning frames, opting to alter their beliefs or behaviors as a means of reconciling their dissonance. The process informs how they participate in the evaluation and legitimation process of the brand or branded product within networked tribe. The following posts from Reddit conversations illustrate this form of reconciling:

> **Kanye's validation of President Trump is disturbing and I cannot wear my Yeezy's in good conscience. I cannot support someone that is publicly pleading on behalf of Trumps movement of bigotry and racism. (u/blowinmoneyfast, 09/30/18, Yeezy, r/Hiphopheads)**

> **So done with this dude. Selling the yeezys too. (u/Confucius_ said, 10/01/18, Yeezy, r/Hiphopheads)**

> **I'm out. Bye Yeezy. (u/ProstheticPoetics, 05/01/18, Yeezy, r/ Hiphopheads)**

In these examples, the community members use the reconciling mechanism to change their behaviors and beliefs. The community member u/blowinmoneyfast explicitly communicates the conflict between supporting Kanye West and the cultural characteristics of the community, considering Kanye's behavior. The statement "I cannot wear my Yeezy's in good conscience" expresses the incongruence between the cultural characteristics of the community and Kanye's behaviors and, by extension, the Yeezy brand. And the two posts from the community members u/Confucius_said and u/ProstheticPoetics communicate an explicit exit from consumption—even a declaration to sell previously purchased products—as a means of resolving any cognitive conflict, which casts a vote for the product's evaluation and legitimation.

## MECHANISM #4—REINFORCING

The reinforcing mechanism is how members of the community engage in the evaluation and legitimation process by signaling their appraisal of an object through repetition. Community members state their position about an object through either implicit or explicit statements. As more members do the same, in unison, it communicates a seemingly agreed-upon collective vote. People observing this are inclined to accept this vote and get on board with the consensus as an act of social solidarity. Here's an example:

> **I don't remember the last time I didn't see someone wearing yeezys—real or fake—at least once (u/Nicefroyo, 09/08/18, Yeezy, r/Hiphopheads)**

> **The amount of Adidas I see on campus vs when kanye was on nike is insane though. Like I feel like I see way more Addidas than Nike now and it was absolutely the other way around (u/ XXX_is_my_granddaddy, 05/03/18, Adidas, r/Hiphopheads)**

> **I'm convinced 95% of the population has airpods (not judging I have them too but wtf They really out here) (u/Bobokins12, 01/13/19, AirPods, Kanye)**

In these examples, community members observe the frequent use of a brand out in the world, which signals an implicit positive evaluation and legitimation. Even when the use of these products by those who could be argued to be nonmembers of the hip-hop community is observed, it provides evidence of agreement when community members engage in conversations with other members about the brand's popularity. The more the brand is worn or used by community members, the more credence the brand or branded product is given as it undergoes assessment of being deemed "good" and "in" by the community.

The fourth mechanism, reinforcing, illustrates that as people visibly present themselves with a particular brand or speak positively about it, they are essentially casting their vote about the evaluation and legitimation of the brand. The more community members wear the brand or talk about the brand in a positive light, the more the brand is perceived by other community members as "cool" and "acceptable" more broadly. As the saying goes, "Nothing draws a crowd like a crowd."

The reinforcing mechanism facilitates what is performed by the individual and observed by other community members, the result of which helps to drive the social coordination that is needed for social contagion to occur within a community. The reinforcing mechanism is heightened thanks to the prevalence of social network platforms— like Facebook, Instagram, and TikTok—that enable greater visibility of the cultural receipts that community members present when their identity projects are on display through the content they post online. We will discuss this further in the next chapter.

## THE PEER FASHIONING SYSTEM

While the fashioning systems that McCracken introduced as vehicles for meaning movement are seemingly exhaustive, the way in which meaning is made in the hip-hop community—and others like it—does not fit well into any of the four fashioning systems. The hip-hop community consists of people, not a third-party entity. Although community members certainly ingest the media messages that are produced by third-party entities (advertising, news, or high esteem), these systems do not capture the communal aspect of meaning making that takes place among tribal members.

To describe the way in which members of the hip-hop community engage in meaning making, there is a need to introduce a more nuanced fashioning system to McCracken's watershed contribution. This modified fashioning system should account for the communal nature of the group and its appeal beyond the shadows of fringe society. My research provides justification for an additional fashioning system that I call the "peer fashioning system." Within the peer fashioning system, meaning is made when community members engage in the negotiation and construction of evaluation and legitimation when social contagion occurs.

Set in 1986, McCracken's work did not account for contemporary technological advances, like social networking platforms and other digitally mediated communication systems, because they didn't exist. However, these technologies accelerate and influence the meaning-making process whereby people collectively evaluate and legitimate brands and branded products and just about every aspect of daily living. For example, consider the 2021 Oscars and what will likely live in infamy, the Will Smith "slap."

What would typically be considered standard fare for an award show broadcast quickly became controversial when the megastar Will Smith walked onstage and slapped the comedian Chris Rock across the face. The altercation arose after Rock made a joke at the expense of Will's wife, Jada Pinkett-Smith, regarding her short hair. This behavior was so uncharacteristic of Will Smith and so abnormal during what anyone would expect of this black-tie award ceremony that I thought the incident was staged. As I watched the show, I was sure it was a comedic bit until the audio of the live broadcast went silent on my television. Of course, we would later find out that it was indeed real. But what I found most interesting was the great sum of commentary that took place after the fact.

From news coverages to think pieces, celebrity weigh-ins and social commentary across Twitter, we watched the country collectively make meaning. Was it real or fake? Is violence an appropriate response when defending a loved one? Does the prestige of an event like the Oscars require a set of norms that forbids this kind of behavior? Was this a demonstration of protecting Black women, or was this an act of toxic masculinity perpetuated by the patriarchy? Have we gotten too "soft" as a country or too politically correct to take a joke? It seemed as though "the slap" was interrogated from just about every possible angle and debated on all sides. All such contributions to the public discourse help us decide whether a behavior is OK (evaluation) and, ultimately, acceptable (legitimation) so we know whether people like "us" do something like "this." This is a microcosm of how we negotiate and construct meaning for practically everything and decide what will be adopted into our cultural practice and what will be prohibited.

Imagine what this means for new products, new candidates, new music, or a new ideas. The conversations we have and the media we consume help us make meaning and decide what to buy, how to vote, what to join, and what to try. Considering the transparency and social proof that are innate to observing peer behavior in the practice of meaning making, the actions of these observed individuals inform and influence the culturally constituted world whereby meaning is established for onlookers. This results in a cyclic relationship in which the act of displaying one's meaning frame serves as a cultural receipt or public progress bar by which the affects, behaviors, cognitions, and desires of community members influence those of other community members. In other words, the reinforcing mechanism is the bridge that connects the meaning-making process—which is inherent to evaluation and legitimation—to the occurrence of social contagion.

## LEVERAGING MEANING MAKING

It is worth noting that the fashioning systems introduced by Mc-Cracken's work (advertising, news and magazines, high esteem, and fringe society), and now the peer fashioning system introduced in my research, all work together as people make meaning of brands. While tribal members move meaning from the cultural world to brands, the meaning associated with the same brands is being informed by advertisements, blogs, and "influencers." These different communication vehicles can sometimes signal different meanings—for instance, an ad may say one thing about the brand, while an article says something different, and an influencer says something altogether different from the other two. This meaning confusion can cause a challenge for community members with regard to ritualizing the brand into their identity because of the ambiguity in the brand's potential meaning and how other members of the community might see it.

It's also important to note that the process of meaning making is not linear. We don't see an ad or read an article, and "just like that," meaning is made and reworked into our identity, like a bowling ball going down an alley to knock over pins. No, this process is much more akin to a pinball machine, where one's identity is constantly bumping into multiple, and sometimes conflicting, meanings that have impregnated a brand or branded product through a host of different fashioning systems. Maybe an ad says the product is great, but an article says it's no good, and although Shaq endorses it, the product has been panned on Reddit but moderately appraised through Amazon reviews. What does it mean? In this regard, the relationship between the different fashioning systems, the subsequent meanings associated with an object, and the individual's identity is illustrated in Figure 3 in

Figure 3. Meaning-identity congruence

what I call the meaning-identity congruence model. People are tasked with the challenge of finding compatibility between these different meanings and their congruence with their identity within the cultural frame of the community.

While this may seem like a daunting and uncontrollable scenario for marketers or anyone who wishes to excite behavior, the situation is actually more empowering than anything else. The multiple fashioning systems that inform meaning create an opportunity for marketers to curate uniformity by the way in which potential meaning is signaled. Each fashioning system can be coordinated to work together such that one system echoes the other, creating a redundant, singular, and salient brand message with a consistent desired meaning. As community members are exposed to said messaging, be it an advertisement or an "influencer" endorsement, the process by which these individuals make meaning becomes easier because they don't have to parse conflicting information. Therefore, marketers and managers alike should consider these fashioning systems as controllable levers that can be used to ease the meaning-making process for individuals and the social negotiation of evaluation and legitimation within their communities.

The reinforcing mechanism presents an opportunity for marketers to invest in the creation of public artifacts that present visible receipts of behavior. For example, consider StockX, the online aftermarket website where buyers place bids on highly coveted products sold by individual sellers. As a brand, StockX believes in transparency, and it demonstrates this conviction by removing the opacity of buying sneakers and streetwear in the secondary market after they have been sold in retail stores. Unlike eBay and other auction websites, StockX provides a manual, proprietary authentication process that uses twenty-seven different indicators to assess whether the product is "real" and not a counterfeit. This is the company's core differentiating value proposition for consumers. Considering the overwhelming number of fake products in the resale market, this is a compelling feature of the StockX offering.

When a product successfully passes StockX's authentication process, it is then validated with an affixed tag that serves as a "Good Housekeeping seal of approval," as if to say, "These are legit." This reduces the normal buyer's anxiety that is typically associated with purchasing products from strangers online. A product purchased from StockX is guaranteed to be the real thing. Because of this transparency, users can shop in a more informed way. This gets right to the heart of the company's conviction: in a world of elitist smoke and mirrors, StockX cuts through the facade and empowers consumers with knowledge and access. So the semiotics of the StockX symbol on a pair of Nike sneakers or any other branded product means it's real—not because the sneakers are necessarily real, but because people have agreed that the artifact means they are. Not to mention, it takes what would normally be unknown to onlookers—where you bought your shoes—and makes it visible to the public, creating an identity project through the retailer by making the private public.

This meaning construction is negotiated and formed by community members as they decide what's cool and what's acceptable. The use of products and the expressed opinion of a brand, for example, act as a public progress bar that signals what is likely deemed "cool" and acceptable by the community at large. The repeated observation of this public progress bar creates a sense of perceived ubiquity within the community and influences the affects, behaviors, cognitions, and desires of other community members. This gets people to take action. As the reinforcing mechanism is at work, it informs the culturally constituted world from which advertisers, magazines, influencers, and peers move meaning to products. Understanding meaning making enables marketers to potentially project artificial public progress bars, like the acquisition of Instagram views or becoming a trending topic on Twitter, that signal to the tribe, "Everyone is doing it." The result of this activity will help forward the processes of evaluation and legitimation, which are critical processes for social contagion.

Moreover, these implications extend beyond a commercial consumption context. There are a host of industries in which marketers spend a large amount of resources trying to get people to recycle, vote, wear a mask, and other nonfinancial behaviors. Our propensity to adopt said behaviors depends on how we make meaning, and meaning is culturally mediated.

## FROM KNOW-WHY TO KNOW-HOW

This is the power of culture. It determines how we see the world and how we behave in the world. If you can harness meaning congruence within the congregation of people who subscribe to the same beliefs and ideologies that you do, you significantly increase the chances of getting people to take action when you preach the gospel. When we achieve that kind of collective agreement, people don't consume or join because of who we are (the brand); they do it because of who *they* are (the community). The brand or organization is now a way by which people express their identity. In these cases, the brand or organization can be elevated from its utility function (more than just a pair of shoes, as in the case of Nike) to become consecrated within the community.

What's more, the things we often assume are innately "of" a particular culture in many cases originated outside said culture. Take Scandinavian culture. Much of what we think of as "Scandinavian" is actually borrowed and recontextualized. Swedish meatballs aren't Swedish. They are Turkish. The pastry we know as the danish isn't Danish; it's Austrian. Our cultures are constructed and reconstructed every day as we interact with and encounter new ideas, new products, and new people. This negotiation and construction exercise that community members undergo is how they make meaning of the world, and it governs how they show up in the world. Evaluation and legitimation are critical processes for making meaning of products, advertising, partnerships, and just about everything around us. Understanding this is the key to leveraging the power of culture to excite collective behavioral adoption. In the next chapter, we'll explore what happens when our understanding of meaning is anemic and we misinterpret the codes of culture.

## CHAPTER 5

# MISSING THE CODES

S TANLEY VINTON WAS BORN ON APRIL 16, 1935, JUST outside Pittsburgh, Pennsylvania. His parents, Stan and Dorothy, encouraged his musical interests at a young age, which paid dividends throughout his life. Playing in bands throughout his adolescence, Stanley saved money from local gigs to pay for college, where he studied music composition. He would go on to pursue a career in music following graduation, adopting the stage name "Bobby Vinton" from his middle name, "Robert," so as not to be confused with his father, who himself was a working musician. Bobby Vinton tried several musical ventures before a short stint in the US Army. His big break came in the form of a lullaby-like pop song that his record label had earlier dismissed called "Roses Are Red (My Love)," which became a number-one hit in 1962—the first number one on Billboard for his record label, in fact. But Bobby had much more up his sleeve. By August the following year, he had another hit on the charts, "Blue Velvet," and another on its way.

In January 1964, Bobby Vinton's rendition of "There! I've Said It Again" reached number one on the Billboard 100 and remained in the top spot for four weeks. Vinton's velvety tenor voice captured the sonic silhouette of contemporary American culture at the time. But that would change drastically in just a matter of weeks when four lads from Liverpool—John, Paul, George, and Ringo—burst onto the scene with their raw energy, clever cheekiness, and peculiar hairstyle. Together, they were known as the Beatles, and their debut on the American airwaves started a cultural phenomenon that would later be known as the British Invasion, where music and fashion exports from the United Kingdom would dominate the popular zeitgeist in the States. The Beatles' "I Want to Hold Your Hand" rocketed to number one in February 1964, usurping Vinton, and changed the musical landscape forever.

This should come as no surprise to anyone reading this. It's the Beatles, after all. They are arguably the best rock band in history. However, that was not the refrain in 1964. The shock to the system that was the Beatles, was for many, er, shocking. The *Chicago Tribune* quipped, "The Beatles must be a huge joke, a wacky gag, a gigantic put-on." The *Boston Globe* dittoed: "The Beatles are not merely awful; I would consider it sacrilegious to say anything less than that they are god awful." The *Washington Post* wrote, "Just thinking about The Beatles seems to induce mental disturbance. They have a commonplace, rather dull act that hardly seems to merit mentioning." And *Newsweek* wrote, "Visually, they are a nightmare. Tight dandified Edwardian-Beatnik suits and great pudding bowls of hair." Even Elvis chimed in, lamenting, "The Beatles laid the groundwork for many of the problems we are having with young people today by their filthy, unkempt appearances and suggestive music." Yes, that Elvis Presley, with the hips and all. Ironic, right?

How could they have missed something that would become so salient in society—and increasingly more prevalent in the decades to come? The answer is quite simple: the obvious typically isn't obvious until someone points it out, especially when it comes to understanding culture. Culture is nuanced, and meaning is unstable. To understand them requires great intimacy. What may seem crazy to some might be normal to others. The people who didn't "get" the Beatles were neither close to the legion of early adopters who caught the wave first nor curious enough to look at the world from their perspective to understand the gravitational pull the band had on them. So they missed it, just as people mistook hip-hop for a fad or social networking platforms as merely an outlet for narcissism. These and many other cultural phenomena like them seem crazy to those who do not possess the cultural framework of the tribes who construct them. The result is meaning incongruence.

## MEANING INCONGRUENCE

As we discussed in the previous chapter, meaning is the interpretation or translation of one's reality. Naturally, this translation is subjective—based on the cultural lenses through which we see the world—so that what seems weird to one person might feel normal to someone else based on the beliefs, ideologies, and norms that frame their worldview. Meaning incongruence, therefore, happens when one person's reality does not align or agree with another person's reality. In these situations, two people can observe the same thing and perceive two totally different meanings. For instance, some people saw the storming of the Capitol on January 6, 2021, in Washington, DC, as an insurrection committed by domestic terrorists and instigated by a treasonous president seeking to overturn a free and fair election. However, other people saw the incident as American patriots taking back their freedom in opposition to a corrupt election that was being stolen from them. While the empirical facts of the matter are clear—these rioters brutally took over the Capitol with the intent to shed blood and erode our democracy—people's interpretation of the event is not objective. Just as beauty lies in the eye of the beholder, meaning lies in the mind of the interpreter. Differences in interpretation help demarcate who we are and to what tribe we subscribe. MSNBC and Fox News are clear demonstrations of this. The two news outlets report on the same political and social events; however, they do so with two different interpretations. Some call it an "angle" or a "spin," but it essentially equates to the meaning frames we use to translate the world.

In 1951, the Dartmouth football team played against Princeton in their annual match-up. These Ivy League battles predated the spectacle that is now Big Ten football and today's Southeastern Conference showdowns, but for the young intellectuals who populated these campuses (and, of course, the alumni), these games were a major source of pride. However, this game was particularly contentious, and two psychologists, Albert Hastorf and Hadley Cantril, wanted to get to the bottom of it. Hastorf and Cantril devised a research project in which students from both Dartmouth and Princeton separately watched footage from the same game and were asked to report what they observed. Even though they watched the same game, each group of students perceived the game differently. The Princeton folks thought Dartmouth had committed twice as many infractions as their team, while the Dartmouth folks saw equal amounts of brawn displayed on the football field. Clearly, these realities were not the same, but each group's version of the game was just as real to them as the opposing group's version. Each group believed they saw the same events objectively, despite their differing recounts of what had taken place. Indeed, things aren't the way they are, they are the way we are, and meaning bends accordingly.

Social psychologists refer to this phenomenon as naive realism, where people believe that their worldview is objective and that people who disagree are misinformed or irrational. The world is as we see it and how we interpret it, and anything that says otherwise is just plain wrong. Naturally, this makes communication a challenge for those who aim to preach the gospel because what you intend to mean in your communications may not be what people receive. As political pollster Frank Luntz said, "It's not what you say, it's what people hear." Therefore, it is critical for marketers, activists, politicians, leaders, and the like to not only understand what they intend to mean but also understand what their communications might mean to people. When these two things are not aligned, we find ourselves in a state of meaning incongruence.

In 2017, everything in the Kardashian-sphere was en vogue. *Keeping Up with the Kardashians*, a reality TV show that chronicled the lives of the Kardashian family, was one of the most viewed shows on television. Kim Kardashian, inarguably the brightest star of the bunch, alone had her own world orbiting around her, from her legions of fans and followers on Instagram to her storied romantic life. But the entire Kardashian family, which also included a blended family from Kim's mother's second marriage to then Bruce Jenner (now Caitlyn Jenner), was featured on the cover of magazines, dominated the media headlines, and remained on the fingertips of users' posts across social networking platforms. The Kardashian-Jenners were easily one of the biggest things in the pop-culture zeitgeist. To capitalize on the Kardashian-Jenner fame, Pepsi tapped Kendall Jenner to be the bright-wattage face of its newest marketing communication. Kendall, a star in her own right, was a high-demand supermodel who typically kept a lower profile than her sisters.

The Pepsi ad positioned Kendall as the protagonist who leads a standoff between a crowd of protesters and the police. As Kendall approaches the police in the ad, with a sea of protesters behind her, she confidently hands what appears to be the commanding police officer a can of Pepsi. The intensity mounts as the viewer awaits the White police officer's reaction with anticipation. The officer opens the can and takes a sip, and his once intimidating stance melts away as his face beams with glee from the refreshing taste of Pepsi. The crowd erupts in celebration, and the ad ends with jubilation.

Without question, the outlined scene closely mirrored the heightened social unrest at the time between the Black community and the police, an authoritative institution with a long history of systematic racism and brutality against Black bodies. But, unlike the Pepsi ad, Black people didn't have Kendall Jenner to intercede on our behalf and offer the police a can of Pepsi to cool things down. The backlash was immediate. Certainly, the intent of the Pepsi executives who approved the ad was not to offend anyone—at least, I like to imagine so. They made an ad that was an optimistic reflection of the times starring one of the "it" girls of the moment. How could it go so wrong?

The meaning frames through which the public interpreted the Pepsi ad reflected an altogether different reality. Through the meaning-making frames of the public, Pepsi hired a celebrity—whose family had historically been accused of appropriating Black culture (more on that in Chapter 7)—and depicted her as the "White savior" archetype that was rescuing the Black community—a common trope in American mass communications from film to literature, mythology, and advertising. This was a clear case of meaning incongruence, and with it came a lot of headaches for the folks at Pepsi.

Those who study and practice the art of communication know this all too well. What we intend to mean in our communications and what they actually mean in the minds of people oftentimes do not align. Effective communication requires that the intent of the messenger be in sync with the interpretation of the receiver. This dynamic harkens back to one of the most foundational models in communications literature known as the Shannon-Weaver model, shown below. The model takes a snapshot of the relationship between message senders and message receivers that results in effective communication.

The sender or the information source, is the person—company, organization, or entity—who has information to communicate. This

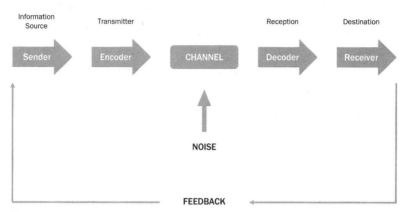

Figure 4.
SOURCE: Claude E. Shannon and Warren Weaver, *The Mathematical Theory of Communication (1949).*

could be a politician who wishes to state her position on a particular topic or maybe a brand that intends to communicate its conviction to the congregation of people who hold a similar ideology. The sender encodes the idea through a transmitter, or an encoder, like an advertisement.

The message is then delivered through a channel, or a medium, to reach the desired audience. The medium serves as a vehicle that transports and delivers the message on behalf of the sender. This could be television, print, billboards, podcasts, social networking platforms, or any other communication technology. Even face-to-face communication counts. Noise can enter the channel, either literally, by way of interruptions in a broadcast or a failed Internet connection, or figuratively, in the form of voices of detractors muddying the message.

Once the encoded message is delivered from the sender through the channel, the message is then decoded to make sense of what was received. When people receive a message through the channel, they translate the meaning of what they just heard, saw, or experienced into something understandable based on their worldview. Naturally, this is where meaning incongruence happens as well.

We all know this intuitively, which is both the beauty and the challenge of the social sciences. We've experienced this process of communication from birth, since we were able to make meaning, and we go through this dynamic thousands of times a day, both as a sender and as a receiver. However, we rarely stop and assess the phenomena that we experience so frequently in our lives. That's why the social sciences are so critical to understanding "us."

Say, for instance, my wife, Alex, asks me to take the clean dishes out of the dishwasher and put the dirty dishes from the sink into the dishwasher. I (the sender) may reply, "Yes, dear," verbally (the encoder) with the intention of communicating my acquiescence in changing the dishes in the dishwasher. Although the tone of my voice (the channel) might sound sweet and loving, my facial expression (the noise) might betray me by conveying how much I don't want to do it. While Alex (the receiver) may have heard my words, she likely also factored in my facial expression, and her translation of my overall communication might be that I'm annoyed that she asked me, even though that was not what I intended to communicate. This is meaning incongruence, the result of which might easily lead to an argument in most households—including mine.

While these sorts of misunderstandings might be settled through a few rounds of back-and-forth between husband and wife, or in any other social relationship between friends or family members, the market typically isn't as forgiving or tolerant of meaning incongruence. People just aren't invested enough to give most brands, with which they have only a transaction-based relationship, a "second chance" to explain themselves when what was translated by the receiver is out of step with how the receiver sees the world. The result can be consumer backlash, public ridicule, and—in some cases—a demotion of brands, public figures, and institutions from consecrated status to excommunication. Take the former governor of Vermont, Howard Dean, for example.

Dean was once the front-runner for the Democratic primaries in the 2004 presidential election. He had obtained coveted endorsements from the former vice president, Al Gore, prominent senators, ambassadors, and politically influential organizations. Everything was going his way, and he was projected to secure his party's nomination. After a surge from two other favorable opponents, Dean slipped into the third spot in the Iowa caucus, a local electoral event that is typically seen as an indicator of how a candidate might fare in the national election. Candidates who perform poorly in the caucus are likely to drop out of the race, so a third-place finish was a dangerous place for Dean.

To rally his supporters for the next primary event, Dean gave an impassioned speech, encouraging his people that despite the setback, there would be much more opportunity to make up the lost ground. Dean assured his supporters, "If you would have told us one year ago that we were going to come in third in Iowa, we would have given anything for that. And you know something, not only are we going to New Hampshire, we're going to South Carolina! And Oklahoma! And Arizona! And North Dakota! And New Mexico! We're going to California! And Texas! And New York! And we're going to South Dakota! And Oregon! And Washington and Michigan!"

This all seemed commonplace for a political speech, but the ending was where things went awry. At a microphone-distorting volume, Dean capped off his emphatic refrain with a final declaration: "And then we're going to Washington, DC, to take back the White House. Yaaaaaaaay!" This moment would later become known as the "Dean Scream," where what was intended to be a verbal expression of enthusiasm—which matched the energy of the crowd, as reporters on the ground have attested—was translated by television audiences and online viewers as a man gone nuts. At the very least, the interpretation of his actions was that here was a man who was unfit to be president. Dean became a viral meme (before there was ever a Facebook or YouTube) and the butt of jokes among talk-show hosts, political pundits, and stand-up comedians. The result of this meaning incongruence put Dean in the eleventh spot of the Democratic primaries, which ultimately ended his presidential run and led to his political excommunication.

Like consecration, the term "excommunication" comes from the religious world, and it refers to an exclusionary practice where an institution removes a person or group of people from the community. It's essentially an act of shunning someone from the group when they break the social norms of the group. While this practice may have originated in the Christian church, it is a customary occurrence within our contemporary social groups. Look no further than the cult classic movie *Mean Girls* for an illustration.

Based on the 2002 self-help book by Rosalind Wiseman, *Queen Bees and Wannabes*, and the experiences of the film's writer, *Saturday Night Live* and *30 Rock* star Tina Fey, *Mean Girls* chronicles the lengths to which a group of girls is willing to go to be accepted and avoid social alienation—i.e., excommunication. The mean girls are led by Regina George, who is the envy of the school and ruthless in her ability to cut down anyone she deems unworthy of "fitting in." The mean girls live by a set of unwritten rules and other social facts that mandate how people like "them" (the "Plastics," as they are referred to in the movie) should dress, behave, talk, date, and just about every dynamic of social life. At its core, *Mean Girls* is a story about the dynamics of high school social groups, school bullying, and the inherent desire to fit in with the "right people." While this might seem far removed from adult life, it is very much the same as our tribal associations today. Nowadays, we might call this being canceled, or, as Black Twitter would affectionately say, "they are no longer invited to the barbecue." It is the same for brands, leaders, institutions, and the like. If the interpreted meaning of your actions and your words is out of sync with what is deemed acceptable among the congregation, you run the risk of no longer being able to sit at the cool kids' table.

## MISSED NUANCES

So how do we avoid this incongruence? It's tricky because there is a far greater degree of difficulty in making sure your message connects with your target. It requires understanding how other people see the world and make meaning of it, which is very nuanced. Remember the "OK" sign? Or the phrase "you straight"? The shades of meaning that differentiate the "OK" sign from the "White supremacy" sign are very subtle. The difference between "You straight," as in "You're welcome," and "You straight?," as in "Do you need anything?," is totally dependent on context and precision. It's like the many shades of white paint: they are very subtle and can easily be mistaken for one another.

The ability of a sender to embed meaning in a message so that it is interpreted as intended by the receiver when decoding the message requires an uncanny ability to understand the mind of the receiver. Not only does this mean that the sender has to know the likely interpretation of the message that the receiver will choose, but the sender must also know the different permutations of meaning that could be chosen by the receiver in order to avoid them when signaling. Review the work of any playwriter or screenwriter, and the complexities of this exercise will become quite clear.

Screenwriters write stories about characters that are interpreted through the meaning-making lenses of the audience. To do so successfully, writers make precise decisions about the setting (context), the dialogue (language), and a host of other semiotic cues that the viewer uses to decode the meaning of what they are observing in the film. The smallest flaw could be the difference between someone "getting it" and not understanding what the scene or film is "supposed" to mean. Naturally, understanding how the audience will interpret what they see or hear is vital to preaching the gospel in an effort to get people to move.

Unfortunately, however, far too often, companies and leaders miss the subtle nuances that shape meaning for people, and subsequently, these entities find their intentions out of sync with people's interpretation. The result can be unfavorable outcomes. How many times have we seen politicians issue an apology because their "words were not a reflection of their intent"? These faux pas reflect incongruity due by and large to the missed nuances of meaning. They are avoidable, but avoiding them requires understanding how people make meaning.

In the holiday season of 2019, Peloton, the fitness and media company, debuted an advertisement for its high-end stationary bike. The thirty-second commercial, called "The Gift That Gives Back," features a woman who is given a Peloton bike by a man who appears to be her husband. She seems quite surprised by the gift—with a $2,000 price tag, who can blame her? Nevertheless, as the story goes on, she begins to document her rides on the Peloton through videos that she films on her mobile phone. She narrates the first video sitting on the bike, looking directly into the camera, saying, "Okay, first ride. I'm a little nervous, but excited. Let's do this." In another video, she rushes through the front door, dressed in business casual as if she just got home from work, and says to the camera, "Five days in a row. Are you surprised? I am." It is not quite clear to whom she is addressing her video entries, but there is little doubt that these vignettes are meant to signal progress. There's a video of her waking up at 6 a.m. to unexcitedly get on the bike. Another video of her triumphant, saying, "That was worth it." After some time has passed, we gather, she gets a shout-out from one of the instructors, and we learn that her name is Grace—from Boston.

The commercial then reveals that her short video entries were, in fact, small clips of a larger "thank you" video that Grace created. This reveal happens as we see Grace and her partner, together, watching the video after a year of her chronicling her experience on the Peloton bike. Grace then says to the camera, "I didn't realize how much this would change me. Thank you." At this point, we realize that the intended audience for her videos was her husband. A voice ends the film, saying, "This holiday, give the gift of Peloton."

On the surface, the commercial seemed harmless. However, that was not how many people interpreted its meaning—and the result was a massive backlash from the general public across the Internet, the news, and commentary from other cultural producers. The masses perceived the commercial as a man telling his already-in-shape wife that she needed to get in better shape. One Twitter user wrote, "Nothing says 'maybe you should lose a few pounds' like gifting your already rail thin life partner a Peloton." This is clearly a case of meaning incongruence. I have worked with the folks at Peloton on a few projects, and I can say—unequivocally—that all of those with whom I had the privilege of working were well-intentioned, good people. Unfortunately for Peloton, meaning incongruity has nothing to do with intention but everything to do with the nuances of meaning. And in the minds of many, the ad came off as sexist and body shaming.

Peloton's holiday commercial aired at a time when the discourse in the cultural zeitgeist was challenging conventions around the patriarchy, the objectification of women, pay disparity, and a host of other social systems that have marginalized women for decades (if not centuries). The prosecution of these systems was happening on the nightly news and just about every corner of the Internet—and rightly so. It was about time for these cultural norms to be reevaluated in this country. The "Me Too" movement, which fought against the sexual abuse and harassment that women experience in the workplace, had really kicked things off just a year or so beforehand. And it was this cultural backdrop that created the frames in which Peloton's ad was viewed and, subsequently, interpreted—much to the chagrin of Peloton, of course.

According to news outlets, the company's stock fell by 9 percent as a result of the backlash surrounding the ad. A statement from the company read, "Our holiday spot was created to celebrate that fitness and wellness journey . . . we're disappointed in how some have misinterpreted this commercial." Indeed, but this wasn't a matter of "misinterpretation," where the audience misread the meaning or just didn't get it. Rather, this was a matter of the company not understanding how the commercial would be translated and meaning subsequently made. The onus is on the communicator to "read the room" and signal meaning in such a way that it aligns with how meaning is made, however nuanced that may be.

A quick sidebar for my marketing friends who are likely reading this story and saying to themselves, "Yeah, but maybe the people who saw the ad differently than what Peloton intended were not the target audience." That would be a fair argument, in response to which I would cite another Twitter user who wrote, "I am one of those weirdos who got a Peloton for Christmas (long story) from my husband and love it. I hate this ad so much it hurts. Just wanted to make that clear. I'm exactly the target demo & I agree w/ you all that this is the beginning of a Black Mirror episode"—referring to the *Twilight Zone*–like science fiction series from Netflix. This and similar comments from across the web strongly refute the "target audience" argument, I'm afraid.

It should also be noted that the public outcry attracted the attention of another marketer who, unbeknownst to anyone, used Peloton's calamity as an opportunity to promote his own products. That marketer, of course, was the international A-list actor and business owner Ryan Reynolds. Reynolds had amassed a reputation for disruptive marketing tactics that capitalized on the dynamism of the social web and led to the success of Marvel's *Deadpool* movie franchise, in which he starred. Among the many memes that people used to make meaning of what they saw in the ad (through recontextualization, as we discussed in the last chapter), the *Get Out* meme, borrowed from Jordan Peele's horror movie about being trapped with no agency over one's body, was one of the more popular choices. People compared "Grace from Boston's" look of despair on the bike to that of one of the characters in Peele's movie whose body had been "snatched." This was just the thing that Reynolds needed to capitalize on the moment.

Hiring the original actress from the Peloton ad (yes, Grace from Boston), Reynolds situated her with two of her "friends," one on each side, at a bar. The camera is dead on Grace as her friends try to search for comforting words. With a drink in front of each of them, Grace breaks the silence and says, "This gin is really smooth." Her friends agree and assure her that "she's safe here." The three women then raise their glasses and toast to "new beginnings." As the two friends take a sip from their glasses, Grace chugs her entire drink while her friends look on with concern. The film then cuts to a product shot of Reynolds's Aviation Gin, the branded product that is benefiting from this moment. And just before the last frame, one of the friends says to Grace, "You look great, by the way," signaling that Reynolds is in on the joke. He understood the meaning associated with the original ad, and his "ad" is not merely an advertisement but a contribution to the cultural discourse. We'll talk more about this and how it's done in greater detail in the next chapter.

The unfortunate part of this Peloton story is that much of it was avoidable. A slight tweak of the script could have made all the difference in the world. If Grace's husband had said something like "Hey, I got you the Peloton you wanted" or "Here's the gift you've been asking for," the interpretation of the ad would likely have been different, if for no other reason than the fact that this adjustment to the script would have given Grace agency, the lack of which contributes to the social system that marginalizes women more broadly. Though the change is slight, its impact on the meaning is substantial, and for those who seek to get people to take action, realizing these subtle differences in hues will make all the difference in the world.

All that said, there is no question that understanding the nuances of meaning is difficult. It's much easier to play "Monday-morning quarterback" and critique when meaning incongruence occurs than it is to actually create messaging (i.e., preach the gospel) that successfully achieves meaning congruity. It takes a lot of courage for people to get onstage and share ideas or put music into the world, or release a film, or even send a tweet knowing that their intended meaning might not be what people interpret. What's more, the interpreted meaning might lead to excommunication, which is something that we—as social animals—all fear, not to mention the possible economic and PR consequences for our brand or organization.

When I think back on some of the best advertising campaigns that I saw in the wild, Sprite's "Obey Your Thirst" ranks high on my list of favorites. If you're not familiar with the campaign, let me take you back to the 1990s, way before hip-hop was ever embraced by the masses as a legitimate art form, let alone the most consumed genre of music in the country. At the time, the prevailing cultural product in mainstream television that appealed to American youths had prototypical archetypes that represented young teens. There was the "jock," the "heartthrob," the "nerd," the "pretty girl," her best friend, and, of course, the token Black person—if there even was a Black person in the cast. Basically, teens were portrayed as a snapshot of *Saved by the Bell*. But Sprite, the lemon-and-lime-flavored soda brand within the Coca-Cola Company's portfolio, had chosen to go another route to ingratiate itself with American teens who had otherwise been unrepresented or essentially ignored.

As a niche brand, Sprite found a likely audience in hip-hop. Though Sprite had featured prominent hip-hop artists—like Kurtis Blow, Heavy D, and Kid 'n Play—in previous campaigns, the brand was not representative of the culture. The colors were bright, the music felt like a jingle, and everyone just seemed too happy. It was not reflective of how the hip-hop tribe dressed, spoke, or carried themselves. All that changed when Sprite's brand manager Darryl Cobbin decided to focus on the nuances of the culture. As Cobbin put it, "I wanted to usher in a real authenticity in terms of hip-hop in advertising. We wanted to pay respect to the music and the culture. What's important is the value of hip-hop culture, not only as an image, but as a method of communication." With Cobbin at the reins, Sprite enlisted hip-hop artists who may not have been big in popularity, per se, but possessed the kind of cultural capital that credentialized the brand among the hip-hop tribe in ways other brands could not.

Among these artists were Pete Rock, CL Smooth, Grand Puba, and Large Professor—names which only people deep in the culture would truly understand the significance of. The commercial was shot in black-and-white to give it a certain grit that was not present in previous Sprite ads, and the first thing you see are the words "After another session in the studio . . ." to provide context for what you are about to experience. Just then, a drum beat loops that is reminiscent of the soul samples used in hip-hop music. As the camera pans the room, Pete Rock and CL Smooth are sitting at a mixing board freestyle rapping over the beat, and a Sprite can is sitting on the console as if it belongs there. One of my past colleagues, Abigail Weintraub, once said, "The Sprite can could have been a blunt because it felt so natural in that moment." In another clip, we see Large Professor and Grand Puba rapping over the beat in a cypher—a freestyle improvisation session where rappers display their lyrical abilities among their peers and celebratory onlookers. As the commercial comes to an end, Puba says, "First things first, obey your thirst. Sprite, aiight?" And just like that, "Obey Your Thirst" was born.

I remember this campaign so vividly because when it aired, it was the first time I could remember feeling like an ad was talking directly to me. Sprite understood the assignment perfectly. From the casting of the artists to the music, the setting, the language, and the artifacts, everything was spot-on. "Obey Your Thirst" wasn't just a tagline, it was cultural language that represented the ethos of the hip-hop community. To obey your thirst meant to go after what you cared about, even in the face of adversity. Whatever you desire, whatever your thirst, go get it.

This gospel was directly aligned with the ideology of hip-hop culture, and it catapulted the Sprite brand to new heights. By the time

"Obey Your Thirst" really got going, Sprite had overtaken the lemon-lime category leader, 7UP, and broken out of its niche category altogether to become a mainstream soda brand with over $1 billion in sales by 1996. The campaign would go on to include other artists (Nas, KRS-One, A Tribe Called Quest, Common) and athletes (Kobe Bryant, Grant Hill, Anfernee Hardaway). It would later include mixtapes, NBA Slam Dunk Contest sponsorships, and spoofs of traditional advertising that recognized that young teens didn't want to be marketed to. "Obey Your Thirst" took on many iterations over its decade-long run, but somewhere along the line, Sprite lost its way. So in 2013, Sprite reached out to the agency I was working for at the time to help it find its way back.

The brief was fairly straightforward: help Sprite reclaim its position as a cultural icon among contemporary youth by reintroducing the spirit of "Obey Your Thirst." This was a dream come true for me. I had loved the campaign as a kid, and here was my chance to help resurrect it. Our teams worked with the brand managers at Sprite to come up with a campaign that we called "Only for the Thirsty." The idea was to evolve "Obey Your Thirst" from a declaration, where we told people to follow their aspirations, to an invitation that said, "If you go after your dreams, then you're one of us." It made all the sense in the world. The only snag was that the cultural landscape had changed since the original campaign, and the word "thirst" had a completely different meaning and connotation. "Thirst" may have meant your desire or your dreams in the '90s and early 2000s within the hip-hop culture, but by 2013, "thirst" meant desperation for someone to whom you were attracted—as in "Why are you so thirsty? Go find someone else." Thirst wasn't about ambition; it meant you were pathetic.

The sad part is that we all (in the agency) knew that, but we didn't factor that into the equation when working on the new campaign. Just the summer prior, in 2012, the biggest song on the radio (and in the popular culture) had been Kanye West's "Mercy," which underscored the change in the lexicon within the chorus: "Lamborghini Mercy, your chick, she so thirsty, I'm in the two-seat Lambo with your girl, she tryna jerk me." The shift in meaning for the word "thirsty" was clear. There was no excuse. We just weren't paying close enough attention.

Nevertheless, we released the new spot for the campaign, which featured the basketball superstar LeBron James and a host of other noncelebrities who were fearlessly expressing themselves—obeying their "thirst," if you will. At the end of the commercial, the voiceover and copy read, "Sprite. Only for the thirsty," and the Internet had a field day. One tweet read, "You hear that hoes? Sprite got your thirsty assess covered lmao" and another Twitter author wrote, "Sprite for the thirsty. Y'all hoes need to get y'all some." These were the tamer responses, by the way.

It was embarrassing, and the client removed the ad from rotation within twenty-four hours of its debut. We had really missed the mark, not because the ad was bad (per se) but because our intended meaning was not congruent with the way in which it was interpreted. And since people didn't want to be identified as a "thirsty ho[e]," or a pathetic and desperate person, drinking Sprite (publicly, at least) was a "no go" for them.

## SAME, SAME

Thus far, we have examined why culture has a gravitational pull that catalyzes people to collectively take action and how you—with your new understanding of culture—can leverage its influence to get people to buy, vote, compost, donate, and just about anything else. However, so far, we have looked at the influence of culture as a matter of fact—as something that *is* as opposed to assigning value to the ability to utilize it. We have not yet discussed the "good" and the "bad" with regards to wielding the power of culture. Neglecting to do so would be irresponsible and the equivalent of arming someone with a gun but failing to provide the proper safety precautions for using it. The same use of culture that can influence people to support women's rights can influence people to support banning abortions. It's the "same, same."

When my daughter Georgia was in daycare, she learned a phrase that would always tickle me when she said it: "Same, same." Her teachers taught her this phrase to identify when things were very similar. For instance, if my wife was wearing a blue shirt and I was wearing a blue shirt, Georgia would point and say, "Same, same." Of course, our shirts weren't identical, but they were related. Or, more accurately, they were the same but different. Interestingly, the saying has its roots in Southeast Asia, particularly among the people of Cambodia, Vietnam, Singapore, and Thailand. While the exact origin of the phrase is unknown, some theorize that it's an idiom born of the way Thais learned the English language, or what some call "Tinglish." Either way, "Same, same, but different" has become cultural vernacular in Thailand with such popularity that you see it on T-shirts, marketing slogans, and the like. That's cultural production at its finest.

When we think about the power of culture and its ability to catalyze people to do something "good," like save for retirement or donate to a charity, we must also be mindful that the same strategies and tactics can be used to catalyze people to do something "bad," like spend excessively or commit a crime. Regardless of the context, the same underlying physics of culture that influence people to move are at play. Therefore, similar tactics and strategies can catalyze different evaluative outcomes. It's the "same, same." Take storytelling, for example. Marketers, leaders, clergy, and politicians frequently leverage the power of stories to preach their gospel and connect with their targets. Storytelling as a strategic tactic, however, is neither good nor bad in and of itself. But it can be used in different contexts.

When I was in high school, my eleventh grade social studies teacher, Mrs. Allen-Shelton, used the power of storytelling to illustrate

the challenges that Jewish Americans faced as anti-Semitism reverberated throughout the country post–World War II. Like most of my
classmates at the time, I knew about the atrocities of the Holocaust,
but I was not as knowledgeable about its lingering effects. So Mrs.
Allen-Shelton had us watch the movie *School Ties*—a story about a
prep school student who hid the fact that he was Jewish to escape ridicule from his teachers and peers—to not only make us aware of these
realities but also help us make meaning of them through our cultural
frames.

That film was eye-opening for me. As I watched the movie, I lik-
ened the lead character's struggles to those of Black Americans, and I
found myself connected because in some ways, I could see myself in
the story. This was powerful for me, and its effects have been long-
lasting. I often credit that movie, and others like it, for helping me
understand the experiences of people who didn't look like me or come
from similar places. On the other hand, stories can be used to see
people in a much more damning light. Look no further than the White
supremacist hate group the Ku Klux Klan for an example.

The KKK, as it is prominently known, has terrorized and murdered
people of color—particularly Black people—in this country since it
got its start in the 1860s. The organization believes that Whiteness
is divine and that American society needs to be purified of anything,
and anyone, that does not fit the White Protestant national identity.
The KKK had a few fits and starts before it really got its footing in
the 1950s. The first iteration was fragmented, with different chapters
across Southern states, each of which had its own unique set of artifacts (like different-colored robes) and behaviors (different forms of
targeted violence against Black people) despite sharing the same ideology. However, in 1915, the KKK got a story to help mythologize its
existence thanks to D. W. Griffith's *The Birth of a Nation*, the silent film
that egregiously depicted Black people as savage beasts that needed to
be controlled. Griffith's film was the perfect vehicle to help evangelize

the gospel for the KKK, and though it was fundamentally erroneous, it really rallied the troops for the terrorist group—leading to an influx of new recruits. That's the thing about preaching the gospel: it can resonate in the limbic system—the part of our brains that reside in our chests—and evoke people's emotions (in this case fear and pride), which gets people to take action if they see the world similarly.

Watching a film like Griffith's, or any film for that matter, is not a passive act. As the American cultural critic Vivian Sobchack asserted, a movie is always incorporated and lived by the human beings who watch and engage with it. The viewing of a film is done within a structure of meanings and metaphors in which subject-object relations are cooperative, co-constitutive, and dynamic. Unfortunately, to the benefit of the KKK (and the centuries-long horror Black people have experienced in this country), many White Americans shared a similar belief that the White race was a superior race, and *The Birth of a Nation* provided the perfect ideological story to match that worldview.

With the perfect weaponized story in hand, the KKK developed rituals like cross burnings and a new language that introduced words that started with the letter "k" into its vernacular. As you can likely gather, it began to act as a congregation with social facts that governed what it meant to be a part of the tribe. By the 1920s, the KKK had grown to over four million active members across the country and made life a living hell for Black people, Jews, and other Americans through the 1960s.

The stories we tell to help preach our gospel are the stories we tell ourselves and each other, and they shape the meaning frames by which we translate and interpret the world—whether good or bad. Stories are important to culture. We use stories to communicate, propagate, and socialize what people like us are supposed to do. And we have been operating by, and against, the stories that have been told to us for years and years.

We learn about the world (beliefs), who we are (identity), and how we fit in the world (ideology) through storytelling. Stories are how we teach morality (folklore) and help the interpellation of children so that they become citizens in good standing in society. As a child, I learned about my religion through stories like Daniel and the lion's den and the Exodus from Egypt. They were easily digestible, readily available for memory recall, and, consequently, frequently shared. It's no wonder Jesus spoke in parables because stories serve as an incredible vehicle that helps socialize cultural values and foster community cohesion.

Storytelling is a long-standing practice among humankind. It's just what we do. Long before there was science, there were stories, and stories were the way in which we captured and socialized evidence. To this day, sworn testimony by witnesses or victims is used as "evidence" in a court of law to piece together meaning regarding what might have happened in a given situation. Similarly, stories are used among communities to make meaning and understand the world around them and the people who cohabitate in it. The communications literature refers to this as public pedagogy, the way in which we learn about people who are not ourselves through the stories we ingest via media consumption. If you've never been to Saudi Arabia, you probably have some meaning frames about what it might be like to live in Saudi Arabia. If you have never been to Brazil, you likely have a mental picture of what it might be like to live in Brazil. Where do those meaning frames come from? How did you develop that mental picture? It's through the movies you've watched, the television shows you've consumed, the narratives you've read, and the stories you've heard. The media—and its stories—work us over completely.

Here is where it gets interesting. The more we hear the stories, the more we believe them to be true. That is to say, the repetition of the stories creates a sense of reality for us. This is why fake news has such a weighty gravitational pull on the social consciousness: people hear it repeatedly and think that it must be true because so many people have said it. As Daniel Kahneman put it, "A reliable way to make people believe in falsehood is frequent repetition because familiarity is not easily distinguished from the truth. Authoritarian institutions and markers have always known this fact."

Not only does the repetition of stories establish what we consider to be true, it also influences our preference. The more we hear it, the more we like it because familiarity feels good. It's easy, and it reaffirms what we already know. There's a phenomenon in psychology that explains this process called the mere exposure effect, referring to people's tendency to favor a thing to which they are repeatedly exposed, not because of its intrinsic value but simply because they are familiar with it. I always refer to this in speaking to students starting in the MBA program. When folks first get to campus, some women tend to bemoan their disappointment in the lack of cute, available guys in their program. But once the semester kicks off and they start to be repeatedly exposed to the guys in their classes, their tune changes a bit, and they begin to think, "Well, I guess he's kind of cute." Before long, that sentiment changes to "he's really cute," and now they're dating.

But once she takes him home to meet her friends, they don't see the same thing, so they don't get the attraction because they haven't been exposed to him as often and, therefore, have not experienced the mere exposure effect. This is the same reason why you like a song on the radio that you thought was terrible when you first heard it. The radio station plays the song five thousand times a day, it seems, and before long, you find yourself unknowingly humming the melody throughout your day, and now it's your jam. It's not because the song is good but rather because you've heard it over and over again. This is how the media works; it works us over completely. The stories we repeatedly hear are the ones we tend to believe. And the more we hear these stories, the more we prefer them, which is how they ultimately become legitimated.

Yasmin Green is the CEO of Jigsaw, a unit within Google's parent company, Alphabet Inc., that focuses on solving global security challenges through technology. In 2018, Yasmin gave a TED talk in which she recounted her experience growing up in Iran and the research she conducted on violent extremist groups like ISIS (the Islamic State of Iraq and Syria), which is known for committing heinous acts of terror and mass murder.

ISIS is an ultraconservative Islamist organization that holds a violent ideology toward the West and trains militia-like forces to bear arms in pursuit of their cause. As radical as ISIS might seem, especially to those of us in the Western part of the world, the organization was successfully recruiting and converting Westerners to join its ranks and wage war against other Westerners. Headlines were filled with more and more reports of people being "radicalized" online by ISIS and leaving their homes for a new tribe in Syria. The issue was so prevalent that it became a matter of national security in the United States and throughout Western Europe.

Yasmin's research, and subsequent talk, provides a closer look at how something like this can happen, and happen to so many people. Through many conversations with these radicalized citizens of the West, she found that it was the storytelling of ISIS that helped mythologize its ideology and convert so many people. As Yasmin asserted, it's not tech-savviness that allows ISIS to win the hearts and minds of people. "It's their insight into the prejudices, the vulnerabilities, the desires of the people they're trying to reach that does that." They have a clear ideology about righteousness and heroism, and that's the story that they tell—in English, Arabic, German, Russian, French, Turkish, Kurdish, Hebrew, and Mandarin Chinese. They even create marketing material in sign language for the deaf and hard of hearing. Radicalization isn't a yes-or-no choice. It's a cognitive process that starts with ideological engagement. It's that feeling when you hear something and think, "You know, he's got a point there." Or you read a thing and say, "Man, that's so true." It eases you in because it appeals to who you are and how you see the world—not what it is or what it does.

What ISIS realizes about people is exactly what we've been discussing throughout this book. Getting people to move is not about demographics or key selling propositions; it's about beliefs and ideologies, which anchor our cultural subscriptions. So if you want to get people to move, start by finding the people who see the world the way you do—if only just a little—and preach the gospel. The way it has worked for ISIS is the same way it works for brands, the military, and political affiliations. As the American philosopher Charles Sanders Peirce noted, "The function of belief is to commit us to action." Same, same.

The hyperconnectivity of the social web has empowered more media producers—from amateurs to budding professionals—to tell more stories and has simultaneously enabled these stories to proliferate across the Internet at an unbelievable speed and frequency. The result has quickened the tempo of cultural shifts and made meaning making even more difficult for marketers, content creators, or anyone with a desire to communicate. Kevin Roose, a technology columnist for the *New York Times* who studies fringe Internet cultures across the web said that he'd realized that "what unites these groups is their way of finding and processing information." The act of finding information itself has become a cultural act within these groups. You've got to "do your homework," as they say, which often amounts to a Google search or going down the rabbit hole of a YouTube conspiracy trail. Yes, this practice is grounded in the belief that, according to Roose, "the way to figure out what's true isn't to listen to the experts or the mainstream media, but to figure it out for yourself on the internet."

This premise has given oxygen to groups from anti-vaxxers all the way back to the cohort of people who believed 9/11 was an inside job, as depicted in the Internet movie *Loose Change*. There are even tribes of people who have united under the satirical conspiracy movement Birds Aren't Real, which mocks conspiracy movements. Just as there are subreddits for almost anything, there's a tribe for just about everything. This worldview and the proliferation of information have enabled more stories—and more gospels—to fuel the cultural rate of change and further fragment tribal affiliations. The next chapter will explore this further and offer recommendations for navigating these changes as you seek to harness the power of culture to catalyze collective behavior.

### FROM KNOW-WHY TO KNOW-HOW

As we've seen, culture is a realized meaning-making system that influences practically every aspect of our lives, and we can leverage this influence by preaching the gospel to the congregation of people who see the world the way that we do. To do so, however, we must understand how our congregation makes meaning to ensure that what we say and do is interpreted in the manner that we intend. It's not about what we say so much as it is about what people hear. This may seem simple on the surface, but it requires a nuanced comprehension of the social facts that mediate the way the congregation interprets the world, and that's more difficult than it seems.

As you think about how you'd preach the gospel to your target tribe(s), pay close mind to the language and artifacts of the community. These two cultural characteristics, in particular, are more susceptible to change than beliefs and behaviors because of the dynamism associated with words and symbols and their corresponding meanings. A phrase could mean one thing today and another thing tomorrow. A certain kind of garment could be cool this month and dated the next month, so you have to stay close to ensure meaning congruence when you preach the gospel or show up in the world.

## CHAPTER 6

# THE SPEED OF CULTURE

I AM A CHILD OF THE '80S. MICHAEL JACKSON, *BEVERLY HILLS Cop*, Atari, Bart Simpson, Saturday-morning cartoons, and just about every other '80s artifact that you can name bring back fond memories of my formative years. I distinctly remember the Saturday nights when my brother, Eugene, and I would stay up late to watch Kung Fu theater, the debates we'd have as to whether Ric Flair could beat Hulk Hogan (because we believed that pro wrestling was real in those days), and the anticipation we'd have to see our favorite artists' music video on *Yo MTV Raps!* It all felt like an endless loop of awesomeness. Included in our media diet was a not-so-healthy dose of stand-up comedy, which was huge in the '80s.

Somehow or other (unbeknownst to our parents, of course), Eugene got his hands on a copy of Eddie Murphy's HBO stand-up special, *Delirious*, and his subsequent stand-up movie, *Raw*, on VHS cassette. We were too young to get most of the references in the jokes, but the parts we did understand were some of the funniest stuff we'd ever heard. We were mesmerized. The profanity alone was enough to make the film taboo and, therefore, intriguing for two church boys like Eugene and me. Not to mention, Eddie Murphy's impressions of Mr. T, Stevie Wonder, Elvis, Michael Jackson, James Brown, and Jackie Gleason were so over the top—and spot-on—that even without the inappropriateness, the films were hilarious. We watched them repeatedly, so much so that I committed each film to memory and could perform them on demand, though my impersonations were not as convincing.

Fast-forward to 2017. I found myself feeling nostalgic after realizing that both *Delirious* and *Raw* were available for viewing on Netflix's streaming service. I was immediately transported back to my youth, recalling all my favorite bits from these films, which had been enshrined in my mind as the apex of comedic brilliance. I could feel myself smiling in anticipation as I cued up the television to begin my binge. However, a few minutes in, my smile began to fade. In fact, I was practically clutching my pearls throughout the entire viewing. The jokes were the same, but I wasn't. Or, more accurately, the jokes were the same, but the cultural frames through which I experienced them were different, and, therefore, the meaning had shifted. What was funny then felt offensive today—not because of some mandate of political correctness but because of the beliefs and ideologies that I now hold some thirty years later. While I still have fond memories of Eddie Murphy's stand-up classics, this experience evidenced for me that culture, like anything else, changes.

The only constant in life is change, as the ancient Greek philosopher Heraclitus so poignantly noted centuries ago—and it is the same for culture. Culture is in constant flux. Beliefs, artifacts, behaviors, and language are continually reworked as new ideas force community members to collectively negotiate and construct meaning. As an emergent idea is introduced into the community, say, skinny jeans for men or the legalization of marijuana, it sparks conversations and debate about whether and how it fits within the community's social facts.

Do skinny jeans fit the community's conception of masculinity? Is it acceptable for people "like us" to smoke marijuana? In the case of Will Smith and Chris Rock, is it OK to slap someone on national television because they offended your spouse at a black-tie event? Is it good or bad (evaluation)? Do people "like us" do something like this (legitimation)? As we discussed in Chapter 5, these are the mechanisms by which people make meaning and adopt behaviors in a contagious manner. These conversations and debates are the forces that push and pull cultural change. They challenge us to rethink the beliefs that we hold and the stories we've been told, which subsequently alters our behaviors, language, and use of certain artifacts.

Moreover, these changes in cultural ideology and cultural practice result in a similar change in cultural production—music, film, literature, dance, fashion, and brands. Hence, my reaction to watching Eddie Murphy decades after my first introduction to his films. Societal beliefs and ideologies around sexual orientation, misogyny, and gender had shifted such that a word that was once normal vernacular, like what we now call the "f" word, is equated with the severity of the "n" word.

Naturally, this is reflected in the creation of new cultural products and, likewise, in the reevaluation of previously created cultural works. Oddly enough, the use of profanity has shifted in the opposite direction. It appears as though America was much more conservative back then when it came to what people could say and wear on air but far less concerned about the nomenclature used to describe certain groups of people. The Federal Communications Commission (FCC), which regulates broadcast television, did not allow the use of swear words on television due to the offense it would cause the American public. But today, even the past president of the United States, Donald Trump, has used profanity on air—among other vulgarities. Indeed, in some ways, Americans have loosened our tie when it comes to language, but in other ways, we've tightened things up, all of which is represented in our cultural production.

Cultural product, as discussed in Chapter 2, is the creative output of the community that expresses its shared perspective. This often starts as a shock to the system—the reaction to something that happens outside the group, like a new product release, new music, new campaign, or breaking news in the media, that has not yet been legitimated by the community. Once introduced to this shock, the tribe collectively enters the negotiation and construction process to make meaning of it. Of course, this meaning is not stable; therefore, what is intended by the cultural producer (i.e., what is encoded in the media) is not always what is interpreted (or decoded) by members of the tribe.

For instance, in April 2020, the hip-hop artist Travis Scott held an unexpected—and unprecedented—concert inside the virtual world of Fortnite. News about the concert created an exogenous shock to the system for both the hip-hop community and the gaming community, which catalyzed conversations among their members and, subsequently, helped construct meaning within their respective cultures. When I was a child, I blew sugar dust that mimicked smoke while eating candy cigarettes and stuffed wads of Big League Chew Bubble Gum in my mouth that was made to imitate chewing tobacco. These acts were commonplace during those times. However, through debate and reevaluation over time, these products were assigned different meanings and have now been delegitimated, a topic we'll expound on later in this chapter.

These shocks to the system extend beyond social morals and product consumption; they even include currency itself, like the dollar bill. The dollar has value only because we—collectively as a global society—have all "agreed" that it does. The dollar is just paper that we exchange as a representation of something else. It is a signifier that stands in for a monetary value that is negotiated and constructed twenty-four hours a day through trade. Just like culture itself, currencies remain in constant fluctuation as people and institutions around the globe decide on their meaning.

However, new currencies like bitcoin have introduced an exogenous shock to the system, and now, through discourse, exchange, and observation, society is negotiating what they mean and whether they have "value." Jack Dorsey, cofounder of Twitter and founder of Square, predicted that Bitcoin will replace the US dollar in the future, which would certainly signal a huge cultural shift, one far greater than colloquialisms and fashion fads. These shifts generally happen beneath the surface, building slowly and quietly as our beliefs and values change the meaning of the object. This is called "slow culture."

## FAST AND SLOW

Slow culture is what causes us to behave the way we do—our shared beliefs and values—and fast culture is a reflection of a community's beliefs displayed in how society functions (most often seen in rituals, language, art, music, and film). Fast culture is typically ephemeral (a new diet trend or slang word), and slow culture occurs over long stretches of time. This is where trend watching goes wrong. Consider your favorite marketing publication or pop-culture periodical, and you will certainly find what is in vogue at the moment—the popular hairstyle, the in-demand artifact, the latest [fill in the blank] that's so hot, everyone's doing it. While there is great value in understanding the observable cultural expressions that diffuse throughout a population, these trends tell us only "what" people do, whereas slow culture tells us "why" they do it. That said, understanding the characteristics of fast culture can help us better understand the functions of slow culture.

It's also worth noting that these changes in culture, be they fast or slow, are products of conversations and cultural discourse that take place among members of the community, particularly in response to an exogeneous shock to the system. As we navigate the world, we bump into things that make us question ourselves, our people, and the institutions that demarcate what people like "us" should and should not do. These provocations spark conversations among our people—both explicitly and implicitly—which subsequently activates the process by which we collectively decide meaning, whether it's legitimate, and, ultimately, how to behave.

Say it's the summer of 2003, and you're at a barbecue or nightclub, wedding reception or family reunion, and R. Kelly's "Ignition (Remix)" blasts through the speakers. What happens next? Well, if you were me in those days, you'd probably see a rush of folks make a mad dash to the dance floor. That should be of no surprise because "Ignition (Remix)" was a massive hit that year, among a string of hit records from Kelly that extended his successful career from his 1992 debut well into the 2000s. However, if you play "Ignition (Remix)" after January 2019, the response is likely quite different—not because the song has aged or gone out of favor but because R. Kelly has been canceled. He is no longer deemed acceptable due to a number of sexual abuse allegations concerning underage girls, of which he would later be found guilty. Radio stations stop playing his music. Concert promoters canceled tour dates in response to the pressure from "Mute R. Kelly" protests at performance venues. What was the catalyst? A multipart documentary that aired on the Lifetime cable channel in January 2019 that brought Americans face-to-face with R. Kelly's alleged crimes and victims.

But here's the thing: there wasn't necessarily anything new in the documentary that the public didn't already know. Thanks to the explosive journalism of *Vibe* magazine back in 1995, we knew R. Kelly had married the then fifteen-year-old R&B singer Aaliyah when he was twenty-seven years old. That marriage was annulled, of course, due to the legal age of consent. We knew about the leaked tapes of R. Kelly engaging in sexual acts with an underage girl thanks to reporting by the *Chicago Sun-Times* in 2002. Kelly was brought up on twenty-one counts of child pornography as a result of this development, but the charges were dropped a year later. Dave Chappelle reminded us about "the tape" shortly thereafter on his hit Comedy Central sketch show,

*Chappelle's Show*, when he spoofed the music video to Kelly's "Ignition (Remix)" with hyperbole tamtamount to the lewd acts from the leaked tape. Later still, in 2005, the animated Cartoon Network breakout show *The Boondocks* reminded us about the tape and all the alleged crimes of which R. Kelly stood accused. But it wasn't until January 2019 that R. Kelly was officially canceled. The major difference between 1995 and 2019 was that we watched the documentary together—shoulder to shoulder, if you will—and collectively engaged in discourse about it thanks to social networking platforms like Twitter, Facebook, and Reddit.

These technologies allowed us to contribute to the discourse that was taking place among members of the tribes and congregations to which we subscribe our identity. We watched our friends tweet, "Hmmm, I think I'm done with this guy [R. Kelly]." One after another, we saw our people cast their vote, saying they were no longer going to listen to his music or consume anything associated with him. As we observed these statements of evaluation in our timelines and newsfeeds, we collectively made meaning and reinforced what we believed to be "normal"—what people "like us" do. And R. Kelly was canceled just like that. This is the legitimation process in action. If Jane is done, and John is done, and Sally is done, and Henry is done, then I guess I'm done also. This is the social process by which we make sense of the world. Why? Because members who subscribe to a particular culture act in concert to promote social solidarity among themselves.

The act of canceling R. Kelly may appear to have happened "all of a sudden" (fast culture), but the reason why he was canceled was a reflection of long-standing beliefs and ideologies (slow culture). We just didn't have the forum to debate this topic then as openly and concurrently as we do now. New technologies accelerate the speed by which culture (both fast and slow) moves because they provide transparency and record-keeping so that the negotiation process among tribal members is seen by all members and, likewise, democratized so that all members can contribute to the discourse. The Library of Congress has gone so far as to say, "The Twitter Archive may prove to be one of this generation's most significant legacies to future generations. Future generations will learn much about this rich period in our history, the information flows, and social and political forces that help define the current generation."

Observing the discourse that takes place within the congregation helps illuminate the social facts about the community, which enables marketers and leaders to better understand the cultural codes that influence how members of the community behave. Once you understand the cultural codes, you are equipped to engage the congregation in a manner that will activate the limbic system and get them to move. If our aim is to leverage the influence of culture to catalyze collective behavioral adoption, then it will require an intimate understanding of the social facts that govern the community.

In order to understand cultural phenomena, you need to immerse yourself in the particular community of interest. Let's say you want to learn about the cultural characteristics of cosplayers—the people who dress up as characters from works of fiction (like comic books, video games, or television shows)—then you might consider attending Comic-Con, the international comic book convention, to immerse yourself in their cultural practices and observe their behaviors firsthand. To learn about the cultural characteristics of Harley-Davidson motorcycle owners (H.O.G.s), you might go on rides and attend gatherings, subscribe to their magazine and newsletters, and shop at the many Harley-Davidson dealerships, which have as much merch for sale as they do bikes. In fact, two researchers did just that and more.

Curious about the consumption behavior of H.O.G.s, John Schouten and James McAlexander spent three years studying members of the H.O.G. community *as* members of the community. They spoke with H.O.G.s, hung out with H.O.G.s, rode with H.O.G.s, and—in many ways—became H.O.G.s themselves. Observing the community's cultural practices at such close proximity helped Schouten and McAlexander understand the underlying beliefs and ideologies (slow culture) that inform its social dynamics and consumption behavior (fast culture).

Just as investigative journalists "go undercover" to get their story, you, too, must go deep into the community to get the story on who these people *really* are and how they make meaning. This requires moving from being an "outsider" looking in to becoming an "insider" who participates. The study of culture is an interpretive science, one that relies on qualitative research to explore the world through the point of view of the community, not your own. This kind of research is called an ethnography. James Spradley, an ethnographer and anthropology professor at Macalester College, describes ethnographies as a "chance to step outside our narrow cultural backgrounds, to set aside our socially inherited ethnocentrism, if only for a brief period, and to apprehend the world from the viewpoint of other human beings who live by different meaning systems." We ought to view ourselves in this way, too, if we are to truly understand a particular community's culture.

The growing prevalence of digital communication technologies, like forums and social networking platforms, has created new research sites—and subsequent methods. These new innovations in research have made it easier for novices to enter "the field" and conduct ethnographic studies. In 1995, Rob Kozinets, marketing professor at the University of Southern California's Marshall School of Business, brought forward one such innovation that he called a "netnography," and its impact was a game changer.

## NETNOGRAPHIES

Netnographic studies use public information exchanged online—via text, memes, videos, and other multimedia forms—to observe how people "naturally behave" in their social environment. Generally, netnographies are unobtrusive in their ability to observe online communities and their subsequent exchanges as a means of understanding society. They allow researchers to observe consumer interactions in the "wild"—unprompted, unmanufactured, and completely voluntary—and develop a "grounded" understanding of unbiased consumer affects, behaviors, cognitions, and desires. If culture is a public matter, then netnographies offer a realistic look at the dynamics of a community by allowing researchers to act as a "fly on the wall" and observe people behaving as they normally would.

Some marketers refer to this form of research as "social listening," where they observe or "listen" to social exchanges between people across social networking platforms. However, netnographies are a much more rigorous and illuminating undertaking because their focus isn't just on observing behavior. Netnographies are concerned with understanding cultural meaning making. Observing people "in person" does not equate to understanding how they make sense of the world, and neither does observing people "online." Netnographic research goes beyond "social listening" and engages in the process of sociocultural understanding.

Today, people shop, date, exchange ideas, collaborate on projects, and—by and large—live their lives online. There is no such thing as the "online world" and "offline world" anymore. At dinner, people talk about what they saw on TikTok and post what they ate on Instagram. Kozinets furthers these points by saying,

> Online communities are not virtual. The people that we meet online are not virtual. They are real communities populated with real people, which is why so many end up meeting in the flesh. The topics that we talk about in online communities are important topics, which is why we so often learn about and continue to care about the social and political causes we hear about through our online communities. Online communities are communities;

there is no room for debate about this topic anymore. These social groups have a "real" existence for their participants, and thus have consequential effects on many aspects of behavior.

Netnographic research provides the most effective approach to observing social behavior online and understanding people's tastes, desires, and the factors that influence decision making. It allows researchers to study the complex cultural practices of social groups in action, drawing attention to a multitude of grounded and abstract ideas, meanings, social practices, relationships, language, and symbol systems. For example, Kozinets conducted a netnography to understand the cultural characteristics of "Burners," the community members of the Burning Man festival in the Black Rock Desert of Nevada. In his study, Kozinets downloaded and analyzed Burning Man–related photographs, articles, documents, and other cultural data available through mass-media channels and on the Internet. He immersed himself in online communication forums and platforms to observe the discourse among community members. After three years of data archival and analysis, Kozinets even attended the Burning Man event to witness the community's cultural practices in close proximity. By immersing himself in the lives and subsequent cultural practices of these people, Kozinets was able to glean insight into the meaning frames by which this tribe translates the world and behaves in it. This kind of information would be particularly valuable for an organization that wanted to recruit this community to join its cause or a politician that wanted to excite these people to vote. The intimacy of this kind of study enables researchers to pinpoint what matters to the community and what challenges it faces. The results not only help the organization or politician preach their gospel but also inform their offerings and policies to best serve the people.

Although the data of a netnography may be pretty unstructured, there is a systematic way to go about it. Kozinets broke this process into four steps: (1) *data retrieval*—immersion in the online community and cultural context by retrieving data from user statements and content submissions as well as data from the personal observations of the researcher, (2) *data analysis*—analysis of data by way of automated software and manual coding methods, (3) *user privacy*—adherence to the ethical guidelines of social research with respect to user privacy, and (4) *aggregation*—the aggregation of findings and corresponding insights. I have conducted netnographies both large and small in scope, scrappy and robust with regard to resource availability, and short and long in terms of timelines and time horizons. Regardless of the situation, netnographies can be incredibly useful in understanding the social facts that govern a group of people.

When studying the social facts of a community, you have to cast aside the more traditional approaches of market research—learning about people's interests and affinities—because they stop short of detecting the coded signs, faint hints, and glimmers of shadowing that reveal cultural meaning shared among community members. In a netnography, you need to comb through the data, revisiting previous exchanges as new conversations shed new light on older conversations. It's the equivalent of rewinding a movie to better understand what happened earlier in the film after finding new information as the plot is revealed. This continued act of "revisiting" helps the viewer better understand the totality of the movie's intended meaning. Comparably, this type of research helps us understand the broader beliefs and ideology that govern who people are and why they do what they do. As taxing as this sounds, the level of intimacy necessary to achieve cultural understanding is impossible through surveys, big data, and artificial intelligence, though this information may be readily available.

We live in a hyperconnected world where more data are collected than ever before. Every Google search, every credit-card swipe, and every authored tweet leaves behind a bread crumb of information that amounts to reams and reams of data in aggregate. Even something as passive as reading an online article offers up data about your device, geography, time spent, and a host of other inputs. The availability of this vast body of data has increased exponentially over time and has theoretically enabled marketers to better understand people. However, ironically, our ability to extract insight from said data has increased only marginally. This paradox amounts to a simple—yet significant— oversight by most people: we mistake information for intimacy.

Information consists of the factual representations of events. Site traffic, engagement across social networking platforms, purchases, and search queries can reveal quite a bit about a consumer's interests, preferences, and desires. It is no surprise that this kind of information is highly coveted by major companies and entrepreneurs alike. Yet, despite having all this information, we still struggle to understand our consumers. How can that be? It's because search behavior, purchase history, and site traffic are not who people are. They are merely what people do *because* of who they are. To understand who people are, you have to get much closer. You have to get intimate.

Before an important meeting, you might go to LinkedIn to (snoop) learn about the person(s) with whom you will be speaking—their current company and position, previous work experience, where they went to school, and perhaps mutual connections. Despite being armed with these facts, you don't really get to know the person until you've interacted with them, exchanged ideas, or observed their mannerisms. These details are revealed only after you've moved beyond the statistical details. Similarly, a person might look like the perfect catch on their dating profile, but it's not until you meet them that you get a better sense of who they are. To know people requires intimacy, a closeness that traditional data metrics will never provide. We know this intuitively; however, when we get into the boardroom, we take off our "human hat"—in exchange for our "marketing hat"— and leave all our humanity at the door. But we must be more human if we want to understand the social facts that govern a tribe of people.

Netnographies—be they big or small in scope—can help practically anyone better understand people and how they make meaning. But they are just one tool in our arsenal. In order to truly understand people you have to get close to them.

## GETTING CLOSE

Without question, the best market researchers on the planet are comedians. Demetri Martin, Sarah Silverman, Hasan Minhaj, Jerrod Carmichael, and others like them are all essentially expert people watchers. Unlike most people, they watch with purpose and with an insatiable curiosity. They observe the behavior of social actors in their daily lives—watching them unobtrusively—until they notice someone do something unexpected. This gets the comedian's attention and they lean in a little closer to investigate the phenomenon before noticing that more people do that very thing. At which point, they go into social scientist–mode to understand what's happening and why. The comedian then hits the stage and says, "Have you noticed that when you go to the grocery store, you do x, y, and z?" We all fall out laughing, trying to catch our breath, as we reply, "That's so me. I totally do that." Well, of course you do. This truth is revealed through cultural proximity.

As in the case of the comedian, curiosity pushes us to look closer, but theory helps us understand what we have observed. This is likely the hardest part for practitioners—particularly those in marketing—because we've been so conditioned to discount the importance of theory. We often use the refrain "That works in theory," as if to imply that reality and theory do not coexist. This only illuminates our misunderstanding of what theory truly is. Theory is the system of ideas and principles that explains what is and why things are. If reality and theory don't align, then it's often because we employed the wrong theory. The problem isn't the theory; it's our lack of good theory. The kind of theory that most accurately explains the phenomenal world around us. This is one of the driving reasons why I thought it was essential to pursue a doctorate degree. I wanted to deepen my repertoire of theory to better understand people and how they make meaning of their lived experiences. I've found that the deeper my theoretical repertoire becomes, the more vividly I see the world and the better equipped I am to successfully put things into the world that get people to move.

However, no amount of curiosity or theory repertoire can overcome our general lack of empathy. Like culture, empathy is one of those words that we often use but don't really understand. My friend the entrepreneur Michael Venture spent years studying empathy and successfully applied it to his work at the agency he founded, Sub Rosa. There, Michael helped brands like GE and Johnson & Johnson use empathy as an engine for problem solving and ideation. He defines empathy as self-aware perspective-taking to gain a richer understanding of people, places, and things. I love this definition because it is both concrete and easy to put into action. Perspective-taking is the act of taking off the lenses through which you see the world and adopting other people's lenses to understand how they make meaning based on the frames that construct their worldview.

There are three forms of empathy. The first is described as somatic empathy. This is involuntary, like a physical motor response that reacts when provoked, thanks to a part of the brain called the mirror neuron system—a group of specialized neurons that mirror the actions and behaviors of others. This is why yawning is contagious. We see someone yawn, and our brain says to itself, "That looks interesting," and before long, we, too, begin to yawn. That's the mirror neuron system at work. Our thoughts, as Sigmund Freud argued, are actions in rehearsal that provoke us to simulate what we see. It's because of the mirror neuron system that our hearts race when we watch horror movies or my wife cries when she watches the movie *The Notebook*, even after watching it for the fifteenth time. Through mirroring, we share the experiences of others, which enables us to see the world from their perspective. Somatic empathy is the body's response to observing people.

The second form of empathy, known as affective empathy, involves understanding another person's feelings. With affective empathy (or what some call emotional empathy), we feel with other people. Like crying at a wedding or during a movie, the mirror neuron system enables us to feel with someone. This form of empathy allows us to walk a mile in someone else's shoes. The renowned psychologist and emotional intelligence scholar Daniel Goleman referred to affective empathy as an emotional contagion that is transferred from person to person, fostering connections between humans that can form strong covalent bonds between them.

The third form of empathy is cognitive empathy, which concerns itself with knowing how the other person feels, not just through feeling but also through intellect. Goleman called this kind of empathy perspective-taking, which allows us to understand the diverse viewpoints of others. With cognitive empathy, we don't "walk a mile in someone's shoes" as much as we see the world through their eyes to gain a better understanding of their experience. The combination of affective and cognitive empathy makes a researcher quite powerful when studying culture and the tribes that practice a particular set of cultural characteristics. Walking a mile in someone's shoes helps us feel their pain. But it's not enough. We must also understand how they make meaning of their experience—based on how they see the world— because this will ultimately inform how they will behave in the world.

Likewise, this is exactly how we ought to examine consumers, voters, and any other community of interest during a netnography to understand the meaning embedded in the cultural texts exchanged among members of the tribe. We are, after all, examining fast culture to better understand slow culture. To do so, we must consider our-selves—the researcher—as the actual research instrument to interpret cultural meaning. John Sherry, an anthropologist and professor of marketing at the University of Notre Dame, referred to the researcher as the "forgotten instrument," stressing the need for the researcher him-/herself to be well versed in the cultural nuances of the research subjects. This, of course, requires a tremendous level of cultural intimacy and empathy. Gillian Tett, an anthropologist and *Financial Times* journalist, underscored this idea by urging researchers to find the familiar in the strange and find the strange in the familiar so that they might set aside their biases and see the world through the lens of others.

If we harken back to the way we described culture in Chapter 2, culture is the realized meaning-making system, and it's through the lenses of culture that we see and translate the world. Culture and meaning making are intrinsically connected, like the interwoven yarns of a sweater. We hold certain truths about the world, and the ideologies that we construct are the stories we tell ourselves about how the world works and what things mean. The German philosopher Martin Heidegger describes humankind as being "thrown" into a world that does not explain itself. Thus, we (humankind) tell ourselves—and each other—stories to make sense of the world around us. But when a brand's story (message or gospel) does not align with our story, we often reject it—both the brand and its story. Therefore, in order to successfully achieve meaning congruence in an effort to get people to move, we must understand the cultural lenses by which the collective makes meaning. This level of understanding is possible only when you can see the world through the perspective of others.

As I observe people participating in their cultural practices, I ask myself three questions before drawing a conclusion about what's happening. The first question is "Why?" Why do they behave in this manner, or why do they see things a certain way? When you ask, "Why?" the answer typically brings your biases to the surface regarding what you think about the people. It's important to get those out in the open so that you can move past them. To go beyond your biases, consider asking yourself the second question: "What?" What are these people feeling that provokes them to act in this manner or see things a certain way? This will help you begin to move outside yourself and stand in their shoes. Finally, ask yourself, "How?" How do they see themselves in the story of life? How do they view the world around them? This is not about what is factual; it's about what is perceived. This will help you see the world through their eyes. You don't have to agree with it. That's not what empathy is all about. Instead, the aim is to understand it because the better you understand it, the better equipped you are to leverage it.

In July 2016, Netflix debuted its sci-fi horror drama *Stranger Things* about a group of young friends who set out to uncover various mysteries amid a series of supernatural events that take place after one of their friends goes missing. The show is set in the fictitious town of Hawkins, Indiana, in the 1980s, and the showrunners—Matt and Russ Duffer—paid great attention to the details to ensure that the '80s-inspired series conjured all the nostalgia from the decade. From *Goonies* to *Stand by Me*, Dungeons and Dragons to *Ghostbusters*, the '80s themselves were practically another cast member of *Stranger Things*. Among the cultural artifacts of the '80s were brands like Members Only jackets, Schwinn bikes, and Eggo waffles. And Eggo waffles were more than just situational product placement; they were a go-to favorite of one of the beloved lead characters of the show, Eleven. The brand was so beloved by Eleven that another lead character, Mike, often gifted her with Eggo waffles left outside her door as a sign of affection—all of which was unbeknownst to the folks at Eggo until the first season aired.

To the surprise of the marketing managers at Eggo, the show's popularity caused an uptick in sales of Eggo waffles, which encouraged the brand to participate in the promotion of the *Stranger Things* season two's advertisement that premiered during Super Bowl 2017. As with the launch of season one, Eggo saw an increase in sales with the release of season two, but not to the degree to which it had hoped. *Stranger Things* had become a global phenomenon, so the brand was expecting a greater impact with the official partnership, but that was not the case. Eggo had to do something more than "advertising" to benefit from the cultural wake that *Stranger Things* created. The brand would have to do more than create an ad; it would have to create cultural production.

With this in mind, Eggo set out to create an experience that would get *Stranger Things* fans excited about the launch of season three and the Eggo brand. However, this time, Eggo didn't have an official relationship with Netflix and, therefore, was restricted from using the *Stranger Things* intellectual property (IP)—unlike other brands like Burger King, Baskin-Robbins, and Coke that paid a small fortune to be integrated into the show and cash in on its success. Knowing my work, the brand manager of Eggo at the time (and longtime friend), Amani Brown, reached out to me to help Eggo tap into the fandom of the show and the culture associated with it.

I had previously watched both seasons of *Stranger Things* and recommended it many times over. But I wouldn't call myself a hard-core fan. For fans, the center of their devotion is consecrated, and they often develop a subcultural community with others who share their enthusiasm. While my team and I loved the show, we didn't meet the criteria of true fans, which meant we had to get much closer to understand who these people were and what made the community tick. Of the many places where this community assembled and engaged in exchanges, Reddit seemed to be the best place to observe them.

With this in mind, we identified all the subreddits related to *Stranger Things* across the Reddit platform and earmarked the other subreddits that these community members shared in common to help us learn about the intricacies of the tribe. It was no surprise that hardcore *Stranger Things* fans were also deep fans of shows like HBO's sci-fi drama *Game of Thrones* and Netflix's dark series *Black Mirror*.

However, what we did not know was that these people were not only deep viewers of the show but also sleuths—minidetectives who analyzed the show, frame by frame, to identify all the Easter eggs and hidden meanings. They were able to reference a scene from season two, episode nine—at the 26-minute, 13-second mark—and connect it to season one, episode seven, to predict what might happen in season three. The ability to do this demonstrates a community member's commitment to their fandom, which provides them with what the sociologist Pierre Bourdieu called embodied cultural capital—the assets that help promote social mobility in a society. The better you were at putting the pieces together, the more clairvoyant you seemed and the more cultural capital you earned. This truth about the tribe unlocked an interesting opportunity that Eggo might pursue to activate the community by contributing to it.

We decided to start in Hawkins. Not the fictional Hawkins of the show but the eleven real Hawkinses that exist throughout North America—like Hawkins, Georgia, and Hawkins, Wisconsin. We took Google Earth images from these ten locations and photoshopped them with billboards of retro Eggo packaging from the '80s, featuring the character Eleven's signature nosebleed dripping from the "E" in the Eggos logo. We then took these images and scattered them across Facebook, Twitter, and Instagram. Along with the faux billboards, we included a cryptic message: "Strange things are coming," knowing that the hard-core *Stranger Things* fans would take notice and start putting the pieces together like the sleuths that they are.

Sure enough, they did, which sparked discourse among the community as members collectively began constructing meaning out of the organically posted images. Images of the billboards made their way onto Reddit, where *Stranger Things* fans arc the most rabid and discerning. The cryptic billboard images were well received within the fan network on Reddit, resulting in thirty-five times more up-votes than any fan-posted content from Coke, Nike, Baskin-Robbins, or Burger

King's paid *Stranger Things* campaigns. With a captive audience among the tribe, we then placed "Easter Eggos" inside what appeared to be lost '80s ads from the brand, inviting hard-core *Stranger Things* fans into the Eggoverse on Instagram to satisfy their inner sleuth. Once a fan found one Easter Eggo, it led to another, which led to another, and another, all of which gave fans a badge of honor for making it to the end.

In all, the campaign generated a 6,000 percent increase in followers on Instagram, an 11 percent engagement rate, and over 500,000 fan interactions. But most importantly, it helped solidify Eggo's rightful place among the show's fandom and drove a 30 percent spike in Eggo purchases at Kroger and Walmart—much higher than the increases from prior seasons. This would not have been possible if we had not immersed ourselves in the world of *Stranger Things* fans so that we could see the world the way they did. For them, the world is full of mysteries, and the ability to solve them is highly valued. Understanding this truth about who they are created an opportunity for the brand to connect with the community in a meaningful way.

This is the power of collective perspective and meaning making. People who subscribe their identity to a community act in concert with the cultural characteristics of the community because they see the world similarly. For managers and leaders with a rich understanding of a community's worldview and corresponding cultural characteristics, there is great opportunity to get these people to move. These kinds of communities exist for TV shows, musical artists, branded products, sports teams, and just about anything you can conceive. This association is not just an allegiance to a team; it's a tribal affiliation to which we assign our identity, and subsequently, we adhere to the beliefs, ideologies, artifacts, behaviors, and language of the community. These tribes help us project who we are and help us find people who are "just like us" through the exchange of cultural product.

With its roots steeped in skater culture, the New York City streetwear fashion brand Supreme has become a powerful, global brand with an identity built on style, rebellion, and authenticity. Supreme is a darling of hypebeasts—the people who avidly follow trends and collect clothing, shoes, and accessories that are considered to be on the bleeding edge of what is, or will be, considered cool. These people are willing to pay a significant premium to don the Supreme logo on an article of clothing or visible artifact. Knowing this, Supreme borrows a page from the art world by creating limited supplies of its products and releasing them online on a first come, first served basis.

In the hypebeast world, this is referred to as a "drop." According to a spokesperson for the brand, traffic on its site can increase by as much as 16,800 percent on the day of a product drop. According to LSN, "Brands such as Supreme have mastered drops where limited product releases cause people to make impulse purchases that they normally might not have made if there was not this constant now-or-never in the back of their heads." The drop is the mechanism that facilitates this FOMO (fear of missing out) scenario in the minds of hypebeasts, and though I do not consider myself a hypebeast, one particular drop got my attention and created a whirlwind for my client Farmland.

In August 2018, Supreme was preparing for its latest drop of new products while hypebeasts and streetwear fanatics waited with bated breath. Among this collective of anxious consumers was Nick Navetta, a twenty-something with an affinity for cool sneakers and streetwear fashion who had frequented drops from Supreme in the past. There was no indication that this particular drop was going to be any different for Nick. Maybe he'd be one of the fortunate few to buy a shirt before supplies ran out, which they tended to do in a matter of minutes once the products were released. No, this day did not feel novel by any stretch. Nick sat in his cubicle at Doner—a full-service advertising agency in Detroit where he worked as a social media strategist—and waited for the drop. Little did he know that this was one time his expensive habit of chasing drops was going to pay off for his day job.

Once the products went live, Nick noticed something eerily familiar about one particular item, a baseball cap. The five-paneled, brimmed cap sported the logo of our client Farmland (a pork manufacturer) on the center patch. But instead of the word "Farmland" across the horizon backdrop of the logo, the brand name had been replaced with "Supreme." Nick was stunned and immediately ran to the creative director of the account to let her know. Unaware of Supreme's cultural gravity, the creative director blew him off and suggested that he let the client know that someone was infringing on its IP. She didn't see the potential of the cultural opportunity at hand, so Nick came to me.

As the chief consumer connections officer at Doner, I ran a department of interdisciplinary marketers that collectively leveraged data, a deep understanding of the behavioral sciences, and an intimate proximity to culture to help brands create marketing campaigns that inspired consumers to move. This situation with Supreme was just the sort of thing that my department was meant to tackle, so Nick knew that I would be the guy to set things in motion. As Nick brought me up to speed on the situation, my first words were "This is the coolest thing that has ever happened to Farmland. We have to do something around it!" I rang the alarm to the rest of the agency leadership, impressing upon them how significant this moment was for our clients and for the agency, and the team got to work.

While this was new territory for Farmland, it wasn't the first offense for Supreme. The brand had a long history of illegally co-opting others' IP. The Supreme logo itself is actually a rip-off of the artist Barbara Kruger's work. Kruger was working as a graphic designer in the 1970s when she first used the Futura font and paired it with snapshots of consumer life to imply people's motives, which inspired her most famous work: "I Shop Therefore I Am." Supreme took her entire design aesthetic and appropriated it as its own. In these cases, the victim of Supreme's IP liberties had essentially three choices: (1) take action by way of cease and desist, (2) do nothing and move on, or (3) choose to provoke cultural discourse—which was exactly what we did.

First, we responded with a tweet just moments after we noticed the offense, saying, "Hey @Supreme, that logo looks super familiar. We missed the drop—what do you think about sending a few our way? #FARMLANDxSUPREME." Within twenty-four hours of going live, the tweet garnered over 13,000 likes, more than 200 replies, and 4,000 retweets—a notable uptick for a brand that rarely sees more than ten interactions on a post. Influencers in the streetwear community weighed in: "Classy move, Farmland." Farmland earned more than ten million impressions across accounts, even engaging actor Seth Rogen and YouTube influencer Casey Neistat. The impact could even be seen on the "stock market of things," StockX, with a notable increase in aftermarket sales—at $44 retail, the demand for this piece started bringing asking prices of up to $149, according to the site's reported sales data.

We then took another step forward and created a lookbook unlike any other, timed with the next week's Supreme drop, featuring the perfect models—our farmers. The lookbook featured glossy, high-quality photos of old farmers with sun-weathered skin, perfectly decked out in the new Supreme gear with the Farmland logo and styled with impeccable coordination with items from previous seasons. Imagine your grandfather standing in a barn wearing a yellow neon box logo Supreme hoodie, flat-brim denim Supreme snapback baseball cap, and jeans, and you'll get a sense of the lookbook's theme. The juxtaposition of old farmers and contemporary streetwear caused the Internet to explode, particularly among the hypebeasts. Our response garnered 1.4 million retweets, a 20 percent increase in search traffic, and a 736 percent spike in online conversations. The press ate it up. Our lookbook was on the front page of all the major advertising trades and got covered by culture sites like *Complex*, the *Fader*, and *Esquire*.

What I loved most about this campaign was that there was so much truth and honesty in it. Supreme did what it does, co-opting IP to create coveted products. Farmland did what it does, working with farmers. And we, as an agency, did what good marketers do: figuring out how to create cultural catalysts that spark conversations and, ultimately, get people to move.

How could something as "unsexy" as a pork producer make such a wake within the culture of this congregation? The answer is simple: to impact culture, you must operate at the ever-changing speed of culture with a keen understanding of the social facts that govern the community. We didn't try to make Farmland cool; that would have been immediately rejected by hypebeasts, who tend to be very discriminating about brands that try to fit in. In fact, we did quite the opposite. We tapped into the "don't mess with us" ethos of the skater culture that had fueled the birth of Supreme and demonstrated a rich understanding of the hypebeast culture in the way that we styled our farmers. This gave us license to participate in their culture by contributing to their culture with a catalyst that brought them together through discourse. We didn't create an ad; we created a cultural product—a means for community members to express their cultural subscriptions. Weighing in on our response to Supreme allowed community members to project their identity and show just how "hypebeast" they were, furthering the back-and-forth exchanges that help foster community.

We got lucky with the Farmland x Supreme campaign thanks to Nick's proximity to the culture. His intimate understanding of its nuanced characteristics, and his participation in the culture, enabled him to catch the drop when it happened. However, research methods like ethnographies and netnographies provide ways in which we can systematically observe cultural happenings and understand these nuances ourselves to create the kind of cultural product that gets people to move. Furthermore, we can go beyond merely reacting to the behaviors of cultural producers—like fashion brands, artists, and celebrities—and instead lean into the networked tribe itself to create the objects—ads, branded products, artifacts, etc.—that its members can use to make their culture material. From Barack Obama's 2008 "Hope" posters to Donald Trump's MAGA hats, Black Lives Matter yard signs to Lance Armstrong's Livestrong bracelets, we, too, can proactively create cultural products that act as receipts of identity and inspire people to act by listening to the community and understanding what makes it tick.

## FROM REACTIVE TO PROACTIVE

Since its founding in 1955, McDonald's has become one of the most recognized brands in the world. Its ubiquity practically established the fast-food industry and gave it a home in the hearts of Americans as a destination for happiness. As a child, few things brought more joy to my life than having McDonald's for dinner or stopping at the golden arches on a family road trip. Our elementary school basketball team would celebrate victories at McDonald's (shout-out to Mr. Jim Thower's McDonald's on Mack and I-75 in Detroit, Michigan), school field trips would often make pit stops at McDonald's, and some kids actually celebrated their birthdays in the playscapes of McDonald's. Even when I graduated from Happy Meals to the Quarter Pounder combo, McDonald's always felt like a slice of joy. Of course, these experiences are not unique to me. As you read this, you're likely recalling some of your own personal moments at Mickey D's and feeling the wave of nostalgia take you back in time like a cognitive DeLorean. Suffice it to say, McDonald's was a special place for many of us. But that feeling began to fade after 2004 thanks to a low-budget film called *Super Size Me.*

*Super Size Me* was a documentary created by the first-time filmmaker Morgan Spurlock, who recorded his experience eating at McDonald's three times a day for a period of thirty days. According to the film, Spurlock gained twenty-five pounds, increased his cholesterol count, and damaged his liver. However, the account of these results has been called into question since Spurlock never produced a food log to substantiate the results of his experiment. Nevertheless, the narrative fit perfectly with people's heightened awareness of the increasing spread of obesity in the country and a pending lawsuit brought against McDonald's by two teenagers, Ashley Pelman and Jazlyn Bradley, who accused the brand of making them obese. *Super Size Me* took an idea and made it tangible for the world to see, and for people to spread, by giving it a story.

Obesity was an epidemic plaguing our nation, according to the surgeon general, fast food was the pathogen, and McDonald's—the biggest player in the category—was the perfect host. Spurlock's film positioned McDonald's as the villain of the obesity epidemic, and consequently, the country's affinity for the brand waned, which resulted in the decline of store traffic and year-over-year sales. This was the case for McDonald's throughout the rest of the decade and on through the 2010s. The outlook at the start of 2019 didn't seem promising for the brand, either, and that was when we—Wieden+Kennedy New York—met McDonald's.

For years, McDonald's had been battling hate on every side—from the press, from the public, and seemingly from everyone in between—but the fight never seemed to let up. The brand became the shortcut for fast food, writ large, and the target for health-conscious critics, all of which proved to be a losing proposition for McDonald's. With hopes of curbing the hate among its detractors, McDonald's tried enlisting new marketing campaigns that provided transparency about how its food was sourced and made, as well as updating menu items with healthier choices like salads. But the results were not unlike those in prior years. The situation was not great, to say the least, but there was one truth that the brand failed to consider: although there was a lot of hate for McDonald's, there was a lot more love for the brand.

Despite all the villainizing and public vitriol, tens of millions of people eat at McDonald's every single day. That's a lot of love. So why not focus on them? Why not focus on the people who love you instead of the ones who hate you? Why not focus on the fans? And that was exactly what we did. We partnered with McDonald's to create a platform that would change the way the brand showed up in the world and, subsequently, inspire droves of people to take action—and it all started with what we called "fan truths."

The pitch group from Wieden was a rotating cast of brilliant practitioners, but the core team consisted of Neal Arthur (then managing director), Karl Lieberman (then executive creative director), Dan Hill (head of strategy—my predecessor), Jacq Steele (then head of new business), and Jac Crowley (then creative director). Together, this crew revealed to McDonald's that just like fans of *Stranger Things*, members of the hypebeast community, and any other network tribe for that matter, McDonald's fans all share a set of cultural characteristics that have been collectively negotiated and constructed through discourse and social observation. Understanding these "fan truths"— the social facts of the McDonald's fandom—would help us engage fans like a fan, so we had to get close.

Fortunately for us, we had recently hired an advertising neophyte, Genet Klasek, who spent years conducting field research for NGOs in Kenya, Uganda, and Tanzania. Genet is the kind of person whom you could drop in the middle of nowhere, and not only would she find her way out, but she would also make ten new best friends along the way. She was the perfect person to help us get to know the nuances of the McDonald's fandom. So she and Tass Tsitsopoulos (a brand strategy director at Wieden+Kennedy at the time) set off on a road trip throughout the heartland of the United States—Illinois, Wisconsin, Indiana, Kentucky, Alabama, and Georgia—to conduct an ethnography by talking to real people in hopes of revealing real fan truths.

They visited 8 cities and 25 towns over a 1,300-mile stretch and talked to 60 people while consuming 14 McCafés, 140 Chicken McNuggets, 1,100 World Famous Fries, 3 Filet-O-Fishes, 4 Quarter Pounder Combos (2 Deluxe, 1 with no bun), 2 Big Macs, and 3 McFlurries (when the machine was working). Their research produced a bible of sorts that chronicled a series of beliefs, artifacts, behavioral rituals, and language that constitute the McDonald's fandom—*A Book of Fan Truths.*

Here are a few truths that might sound familiar: (1) your friend will take a fry even after they said they didn't want any, (2) ordering tap water but filling your cup with soda is an act of living on the edge, and (3) who doesn't eat the cheese off the wrapper? Of the many fan truths that the team uncovered, perhaps my favorite is that despite the innumerable times you've been to McDonald's, when you reach the counter and it's time to order, your response is almost always "Can I get uhhhhhh . . ." I love that one the most because it's so unwaveringly true, which makes it so undeniably compelling.

When truths about cultural practices are identified and revealed to members of a community (be they formal or unspoken), they feel seen, especially when these practices are so subconscious that they happen unbeknownst to the members themselves. It's like the moment when my then girlfriend, and now wife, would pick up on one of my habits and ask, "Have you ever noticed that you [fill in the blank: some behavior]?" I would think, "Do I really do that? Yeah, I totally do. Wow, I'm surprised she even noticed that." And in that instant, we would grow closer because I would realize the intimacy required to understand my idiosyncrasies with such nuance.

This kind of revelation can feel endearing because we feel that someone "gets us." Just as the comedian observes, understands, and reports back, the marketer observes social phenomena, understands the cultural codes, and signals accordingly through the cultural product they put into the world. If you're a McDonald's fan, you read these fan truths and think, "That's so true," and you lean in just a bit closer. At Wieden+Kennedy, we often say, "In the specific, we find the universal." The truth about the cultural practices of a tribe has a gravitational pull that reverberates throughout the broader congregation, and on to potential converts, in a cascading fashion that catalyzes the community's growth. That's the power of the truth.

Fact: if you assembled one hundred strangers across the country and asked them what they all have in common, beyond biology, the chance that they have all eaten at McDonald's is probably about 99.99 percent. In the rare instance that someone reports the contrary, we would likely look at them with disbelief. I mean, who has never been to a McDonald's? It's the great democratizer. Whatever the public discourse about the brand might be, we've all eaten there. Right? In fact, we probably all have our go-to order—mine is a Double Cheeseburger meal with extra pickles and a Hi-C Orange.

That, in and of itself, is a fan truth: we all have an order. No matter how big or famous you are, everyone has an order. With this fan truth in hand, we launched a Super Bowl spot aimed directly at McDonald's fans, spotlighting famous orders from famous fans like Kim Kardashian, who dips her chicken nuggets in honey; Magic Johnson, who eats a Filet-O-Fish; Joe Montana, who orders a Quarter Pounder; and Whoopi Goldberg, whose go-to is a Big Mac, among others. The reaction to the commercial was overwhelming. People took to social networking platforms to echo their go-to order and debate the merit of other people's orders, including those of the people in the ad. "Famous Orders" had a democratizing effect on people. Seeing that some of the biggest superstars in the world might very well share the same order as you made people feel connected and, subsequently, made McDonald's feel communal.

As Brandon Henderson, executive creative director at Wieden+ Kennedy, described it, "The reactions were crazy, people defending other people's meal choice. We looked back on the success of that

["Famous Orders"] and said, 'Well, maybe there's something more here.'" Our partners at McDonald's could feel the kinetic energy brewing. So we took it a step further and partnered with celebrities to turn their go-to order into actual menu items available for purchase for a limited time. We weren't looking for celebrities who ate McDonald's food because, well, we all do. Instead, we were looking for legit McDonald's fans who were unabashed about their fandom. The kind of fans whose meals weren't just regular menu items but consisted of a signature uniqueness to them. Jennifer "JJ" Healan, vice president of brand content and engagement at McDonald's US, reminded us, "That's what makes this idea really special, the twist in every order that is personal to each of our partners."

Our first partner was Travis Scott, a Houston-raised hip-hop artist and creative savant whose impact on the hip-hop and street wear communities cannot be overstated. While Travis Scott may not be as "popular" as Jay-Z or a household name like Eminem, his influence was unparalleled. Furthermore, a famous 2019 photo of Travis Scott eating McDonald's on the wing of his Bugatti told us he was the right pick. His order was the same as it had been back in his hometown of Houston, Texas: Quarter Pounder with cheese, extra bacon and lettuce, fries and barbecue sauce, and a Sprite. This meal could have been ordered by anyone at any time, but for a limited time, you could order it as the Cactus Jack meal—Travis Scott's signature meal. The genius of the meal was that the Cactus Jack could just as well have been "the Marcus Collins," furthering the sense of democratization within the McDonald's fandom. To accompany the meal, we launched a collection of branded artifacts, uniquely designed by Travis himself, with a visual aesthetic that tapped into the rich nostalgia of McDonald's and evoked the edge of contemporary streetwear.

Once the campaign launched, the floodgates opened, so much so that the demand for the menu item caused a shortage of beef, onions, lettuce, and even Sprite at McDonald's restaurants across the country.

Quarter Pounder sales doubled in the first week, and sales grew 10 percent in four weeks, with a $50 million revenue increment. Even Wall Street analysts recognized the impact of the campaign, seeing McDonald's stock price soar and adding $10 billion to its market cap. The Cactus Jack was so coveted that fans stole in-store signage promoting the signature meal and resold the posters on eBay. Indeed, Henderson was correct; there was definitely more here.

"Famous Orders" became an ongoing platform idea that celebrated signature orders from famous fans. After the success of our Travis Scott partnership, we tapped the "Prince of Reggaeton," Latin music superstar J Balvin, whose go-to order is a Big Mac with no pickles, medium fries with ketchup, and an Oreo McFlurry. We followed this collaboration with another signature order partnership, this time with the K-pop global phenomenon BTS, and another later still with the breakout hip-hop artist Saweetie.

"Famous Orders" was a runaway success for McDonald's, inspiring imitation from other QSR brands, like Burger King, which made their own copycat partnerships, only without the fandom. But that was the crux of the "Famous Orders" campaign. It wasn't about the celebrity per se; it was centered around the fandom of the community. Though the trade press referred to "Famous Orders" as a "celebrity meal," that was not an accurate description. As Neal Arthur put it, "It wasn't a celebrity meal, it was a community meal." It was a meal that combined the fandom of McDonald's and the fandom of the celebrity partners, all of which was facilitated by the brand, which engaged fans like a fan—interacting from a fan-to-fan perspective versus a corporation-to-consumer perspective.

Fans subsequently used McDonald's marketing (ads, menu items, signage, and merch) as cultural products to communicate their identity and find other people who subscribed to the same community. It's a phenomenon that psychologists refer to as homophily, the tendency for people to connect with other people who are like themselves. Collectively, fans of McDonald's constructed communal and consumer identities—like meaning making, ritual practices, and consumer attitudes—through conversations on social networking platforms and the transmission of images, videos, memes, and other cultural text. "Famous Orders" was an exogenous shock to the system that catalyzed the congregation of McDonald's fans—and all the many tribes that make up the congregation—to take action by leveraging the pervasive influence of culture.

It's the truth about McDonald's fandom that has made our work with the brand—and its amazing marketing team—so successful. An intimate understanding of the fan truths—i.e., the social facts that constitute the communal practices of McDonald's fandom—armed us with the ability to activate fans by facilitating their fandom. As with the Beyhive, we didn't create the community; instead, the team helped the community come together by getting close. They observed them. They spoke with them. They listened to them. And, most importantly, they understood them—or, more specifically, they understood the way the tribe made meaning and exercised their fandom.

This wasn't about information; this was about intimacy. Fans, tribes, neotribes, community, networks, cultures of consumption, and all the many monikers that go by different names all amount to the same thing: people. If you want to get people to move, then you must focus on people and their proclivity to connect. These connections, of course, are fostered and fortified by the cultural characteristics that govern said people. Adoption into these cultural characteristics catalyzes collective behavior and inspires people to move.

As we discussed in Chapter 2, the first established brands served as a way in which consumers could distinguish which products belonged to which company. The brand mark served as a "legal mark" of ownership. Over the years, marketers used value propositions and positioning statements from psychology research to differentiate their products from those of their competitors, which evolved a brand from a legal mark to a "trust mark"—a mechanism that absorbed uncertainty for consumers. In this case, the brand mark provided consumers with a Good Housekeeping seal that assured them that the product could be trusted to perform. In this way, the benefit of brand was a mark of trust. Later still, marketers would work their wizardry to evoke emotions among consumers to elevate the brand from a transactional relationship, fortified by trust, to an affinity-based relationship built on love. Kevin Roberts, chairman and CEO of the Saatchi & Saatchi advertising agency, aptly referred to these brands as "love marks." But the brands that dominate culture (and, subsequently, commerce) today have evolved into "identity marks"—the marks we use to communicate who we are, what we believe, and where we reside within the stratified social world. These signifiers—like Apple, Supreme, Nike, Carhartt, Ben & Jerry's, Patagonia, or even Bernie Bros, MAGA, and QAnon—are more than just legal marks, trust marks, or love marks. They are receipts of identity that people use to project themselves to the world based on the meaning and ideological associations these brands carry, and their congruence with the people who consume them. The literature refers to this as self-concept theory, where people purchase brands that are consistent with, enhance, or in some way fit well with their conception of themselves.

The resulting effect of this phenomenon will no doubt drive the next evolution of brand or—dare I say—the future of brand: brand as a "tribal mark." Naturally, the brands that people use to communicate their identity are ripe to be elevated from an "identity mark" to a "tribal mark" by fostering and facilitating the people who subscribe to the brand's ideology. You don't need a crystal ball to predict this; it's written on the walls. The longest-standing institutions in the world—government, military, and religion—have understood this since the beginning of time, and they've leveraged the culture of the tribe to keep their members engaged and catalyze collective behavior among them. We're not in a state of identity-based politics. We're battling tribal politics, where people congregate and act in concert with people like themselves.

At its core, the notion of people subscribing to communities based on shared interests and consumption activity is not a new phenomenon. People have long congregated within groups that share similar cultural characteristics, all within the context of commerce—think H.O.G.s, Trekkies, sneakerheads, the hip-hop community, the Beyhive, Swifties, or even fans of the movie *Twilight*, where people claimed membership on Team Edward or Team Jacob. This is quintessential human behavior; we are social animals, after all. The difference today, however, is that contemporary technologies like social networking platforms—and even those to come, like nonfungible tokens (NFTs) and other Web 3.0 technologies—create greater opportunities to operationalize intrinsic human behavior.

While Jack Dorsey makes predictions about the future, I don't presume to be so clairvoyant. There are no crystal balls at my disposal that allow me to see what's ahead, but the future is crystal clear—the brands, companies, organizations, and entities that will win will be the ones that activate their tribes. Likewise, the future of NFTs is intrinsically connected to the future of brand because they provide an operationalizable receipt of membership into the tribe that enables the brand to facilitate the community and foster loyalty among its members. On its surface, the "token" constitutes ownership of a unique digital asset. However, this receipt of ownership also provides access to something far greater. Like the gold coins that grant entry into the New York Continental Hotel of the John Wick cinematic universe, the token empowers its owner with membership within a community. It is, ostensibly, a cultural artifact of authentication that signifies that you are "one of us"—cue the Gooble Gobble scene from *Freaks*. This isn't about masses; it is about subcultural communities.

This is where things get interesting. The "T," in this case, isn't really for "token"; rather, it's better suited for "tribes." NFTs arm marketers with a technology that facilitates tribal membership such that brands can design road maps that benefit token owners. The actual asset is inconsequential relative to the possibilities that come from fostering community, especially for brands or organizations that already have tribal associations, like Apple, the Ford F-150, Patagonia, sports teams, nonprofits, or even political parties. Imagine a Lakers NFT that grants postgame access to the court whether your seats are courtside or nosebleed. As of this writing, Coachella just announced an NFT collectible that gives fans front-row access to Coachella for life. The opportunities are truly endless—not just the perks per se but the way in which brands, artists, or institutions activate a tribe of people who see the world the way they do. Not only is this the true opportunity for brands and NFTs, but it is also the future of brand writ large.

The best marketers in the world understand this better than most. But these marketers don't have "marketing" in their title. Oh, no. Instead, they come from the world of politics, and they leverage the cultural influence of tribes (particularly the GOP) to get people to move—to vote, to adopt and villainize new language (like critical race theory), to accept and defend a lie (the Big Lie), or to refuse to wear a mask or take the COVID-19 vaccine, even if it kills them.

That's not hyperbole, either. According to NPR research, the counties that voted 60 percent or higher for Trump in the 2020 presidential election had 2.73 times the COVID death rates of those who voted for Biden. The counties with even higher proportions of votes for Trump saw even higher COVID-19 mortality rates. Why? Because the cultural norm for the current GOP was to rebel against wearing masks and getting vaccinated. This was the expectation of members of the tribe of the GOP. Once the tribe adopted these cultural practices, even Donald Trump himself could not change its course despite being the mouthpiece that preached the gospel of the tribe. The gospel must be congruent with the way that people see the world if you are to connect with them and get them to move. During a postpresidential tour with the fired Fox News host Bill O'Reilly, Trump told a crowd of conservatives that they should get vaccinated in an attempt to take credit for the efficacy of the vaccines' protection amidst all the public discourse surrounding them. The crowd immediately began to boo him. The tribe had spoken.

This is not the future; it is today. The writer William Gibson is famously quoted as saying, "The future is already here—it's just not evenly distributed." This is, by and large, the ambition of this book: to provide everyone with the ability to harness the power of culture and leverage its influence to get people to move. Doing so, however, requires a conversation about responsibility—a thought I will address in the next and final chapter.

## FROM KNOW-WHY TO KNOW-HOW

The world is constantly moving, and everything in it continues to change. Today's technology has accelerated these changes in ways that were once unimaginable. People's ability to connect, learn from, and influence each other has had a significant impact on culture and its subsequent practices. These technologies have also created a tremendous opportunity for business leaders and idea creators to observe and study other people's culture and all their dynamism in hopes of learning about what makes these people tick and how best to reach them. There are many ways to do this, but here are a few tips to get you started.

I typically start my exploration of a new culture by first getting a sense of the language and general interests associated with the community. For that, I use Twitter Advanced Search, a free tool that allows you to tailor search results on Twitter for specific topics, words, hashtags, people, and dates. Considering the millions and millions of conversations that happen on Twitter across a seemingly endless array of topics, Twitter Advanced Search helps narrow the conversations to those that are most relevant to your research. I usually search by topic or hashtag, so if you wanted to learn about the vegan culture, I'd recommend searching for #vegan or "going vegan." Once the search results come back, you can start looking through the authored tweets in chronological order to get a feel for what's being said about veganism and what other things are mentioned in relation to it. You might have to read hundreds of tweets before you're able to glean any overarching themes about the vegan culture. But once you do, you'll have a general idea of what's being talked about around the topic, and you'll be ready for the next step: Reddit.

Reddit can be a little intimidating and potentially difficult to navigate if you aren't familiar with the platform, but don't let that discourage you. It's a vibrant environment with rich cultural information just waiting for you to extract it. The purpose of using Reddit in this way is to observe the community practicing its culture subscriptions and to "listen in" on members of the community engaging in discourse as they collectively make meaning. To get started on this step, look for subreddits that are associated with the community you're studying. If it's vegans, then you'll find many different subreddits that fit the bill, like "Vegan," "PlantBasedDiet," "VeganFitness," and "VeganFoodPorn." Click into each of these subreddits and immerse yourself in the back-and-forth that takes place among the community members. Take note of some of the themes, language, and related topics that you found through Twitter Advanced Search and how these items are discussed in conversations within the community.

Keep in mind, the idea isn't to just observe and listen; it's to internalize and understand. As you read through the exchanges of the community members, remember the three questions to ask yourself: Why are they doing this? What are they feeling? How do they view the world around them? The goal of this undertaking is to glean understanding, and that is possible only when we're able to see the world through the lens of a community, not just our own. The more you do this kind of research, the faster you'll become at doing it and the better you'll become at learning from it, so I recommend doing it often.

## CHAPTER 7

# THE IMPLICATIONS OF CULTURAL PRODUCTION

I N THE WINTER OF 1785, A GROUP OF CHILDREN LIVING IN A Maryland village accused a fifty-six-year-old Irish woman named Elly Kedward of practicing witchcraft. The locals were enraged. Although their misgivings about witchcraft had been tempered since the Salem witch trials nearly a century earlier and roughly four hundred miles north of the village, witchery was still perceived as demonic and was, therefore, unwelcomed. According to reports, Kedward was banished from the village, tied to a tree, and forced to bear the extremities of the winter with no shelter or defense. She was left for dead and presumed to be so.

Just weeks after what can only be described as an execution, all of Kedward's accusers and half of the children in the village mysteriously vanished with no indication as to why. It was believed among the villagers to be a curse from Kedward in revenge against those who had put her to death. The remaining residents packed up their things and abandoned the village, vowing never to speak of what had taken place or to utter the name Elly Kedward again.

The village was resettled thirty-nine years later and established by its new residents as Burkittsville, Maryland, a departure from its original name: Blair. For years and years following its founding, Burkittsville experienced a string of mysterious deaths among its children, heinous deaths that could not be explained beyond the eyewitness account of a witchlike presence. The lore was that this witch was the spirit of Elly Kedward, and that these deaths were due to the curse of the Blair Witch.

Curious about the legend, Heather Donahue, a film student at Montgomery College, enlisted two friends, Joshua Leonard and Michael Williams, to make a documentary that would uncover the truth about the Blair Witch. In October 1994, Heather, Joshua, and Michael entered the Black Hills woods of Burkittsville, Maryland, and never came out. One year later, their equipment and belongings were recovered with no sign of the three's whereabouts. No one knew what had happened to the three filmmakers until their footage and field notes revealed what had caused the people of Blair to flee their village back in the eighteenth century and caused the people of Burkittsville to live in fear ever since. This was the doing of the Blair Witch and the plot of a fictional movie, called *The Blair Witch Project*, that served as a found-footage documentary that archived the three filmmakers' work.

Yes, there was no Elly Kedward. There were no missing children who vanished. There was no documentary. There was no Heather or Joshua or Michael who went missing. And there was no Blair Witch. However, the directors of *The Blair Witch Project*, Daniel Myrick and Eduardo Sánchez, who concocted this elaborate backstory for the film, certainly wanted us to think so. Their meticulously fabricated fable of the Burkittsville Blair Witch certainly delivered, as it caused tens of millions of people to question, "Is it real?" And I was one of them.

I remember first seeing the trailer for *The Blair Witch Project* in the fall of 1998. I was a sophomore in college with a full tray of nachos on my lap and a large soda in my hand, preparing to watch a movie that would prove to be insignificant once the previews to the main attraction aired. The second that the *Blair Witch* trailer hit the screen, I was hooked. For as long as I can remember, I've loved horror movies. It's my favorite movie genre, with no close comparison. However, by the late 1990s, the horror movie genre had lost its way. One of the greatest horror moviemakers, the late Wes Craven, critiqued the genre with the brilliance of his teen slasher film, *Scream*, which ironically played against the tropes of traditional horror films that he, himself, had once created. However, instead of taking a cue from Craven to continue reinventing the genre, other horror moviemakers seemingly hadn't received the memo. It seemed as though the genre had become a breeding ground for copycats. *The Blair Witch Project*, however, completely subverted the genre. Where beautiful, sculpted A-list actors, like Jennifer Love Hewitt and Josh Hartnett, were starring in Hollywood's horror movies, *The Blair Witch Project* featured three no-name actors. This, of course, complemented the lore that Heather, Joshua, and Michael might indeed have gone into the woods and never come out. If they had been famous actors, there was no way the backstory would have held up.

To further the intrigue, a website was launched with faux police reports that chronicled the search for the three documentarians. "Missing" posters of the three were put up on bulletin boards in college dorm rooms and stapled to telephone poles around college campuses with the prompt "Evidence Exists . . . log on to www.blairwitch.com to see and hear." These were the early days of the Internet, when most people accessed the web via dial-up—except on college campuses, where students had high-speed Internet access and tons of disposable time to surf the far corners of the web.

When people visited the site, they saw the police reports, news-reels, television interviews, damaged canisters that had contained the students' footage, and the soiled notebooks that documented their field notes—all of which made the tale seem . . . well . . . real. To further the uncertainty, the fabricated backstory of Elly Kedward and the missing students was detailed in a mockumentary (a documentary-styled film that details fictional events as if they were real) called *Curse of the Blair Witch* that was broadcast on the SciFi channel (a cable network that was known for creating horror content) just two days before the theatrical release of the movie. By August 1999, a month after *The Blair Witch Project* hit movie screens, www.blairwitch.com had had over 160 million visits, and it seemed as if everybody was in full debate as to whether the lore was fact or fiction—which drove people to the movie theater to see for themselves.

George Lowenstein, an economics and psychology professor at Carnegie Mellon who is also the director of the Center for Behavioral Decision Research, referred to this phenomenon as the gap in knowledge. He said, "Curiosity acts as a form of cognitively induced deprivation that arises from the perception of a gap in knowledge or understanding—this, subsequently, drives us to close the gap." It's the same reason why we continue to watch a show or movie that we aren't really enjoying. We just have to see how it ends. We have to close the gap in knowledge. Likewise, as increasingly more people talked about *The Blair Witch Project* and debated the authenticity of its backstory, it catalyzed people to go see the movie so that they could be socially included and participate in the cultural discourse (i.e., conversation) among their people. As the saying goes, "Nothing draws a crowd like a crowd."

The most interesting part, however, is that people actually believed that the legend was real. Perhaps it was a combination of the backstory, the SciFi mockumentary, the website, the missing posters, and the faux police reports—or maybe a few permutations of those elements, depending on what you were exposed to when these artifacts were in the wild. Whatever it was, people really fell for it, including yours truly, so much so that I bought my tickets early so that I could be there to witness it myself on opening day.

*The Blair Witch Project* debuted on July 14, 1999. It starred no-name talent. The directors weren't acclaimed. It was shot on what appeared to be a shaky camcorder, which was meant to signify the found-footage aesthetic of what was supposed to be a documentary. Needless to say, the movie didn't have a whole lot going for it in terms of the conventional wisdom of what makes a movie a Hollywood success. The movie opened opposite the legendary film director Stanley Kubrick's swan song, *Eyes Wide Shut*, which starred the then "it" couple, Tom Cruise and Nicole Kidman. *Eyes Wide Shut* played on over 2,400 screens on its opening weekend, raking in $21.7 million in ticket sales, which was pretty impressive for a movie rated NC-17, which heavily restricted the population of people who could see it. *The Blair Witch Project* played on only 27 screens its opening weekend and brought in $1.5 million. By the end of its run in cinemas, *Eyes Wide Shut* had made $162 million in worldwide box office sales for a film that had cost its producers $65 million to make. *The Blair Witch Project*, on the other hand, cost $60,000 to produce and made $289 million in worldwide box office sales—a 78 percent differential in revenue despite a 1,080 percent delta in production costs. Conventional wisdom would say that the lower-budget, no-name film should have been bested by the high budget, A-list film. But that wasn't the case. This wasn't due to the film's merit; rather, it was because of the storytelling that surrounded it. That is to say, the content didn't get people to move; it's people who get people to move—particularly people who are like ourselves: our networked tribes.

As Marshall McLuhan argued, the media works us over completely, leaving no part of us unaffected or unaltered. Indeed, media can be quite influential, but there is no media vehicle more influential than the media of people. Instead of hearing it on the radio or watching it on television or reading it in an article, I heard it from my friend Terrance, and because of our relationship, I was more inclined to trust it—and, subsequently, be influenced by it.

We trust people over any form of marketing communication. We trust the word of our tribe more than we do print, radio, television, or billboards because there is an implied credibility associated with the word of our people. Advertising gets our attention; people get us to move. The combination of the two is super powerful and, therefore, should work in concert. This is why savvy advertisers aim to "get their ideas in culture" so as to leverage the influence of our people through the discourse created by exogenous shock to the system (the ad) that gets our attention.

If you took inventory of everything new that you consumed over the last two years, be it a new show you watched or a new technology you adopted, it probably wasn't due solely to advertising you saw. Instead, it's more likely that the ad made you aware and a recommendation (be it direct or indirect) from another person pushed you over the edge. I spent almost ten hours of my life watching *Tiger King* and another swath of hours watching *Squid Game* for the very same reason. Not because of any ad but because my people were talking about them, and I wanted to be socially included. I wanted to know what the talk was all about. I wanted to close the gap in knowledge. People would often say, "I heard about it on Facebook" or "Twitter said thus and so." While this may be true on one level, I think the more accurate description would be "I heard about it *from* Jane Doe while on Facebook."

That may seem like a nitpicky nuance, but its implications are significant. Facebook is a platform that is constructed by a computer coding language. This language forms an environment where people come to interact, much like the physical environments we frequent, like the pub, church, or park. Our human tendency to connect leads us to anthropomorphize the world around us, i.e., attribute human characteristics or behaviors to nonhuman things, like animals, objects, and events.

In his medically reviewed article for the Association for Psychological Science, "Why Do We Anthropomorphize?," Dr. Rick Nauert detailed the entities that are more likely to have these human characteristics. It was no surprise that he suggested that these entities are the ones that appear to have traits most similar to those of humans. We think of our pets in human frames. We give tropical storms and cars human names. We even fashion deities in human form because when we think of these entities as humans, like us, our minds find it easier to connect with them, understand their intentions, and predict their behavior.

The same goes for technology. I cannot begin to count how many times I've heard people say, "Well, according to Google" or "Google said," with regard to Google's search technology. Google Search is a computer code that indexes web pages on the Internet so that information can be easily searched and acquired. Google is not human; it didn't "say" anything. Instead, Google presented information that was authored by people. We anthropomorphize Google because the information that Google indexes and curates is authored and disseminated by people. Therefore, it is no surprise that we give Facebook, Instagram, Twitter, TikTok, or any other social networking platform human characteristics because these platforms are environments where people engage in conversations and make meaning through the exchange of culturally mediated text—words, symbols, memes, videos, etc. Phrases like "the Internet for the win," which acknowledges the perfect encapsulation of a situation through a meme or a well-timed retort that bests someone else online, and "the Internet never fails" are all ways in which we anthropomorphize technology and evidence of our dependence on humankind and our need to connect.

This need to connect is so great that it extends beyond our networked tribe—even beyond the congregations of people who subscribe to the same belief—and reverberates with strangers more broadly. Before I decide to purchase a product on Amazon, I look to see what other people (complete strangers, by the way) think about the product to make sure I'm making the right choice. We rely on people.

PowerReviews, a technology company that aggregates user-generated content online, has shown evidence through its research that a product with just one review (again, from a stranger) is 65 percent more likely to be purchased by a user than a product with no reviews. I mean, if no one vouches for it, can it really be trusted? That's the calculus we undergo when we make decisions and, subsequently, take action. This echoes what evolutionary anthropologists have argued since the beginning of the discipline: humankind thrives because of its ability to cooperate. The Beatles sang, "We get by with a little help from our friends." Prince reminded us, "Dearly beloved, we are gathered here today to get through this thing called life." It's true; we rely on people—even more so, we rely on *our* people. And every review from a stranger, every post from a teammate, every tweet from a colleague, and every snap from a friend is a story told, and these stories are the way in which we fortify the covalent bonds that connect us.

## STORYTELLING

Stories are the account of events organized in sequence of time. They are, fundamentally, a retelling of what happened to whom, when it took place, and where these events transpired. It is believed that storytelling dates back tens of thousands of years to when cave dwellers used pigment to draw on walls as a way to record the happenings of their time. Cave drawings would later become oral retelling through stories and mythology. These informational vehicles were so powerful and so persuasive that they were perceived as fact before modern science was invented in the seventeenth century. Yes, "once a upon a time" was the start of our account of how the phenomenal world functions—describing why things are the way they are and why things happen the way they do. Greek mythology led the way in this regard, with stories of gods, deities, humans, and creatures that gave meaning to the chaotic world we occupied. These stories helped us understand the world around us and our place within it. They gave description and causality to randomness and a blueprint for how we should navigate it all through morals and takeaways.

If you grew up with any religious background, then you know this firsthand. We all learned about our respective religions through stories and myths, and we were instructed to tell them to our children and our children's children. The poet and scholar Robert Graves wrote, "Myth has two main functions: The first is to answer the sort of awkward questions that children ask, such as 'Who made the world? How will it end? Who was the first man? Where do souls go after death?' The second function of myth is to justify an existing social system and account for traditional rites and customs." Stories are the way we interpret and socialize the cultural facts of the community. Whether it was the story of David and Goliath that taught me that I could overcome the greatest of obstacles through my faith in the God of Israel or the story of the Hebrew boys in the fiery furnace that taught me to do what's right regardless of what's at stake, I learned about God, my community, and what was expected of me by both.

Throughout this book, I have utilized religious literature, references, and terminology to illustrate the influential power of culture and its ability to catalyze the collective adoption of behavior because religion itself is more than just an act of worship; it's a social function. The word "religion" comes from "religare," which means to bind. It would later evolve into "religio," which means obligation. So when we're talking about a religious person, we're talking about someone who is bound to their faith, or when we talk about someone doing something "religiously," we're referring to someone who is committed to a particular activity. The same goes for culture. Adherence to the social facts of a community commits us to our people and keeps us closely connected, much like adhering to the social facts of our religion keeps us close to the divine and those who worship similarly. Culture is the governing operating system of humanity, and stories are the vehicle through which the codes of the operating system are propagated throughout the community. The sharing of stories from peer to peer, young to old, or generation to generation is all an act of community. It's how we share knowledge and values to help us navigate life in a manner that is aligned with our tribe or congregation.

Of course, these stories are shared and exchanged from person to person through a cultural frame based on the shared beliefs and ideologies that dictate what people "like us" ought to do in such matters. In many ways, the act of storytelling is really an act of community building, a vehicle for sharing the social facts of the community—the shared beliefs, meaningful artifacts, behavioral norms, and coded language.

The telling and retelling of these stories aims to keep us in lockstep with the community and safe from excommunication. This is the function of folklore within a networked tribe. Folklore is the dissemination of knowledge, predominantly through word-of-mouth communication, that socializes the identity, beliefs, and traditions—i.e., the culture—of a group of people. Alan Dundes, the most renowned folklorist, asserted that "folk" refers to any group of people who share at least one common factor—be it occupation, fandom, school, etc.—and exercise their subscription to this group through traditions that they can call their own. They have a set of customs, "a way we do things around here," that indicates whether you're one of them and demarcates whether you're in or out. The lore, a body of traditions and knowledge that is shared among these people through storytelling, ensures that the members of these communities keep the customs.

Dundes described folklore in a broad fashion that expanded the aperture of how we might typically define storytelling. In his 1965 essay,

"What Is Folklore?," Dundes listed a myriad of expressions that constitute the different forms of folklore, which include art, architecture, textiles, mass-produced objects, music, poetry, tales, urban legends, jokes, proverbs, rituals, and a host of other expressions. Of course, this list should look familiar because each of these items is a different form of cultural product, the way in which we express our cultural subscriptions. They each tell a story that gives the expression socially constructed meaning, which helps shape the community's identity. This perspective on folklore allows us to conceptualize the relationship between identity and cultural product through the many forms of storytelling (be it material or word of mouth). And if we revisit the system of systems that constitutes culture, we can visualize the distance between cultural expression and identity to uncover the implications of this delta.

The identities we choose, and those that are bestowed upon us, inform the beliefs and ideologies that we use to frame the world and make sense of its dynamism. These beliefs and ideologies are held within us, unseen to the naked eye. Cultural production, on the other hand, is the most visible expression of a community's cultural subscription. A

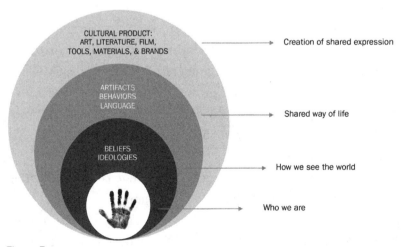

Figure 5.

community's music, film, literature, art, fashion, and materials are all publicly observable and available for consumption. You can listen to gospel music and not be Christian. You can read the Quran and not be Muslim. You can watch a step show and not be in a historically Black Greek letter organization, just as you can eat Greek food and not be Greek. Engaging in each other's culture helps bring us closer together. I suppose this is why the standard convention is that culture is meant to be shared so we can learn about each other.

When I was eleven years old, I spent a summer in Sweden as a participant in a program called the Children International Summer Village that placed kids in delegations of four to represent their country among a dozen or so other delegations. During our time in the village, each day was curated by a different delegation from a different country with the aim of introducing us to their unique way of life. If it was the Romanian delegation's designated day, for instance, we ate their food (breakfast, lunch, and dinner), played their games, learned their songs, and spent our day immersed in their culture. As we learned more about our differences, we also learned about our similarities. It was a powerful experience for my eleven-year-old self that I just recently, some thirty years later, have truly come to appreciate. In that short month, I gained two best friends from Mexico (Sebastian and Fabian), a new brother from Israel (Yaniv), a girlfriend from Brazil (Julia), a big sister from Egypt (Marwa), a big brother from the Netherlands (Ollie), and a perspective that widened my worldview beyond my belief. As I engaged in their cultural practices and consumed their cultural product, and they ours, we learned about the beliefs and ideologies that made these practices and products meaningful. Otherwise, our activities in the village would have merely amounted to cosplay—adopting the artifacts without understanding the meaning.

While the village was designed so that its participants learned about the beliefs and ideologies of the people in whose culture we all participated, our day-to-day lives outside the village are not so curated.

Although we engage in other people's cultures, we aren't always knowledgeable about the beliefs and ideologies that give them meaning. Without understanding the ideologies and shared beliefs evangelized in the storytelling of people's culture, we see only the cultural practices and cultural product without understanding why these people do what they do. At best, this leads to a missed opportunity to learn from each other and grow closer as a society of global citizens. At worst, it leads to cultural appropriation, a topic that has garnered much debate in recent years, resulting in the sharp criticism of some who were deserving and the blunt ridicule of others who likely were not. Many critics of cultural appropriation argue that culture is meant to be shared and, therefore, cannot be "appropriated." However, this argument is narrow in its view and does not account for the complexities of cultural appropriation and the different ways in which it manifests.

Cultural appropriation occurs when members of one culture intentionally or unintentionally take possession or ownership of elements from another group's cultural identity or associated markers. Scholars have categorized cultural appropriation into four types: (1) cultural exchange—the reciprocal exchange of social facts between peer communities of equal power, like the co-creation of hip-hop between Black and Hispanic youths in the South Bronx; (2) transculturation—the cultural elements that are co-created from elements of many cultures, like the heterogeneity of US culture; (3) cultural dominance—the use of a dominant community's social facts by a less powerful community, like hip-hop kids adopting skater culture; and (4) cultural exploitation—the use of a community's cultural practices and products by a dominant community without reciprocity or permission. This fourth form of cultural appropriation—cultural exploitation—is the primary target of contemporary critique.

In the anthology *Borrowed Power*, Bruce Ziff and Pratima Roa curated a collection of essays that investigated this form of appropriation, primarily regarding Indigenous cultures and the dominant Black

American culture. Their collective writing underscored the power dynamic of exploitative cultural appropriation between the privileged and the marginalized, where a privileged community dominates a marginalized community by taking its cultural markers—practices and products—and redefining them through its own meaning frames, claiming them as products of its own curation.

This is most noticeably evidenced when White America appropriates the folklore of Black Americans through the possession of Black musical art forms like jazz, rock and roll, rhythm and blues (R&B), electronic music, and rap. These forms of cultural product have been borrowed, imitated, and reworked through hegemonic frames without the understanding of the beliefs and ideologies from which these practices were created and imbued with meaning. Historically, White artists would mimic the sounds, styles, and gestures of Black artists and sell them to White audiences, without permission or compensation. This exploitation of power differentials created an economic disadvantage for Black cultural producers and a feeling of robbery for an entire community. This fashion of appropriation can be seen more recently on social networking platforms, like TikTok, where Black cultural producers create innovative dances that are then appropriated by White TikTokers and presented as their own. This form of "Christopher Columbusing" the practices and productions of marginalized communities is exacerbated by the systematic racism that rewards Whiteness and villainizes Blackness.

Take cornrows, for instance. This is a style of braiding hair very close to the scalp in a tight, continuous manner, mirroring the rows of field crops for which the hairstyle is named. This cultural practice dates back to the African societies of the early 1500s, which used this hairstyle as an identity marker. In the times of colonialism and slavery, enslaved Black people wore cornrows for their utility and as a symbol of remembrance of their homeland. More recently, however, when cornrows have been worn by Black Americans, they have been deemed as "ghetto" by the dominant culture, robbing the practice of all its cultural richness. And when cornrows were worn by Bo Derek in the 1979 box-office hit movie *10*, the dominant culture came to consider cornrows fashionable. Roughly forty years later, Kim Kardashian would wear cornrows on the red carpet of the MTV Movie Awards, but instead of referring to them as cornrows, she called them "Bo Derek braids," crediting the invention to an exploitative imitation and reworking its meaning through the lens of the hegemony. This is part and parcel of the exploitative fashion of cultural appropriation. Marginalized communities are criticized for their originality, while dominant communities profit from the co-opted creations of the marginalized by calling the work of others their own (explicitly or implicitly) through the assignment of new meaning.

The cultural products that people use to express their membership in a particular community—music, film, television, literature, podcasts, comic books, fashion, hairstyles, dances, brands, and branded products—are all different forms of folklore that tell the story of who they are and how they fit in the world. These creations help them make sense of the world so that they can navigate it in concert with their people. When marketers, leaders, and organizations leverage culture to influence behavior, in many ways, they are essentially leveraging the creations and stories of these communities. In cases where these productions are works of marginalized communities, such leveraging can be easily perceived as an act of exploitive cultural appropriation. Therefore, it is essential for marketers, leaders, and organizations to look beyond the cultural product of a group of people—what might look cool or "trendy" from the outside—and set their gaze toward understanding the meaning that makes the stories significant. Doing so not only keeps a brand out of the crosshairs of offending a group of people and potentially suffering the backlash but also creates an opportunity for the brand to empower the people of said community.

In May of 2020, while the world faced the realities of the COVID-19 global pandemic, the United States of America was simultaneously forced to face the reality of a familiar foe: racism. Through the lens of a bystander's mobile device, we witnessed the brutal murder of George Floyd at the hands of a Minneapolis police officer, Derek Chauvin, who knelt on Floyd's neck for over nine minutes while his fellow officers held down Floyd's handcuffed body. This heinous act was broadcast nonstop across news outlets and newsfeeds. The pervasive retelling of Floyd's death sparked a national discourse that made the country take inventory of the Black experience, particularly with regard to systemic racism and institutional authorities. Debates ensued. Protests commenced. And many brands and organizations that sought to find themselves on the right side of history spoke out on behalf of Black Americans through public statements of allyship and black profile photos on Instagram as an act of solidarity. Some even used their platforms as resources for Black Americans to tell their story. The support was long overdue but generally welcomed and appreciated by the community. However, while this reckoning around race was unfolding on a public stage throughout the summer of 2020, a separate but related topic went largely unsaid despite the many statements, gestures, and campaigns from corporations and organizations. That is, until Beats by Dre used its voice to weigh in on the discourse.

Black people have been the victims of some of the most vicious crimes ever committed in this country since the moment we set foot on its soil. From 1619 to the 1960s, the existence of Black people in America was one of outward brutality, servitude, and subhumanization. Although the Civil Rights movement ushered in great reform that mitigated many of the oppressive realities of the Black experience, it did not eradicate them. Yet the cultural production of Black Americans were consistently adopted by their oppressors and reworked as their own. This act of cultural appropriation can be seen in one of the first forms of White American entertainment that was not derived from European roots: the minstrel show.

Minstrel shows were a popular form of theater that consisted of White actors painting their faces black and caricaturing the singing and dancing of Black slaves for the amusement of their White audiences. Though Blackface minstrel shows waned over time, the White mimicry of Black cultural production continued through the co-opting of music, fashion, style, colloquialisms, mannerisms, and the like. It seemed as though America loved Black culture but not Black people. This was a nuanced argument that did not surface in the public discourse until after the murder of George Floyd, but it was certainly in the hearts and minds of Black Americans.

Against this backdrop, Beats by Dre released a film that posed a question that had long been discussed among Black folks but rarely broached among the broader population—*You love my culture, but do you love me?* The voiceover in the film asks this question with an extended refrain: "You love how I sound. My voice. These beats. This flow. But not me, though, right? You love how I look. My hair. This skin. But me? Nah." In doing so, Beats by Dre tapped into the discourse that took place in the private forums where Black Americans congregated—dinner tables, barbershops, barbecues, sorority meetings, etc.—and used its platform to say the quiet parts out loud on behalf of the community. And when it did, the community acquiesced.

I didn't see the *You Love Me* film on television, nor did I see it posted on any media platform owned or borrowed by Beats by Dre. I didn't hear this story from the brand at all; I heard it from the people—my people. I saw Beat's *You Love Me* video proliferated across my social newsfeeds and the timelines of people who looked like me and self-identified as I do—Black. It was no surprise that I shared it with my network. Not because I love Beats by Dre so much. Rather, I shared it because it reflected my cultural subscription. This story was my story. But it wasn't just mine, it was *ours*, and my sharing it was an expression of who I am, just as others shared it as an expression of who they are. *You Love Me* was more than an advertisement; it was a cultural product that the community used to express its identity and connect with other like-minded individuals. Yes, indeed, this was much more than an ad. It was a form of folklore, and we shared it as an act of community.

*You Love Me* is a clear example of the difference between cultural appropriation and cultural appreciation. Appropriation is the act of taking one's cultural markers, ignoring their original significance, and assigning new meaning to them. Appreciation, on the other hand, is the act of honoring another group's culture, which requires first respecting who they are and learning about what these markers and practices signify. Appropriation is an act of cosplay, like kids wearing feathered headdresses at Coachella or "Pimps and Hoes" parties at White frat houses where White college students dress in exaggerated cosplay as a form of contemporary Blackface.

Cultural appreciation is an act of curiosity, a desire to understand the history and context of a community's cultural work. As we seek to harness the powerful influence of culture, especially someone else's culture, we must approach this sacred ground with a sense of appreciation and a willingness to learn about the culture before we even begin to conceive of how we might leverage aspects of it. As evidenced here, Beats by Dre successfully leverages the power of culture because of its proximity to the community it targets. The brand understands the social facts of the people and what they signify to the community. As such, Beats uses its products and its marketing communications to help community members say something about themselves, which transforms its products and its ads into cultural product.

My friend and social media savant Eric Hultgren often refers to a car ride as a useful metaphor for brands tapping into the power of culture. You can either drive it, ride shotgun, or suck tailpipe. I love this delineation because it helps illustrate and operationalize what might very well seem like an abstract idea—"tapping into culture"— and provides a clear role for marketers, organizations, and leaders who seek to benefit from its power. You can lead culture (drive it) by contributing to its social facts with new language and new artifacts (think Black Lives Matter, Nike's "Just Do It," Bud Light's "Dilly," REI's "Opt Outside," Sprite's "Obey Your Thirst," and *The Blair Witch Project*). Or you can participate in culture (ride shotgun) by joining the discourse and elevating the social facts of a community (think *You Love Me* and *Stranger Things* x Eggo). In most cases, unfortunately, brands follow culture (suck tailpipe) by chasing trends without understanding the underlying social facts that give them meaning, like Pepsi's Kendall Jenner campaign. Of course, the last thing you want to do is suck tailpipe. However, contributing to the social facts of a community comes with great responsibility.

## THE RESPONSIBILITY OF STORYTELLING

According to the 2010 US Census data, Detroit, Michigan, possesses the highest percentage of Black residents of all major cities in the country. However, as any Detroit native can attest, you don't need a census statistician to tell you something so blatantly obvious. When I was growing up in "the D," my classmates were mostly Black, my teachers were predominantly Black, our school board was Black, our city council was Black, our mayor was Black, and our police chief was Black, as was the majority of the police force. I've always taken great pride in the city's Blackness, and I revered the authoritative institutions of the city and the people who occupied these positions of power. They were like local celebrities to me, particularly a group of police officers called the Blue Pigs.

These were no ordinary police officers. The Blue Pigs were a musical band that would visit schools around the city and perform Motown hits and R&B songs that were popular at the time. This was the '80s and early '90s, so their repertoire consisted of songs like New Edition's "Can You Stand the Rain" mixed with the Temptations' "My Girl." They were a big hit at my elementary and middle schools. The band was formed in 1970 as a community relations outreach effort on behalf of the Detroit Police Department to help children understand who the police are and what role they play in the community. It was ingrained in me that the police were our friends and that they were there to protect and serve. I even played basketball in the police athletic league on courts adjacent to the downtown Detroit police station. Each of these experiences with the police served as a chapter in a greater story whose moral was "You can trust and rely on the police." And I did—until a different story was told.

In 1991, camera footage of four Los Angeles police officers, Sgt. Stacey C. Koon, Officer Theodore J. Briseno, Officer Timothy E. Wind, and Officer Laurence Powell, who brutally beat an unarmed Black man to a pulp, surfaced and made its way into the hands of the public. The victim's name was Rodney King, and the video of his beating was played repeatedly on the evening news, satirized by comedians, referenced in rap songs, and discussed in the public discourse. The combination helped my almost twelve-year-old-self make sense (meaning) of what I witnessed in that video. I found myself in a state of cognitive dissonance. The display of brutality exhibited in the video was a complete contradiction of my concept of the police. I remember reconciling this conflict in my mind by telling myself, "Those are Los Angeles police officers, not Detroit police. That would never happen here." This was the story I told myself to make sense of these two opposing stories of an institution I had grown to admire and trust. All was well in the world again—in my world, at least. My confidence in the police was restored. The story I'd been told about the police was still mentally intact. That is, until a year later, when a story broke about another brutal beating of an unarmed Black man, Malice Green, by two police officers, Officer Walter Budzyn and Officer Larry Nevers. However, this time, the beating was fatal, and the incident happened in Detroit, with Detroit police officers.

This did not compute with the meaning frames I had for the police. The stories did not add up, and it forced me to conceive of a new story that I have told myself since then: not all police officers can be trusted, and not all police officers are your friend. Since I've established this new frame, I have seen many proof points that support this new narrative about the police in my mind, despite the many proof points that suggest the opposite. There have been many police officers throughout my life—from family members to family friends and fraternity brothers—who have been quite helpful to me. But in my mind, these officers were different from the others. I could trust them, but not the others.

What's interesting here is how our mental frames are influenced by the stories we're told. As a child, I loved the police because of the stories I was told as a child. As an adolescent, I feared the police because of the stories I was told as a preteen. Today, as an adult, I find myself distrusting of the police because of the aggregate stories I've been told, and subsequently tell myself, about the police.

The stories we tell—that is, the folklore we propagate—frame the way we see the world and how we show up in the world. This should be of no surprise considering that modern-day policing originated in the early 1700s when the institution was established in this country to police runaway slaves. Slave patrols, as they were called in the South at that time, were created to mitigate uprisings among Black people who were enslaved on White plantations. The patrols used brutal measures as a system of terror to control enslaved people and enforce behavioral expectations among them. This institution was later replaced in the South with vigilante and militia-style groups that were sanctioned to deny equal rights to Black people after the Civil War and the Emancipation Proclamation of 1863 that abolished slavery, although it would take another two years for all enslaved Black people to be freed on Juneteenth. Meanwhile, just a few decades earlier, cities in the North, like Boston, New York, and Philadelphia, began to adopt a publicly funded policing model that resembled the British policing institution established in 1829.

This origin story is a far cry from the "protect and serve" story we're told about the police now—a slogan that was ironically originated by the LAPD back in 1955. This story is, however, a testament to just how influential stories can truly be. As we discussed earlier, stories have an uncanny ability to socialize beliefs and ideologies, which informs how we show up in the world. When the stories about the police began to conflict, I adopted a new story and "othered" the police officers who didn't fit this new narrative frame. They weren't like the rest; they were different. The cultural geographer Mike Crang, who studies the relationship between social memory and identity, described "othering" as a process through which identities are established in an unequal relationship where people construct who is like them (in-group) and who is not (out-group). The "othering" process is both exclusionary and inclusionary. We "other" people into categorical groups that have been assigned a set of assumptions and stereotypical misgivings. We either "other" them to exclude them from our group or we "other" them to exclude them from the labels we've assigned to an out-group.

For example, during my undergraduate years, there were instances when some of my White or East Indian American classmates would say that I wasn't like "other" Black people they knew—or knew of. While they thought that they were paying me a compliment, they were essentially saying that I did not fit the frame they had of other Black people. This process excluded me from the assumptions that they assigned to Black people, a set of assumptions and stereotypes that they also excluded from their own identity. Although their intentions were good, their actions—whether they were conscious or unconscious—were quite harmful.

According to John A. Powell, the director of the Haas Institute for a Fair and Inclusive Society at the University of California, Berkeley, "othering" is based on characteristics that one group affixes to another group that it deems unfavorable. These unfavored groups usually consist of people that the other groups don't even know very well. Instead, their assumptions are driven largely by the stories that are told and propagated by media fashions, as opposed to personal experiences. We saw this illustrated in the case of D. W. Griffith's *The Birth of a Nation*, a story that helped White Americans, particularly in the South, establish frames for how they saw Black Americans. Over a century later, these frames would be further fortified by other media producers that tell similar stories today, which led to my being "othered" because I didn't fit into the stereotypical frames assigned to people who look like me.

In some cases, we learn about these "othered" groups through formal institutions like school, museums, and temple. However, considering their prolific nature, we primarily learn about the world and others in it through the media we consume—television, movies, news, journalism, books, and (of course) the media of people, like the stories we propagate from person to person. As we now know from our examination of legitimation in Chapter 7 and the literature on the mere exposure effect in Chapter 6, the more we're exposed to these kinds of prompts, the more likely we are to accept them and favor them.

This is further evidenced in the psychology literature on the classical conditioning of learning, which asserts that repeated exposure to (and reinforcement of) stimuli, like stories, can establish meaning frames and memory structures that catalyze expected and routine behaviors. Therefore, the more we hear a story, the more we accept it, the more we prefer it, and the more likely it is to get people to move. We learn about the world through interpellation (family, tribes, school, religion), cultural production (media, literature, art, marketing communications), and classical conditioning (observations and experiences). These stimuli are all understood and factored through a cultural lens that is often established by the stories we tell ourselves and tell each other. It's through stories that we preach the gospel to the congregation—the collection of people who see the world the way we do. For this reason alone, we bear a great responsibility when we use storytelling as a vessel to preach the gospel.

Rebekah Modrak is an artist and writer whose practice is at the intersections of art, activism, critical design, and creative resistance to consumer culture. She is also a professor at the Penny W. Stamps School of Art and Design at the University of Michigan and a friend with whom I coteach from time to time. I am a huge fan of her work and her ability to see the world through the eyes of the most vulnerable. I've learned so much from her over the years, and I incorporate her work into my teaching at Ross, my leadership at Wieden+Kennedy, and my academic scholarship. Of the many wonderful projects Rebekah has undertaken, perhaps the most famous is her study and critique of the company Shinola, the creation of a venture-capital firm based in Texas called Bedrock Manufacturing. Though known for its run-of-the-mill watch and accessory brand, Fossil, Bedrock founded Shinola in 2011 and placed the company in Detroit. Bedrock purchased Shinola's name from the original Shinola, the shoe polish company, which at one time produced racist ads that featured Blackface characters who spoke in derogatory colloquialisms that perpetuated harmful Black stereotypes, which is ironic considering that the company would be situated in Detroit, the Blackest city in the country.

According to Rebekah's article, "Bougie Crap," Bedrock chose Detroit because respondents to a survey said that they would be more inclined to pay three times as much for a product with the perseverance of being located in a bankrupt city, a reality Detroit would face just a few years later. A "downtrodden" city narrative lent itself to a comeback story from which Bedrock could benefit, so the company set up shop in Detroit and positioned itself as one of the outsiders that was "saving Detroit," as the national news media outlets narrated. This, of course, is a well-worn trope of the White savior who comes in and rescues a community of nonwhite people who otherwise will be left destitute. However, "Rethink Shinola," Rebekah's critique of the company, revealed that Shinola's marketing never used the words "Shinola is saving Detroit." Instead, it portrayed White leaders giving manual-labor jobs to Black employees in Detroit. In fact, at the 2019 Oscars, Peter Farrelly, the director of the movie *Green Book* (which received its own criticism for downplaying historical inaccuracies about racism), gave Shinola a shout-out when receiving one of his awards. Unfortunately, Farrelly said the quiet parts out loud when he proclaimed, "Shinola, they're saving Detroit," which forced the brand to hurry a response on Twitter in an attempt to soften the fallout that would soon come.

Shinola incorporates the city's name, "Detroit," into its products and tells a story of grit and resilience when it speaks about the city as a metaphor for the company itself. It is the gospel it preaches, and people buy Shinola products as an act of supporting (or saving) the city because doing so gives them a sense of altruism and the ability to project their identity accordingly. A $600 watch from Shinola signals to the world that I've done a good thing while also projecting a status of wealth, which excites people to consume. In this way, the receipt of consumption becomes a receipt of identity.

Although the principles that enable us to preach the gospel (through storytelling) and get people to act are neither good nor bad (they, themselves, are valueless), when we consider the community that is being exploited and not rewarded in this particular exchange, Shinola provides a note of caution. It is, if nothing else, an example of cultural appropriation, where the company not only used the city for its storytelling but also co-opted the city's Blackness to make the brand more than just a watch and leather goods company. Moreover, it did this without giving anything of substance back to the Black bodies, faces, and narratives it used to sell more stuff. Again, we see the illustration of Beats by Dre's declaration, *You Love Me*, almost a decade before it debuted.

Whether conspiracy theories that are socialized across the web or news stories that run nonstop or marketing campaigns that run across different media platforms, the stories we tell project a worldview that connects with people, unifies them, and excites them to take action. The pages of this book have provided you with the knowledge and ability to tell these kinds of stories and inspire behavioral adoption on behalf of your company, institution, organization, or cause. Now that you have the skills, you have an implicit responsibility to use them ethically, realizing that the ramifications of our stories can have a long-lasting material effect on people.

To navigate the nebulousness of ethics, which is inherently gray, I try to consider three factors: (1) my intentions, (2) the perspective of others, and (3) the potential outcomes. It's what I call an "IPO" approach to ethics. By considering my intentions, I account for the business objectives and marketing imperatives that I aim to accomplish on behalf of my clients while also being mindful of my morality. Essentially, I ask myself, am I acting in a way that is aligned with my own beliefs and ideologies? Do people like me do something like this? As in my day-to-day living, I use this filter to inform my actions.

However, when I consider the perspectives of the people I aim to engage, I try to see the world through their cultural frames to understand how they might interpret (decode) the brand's storytelling. As you know by now, everything we do has meaning, and understanding that meaning is paramount to harnessing the power of culture, participating in culture, and contributing to the culture of a specific tribe or congregation. Understanding the perspective(s) of the people is vital to inspiring behavior. The better we know the people, and the better we know ourselves, the better we'll be at getting people to move. Likewise, understanding the perspective(s) of the people is the crux to empathy. As we saw with Peloton, when we don't understand the perspective of the people, we risk potentially offending them even if our intentions are good. How many times have you heard someone apologize and say, "I didn't mean to hurt them" or "I didn't mean any harm" after they have hurt or harmed someone? I've seen it far too many times with my children, with my students, with politicians, and with brands. I, too, have been guilty of it. It's not a matter of intentionality alone; we must also factor in the perspective of the people when we preach the gospel.

In the best cases, there will be congruence between our intentions and the perspective of others. However, we must also factor in the potential outcomes that may occur as a result of our actions, even when there is congruence. We saw this in the case of the January 6 insurrection and the legitimation and adoption of smoking thanks to the Marlboro Man storytelling vehicle. However, no matter how well intentioned people might have been and how congruent the perspectives were, the outcomes were harmful and could have been prevented if someone had considered the potential consequences of their actions. Imagine the possibilities if we told better stories. Imagine what we could legitimate if we used this new knowledge to activate people in ways that are for a greater good. Imagine if we told stories that helped delegitimate the parts of society that tend to disproportionately impact marginalized communities, like police brutality on Black bodies, equal pay for women, ending Asian hate, fairer voting policies, and so on, and so on, and so on. The impact would be significant.

Here's the best part. We, collectively, have the power to change these things based on the stories we tell ourselves and the stories we tell each other. These stories help establish new cultural frames that change the way we (and others like us) see others and how we, collectively, behave in the world. This isn't meant to project a utopian society or picturesque outlook on life, but it is the kind of world I want my children—and my children's children—to grow up in, and I know we have the tools today, as outlined in this book, to create it just by harnessing the power of culture.

## BROOKLYN NETS ETHICS

I suppose that's what I hope for most for this book, that it will help people see the world better so that we might all be better—if only just a bit. I want that for marketers, politicians, leaders, activists, coaches, and everyone in between. And who am I kidding—I want that for myself, too.

When I look back on decisions I made earlier in my career, I can't help but wonder how I would have done things differently knowing what I now know about the power of culture and the implicit responsibility of those who engage in it. It's easy to look back at campaign failures and think, "If only I had," and play a version of Monday-morning quarterbacking that would have undoubtably led to financial and industry glory. But these days, I reflect more on the campaigns that have been deemed a success rather than the failures. I find myself taking inventory of these victory laps and asking myself, "At whose expense were these victories won?"

An interviewer once asked me, "What's your favorite marketing campaign?" This is one of the hardest questions for a marketer to answer because each campaign is special in its own way. It's like asking a songwriter, "What's your favorite song that you've written?" Could you imagine asking Babyface to pick just one? It's an impossible question. I once asked the music producer Timbaland a similar question before taking the stage for a panel on which we were both speaking, and he looked at me as if to say, "How do you expect me to answer that?" If you know his catalog, then surely you can understand how difficult that inquiry must be. Although my repertoire of marketing case studies pales in comparison to the endless number of hits Babyface and Timbaland have racked up over the decades, even I struggle to answer that question. However, if I had to pick one, it would probably be the Brooklyn Nets campaign that we unpacked in Chapter 3, for all the reasons we discussed.

By all business measures, it was deemed a success despite the odds we faced during its launch. However, we could have done more. Not more in the sense of making more money, moving more merch, or selling more tickets but more for the people of Brooklyn. While the Nets were celebrating their grand opening, we did nothing to help the Brooklyn residents who were displaced or the local businesses that were uprooted due to the team's arrival in the borough. We won at the expense of these Brooklyn residents and business owners. But it didn't have to be that way. We could have made efforts to help them.

When I teach the Nets case study, I typically task students with making creative suggestions for actions we could have taken to remedy the negative side effects of the launch and incorporate more ethical practices into our marketing activities. Their responses range from donations to strategic partnerships. Sadly, I didn't consider any of these opportunities when we launched the campaign. My creative efforts were squarely focused on commerce alone, with no attention paid to the impact on the community in which we were operating. That's why I think this book is so important, because I believe tomorrow's leaders can be better than today's leaders thanks to the ideas espoused in these pages.

For all its success, the Brooklyn Nets campaign would have been even better if we had considered these issues. Perhaps that's why it has become my go-to "favorite campaign" because its success not only taught me about the power of culture's influence but also continues to remind me that when engaging in culture, we have a responsibility beyond our own self-interest. We have an ethical responsibility to consider the impact of our actions and the possible ramifications for the people at the circumference of the spaces we enter and activate.

Make no mistake, I have no misgivings about marketing and the negative connotations it has inherited over the years. "Marketing is manipulative. It promotes overconsumption. It tries to persuade people to do things they don't want to do." I've heard it all before. And, if I'm being honest, most of this criticism is fair and deserved. Marketers have manipulated people. Marketing can drive people to consume in excess. Marketing has convinced people to do things that they otherwise would not have wanted to do. But marketing has also reduced smoking consumption. It has inspired people to participate in democracy and vote. It has encouraged people to recycle. Now, I'm not trying to justify the merits of marketing or argue in support of contemporary capitalism—that's an altogether different book, one potentially worth exploring, but it is not my current project or intent. I say all of this to point out that good business and doing good do not have to be mutually exclusive. If Patagonia is any indication, doing good is actually good for business.

I wish I'd had this understanding earlier in my career, I would have made some better choices along the way. Lord knows I'm making up for lost time in hopes of being better, and that's what this book endeavors to do for you, too. We have a choice. We can myopically consider what's in front of us or widen our aperture to also consider what's around us and how our decisions affect the unseen and the unheard. We can't rewrite the past, but we can certainly improve for the future. And that's exactly where my hope resides.

## I DO THIS FOR MY CULTURE

Over twenty years ago, Jay-Z made a declaration in his 2001 classic song, "Izzo (H.O.V.A.)," from the *Blueprint* album: "I do this for my culture." It established a phrase that would become a mainstay in the hip-hop vernacular and later propagate out to the greater pop-culture zeitgeist. The implication of these words, however, is far-reaching, particularly with regard to communications and consumption, and is perhaps even more important today than ever before. At one time, the pandemic relegated most of our social interactions to the Facebooks of the world, whose platforms are algorithmically designed to curate our media diets to represent the thoughts, feelings, and behaviors of people like us. The content that our people share essentially acts as receipts of community membership—including everything from political affiliation to sports fandom. Therefore, the extent to which we are introduced to new ideas, new products, and the like is predominantly based upon—and colored by—what our communities deem acceptable. This means that today's idea generators have to be even more mindful of the cultural characteristics that govern these communities if they want their ideas to be discussed and adopted by them. The first step to achieving this requires that we widen our perspective on how we think about culture and deepen our understanding of the tribal members who engage in these cultural acts so that we might tailor our company's or organization's activities accordingly.

The truth is, just like Jay-Z, we are all doing it for the culture—the unique culture(s) with which we self-identify. Every single one of us is operating within our own collective operating systems that govern what we do and with whom we do it. Therefore, as leaders and marketers (in the broadest sense), we have to deepen our concept of culture beyond the colloquial if we are to fully harness the power of culture and its influence on the products we consume, the behaviors we adopt, and the brands we consecrate. The better we understand these cultural characteristics, the richer our insights become, which will ultimately produce the kinds of ideas that inspire people to move in a predictable fashion. Now, who doesn't want that?

# EPILOGUE

S O MUCH HAS CHANGED SINCE I WROTE THIS BOOK, YET some things have remained the same. Powerful women have reigned in the media with the unprecedented success of the *Barbie* movie, Beyoncé's Renaissance tour, and Taylor Swift's global domination. At the same time, women's bodily autonomy has remained at the center of the political discourse following the Supreme Court overturning *Roe v. Wade*, the forty-nine-year-old landmark ruling that legalized abortion. Juneteenth was established as a federal holiday, a national recognition of the end of slavery in the United States. However, while the country acknowledged Juneteenth for the first time 157 years after the last enslaved African was freed in 1865, states around the country were banning books that retold this history from both public and school libraries.

The headlines refer to this ongoing dichotomy as the "culture wars"—the political dissent that results from differences in how people believe society should function based on differences in values and lifestyles. But these contemporary debates reek of a familiar problem that has plagued humanity since the beginning of time, from the wars in Mesopotamia to the Crusades and on to debates about transgender rights today. Despite its naming convention, wars are not about culture, the system of systems that we have defined in this text. They are, instead, a fight for power, with power being gained and maintained by preserving normalcy.

Normalcy is predicated on maintaining the status quo—the way things are—and the associated expectations. When the status quo is enforced, those with power remain in power and the marginalized remain marginalized. Any erosion of normalcy is perceived as a disadvantage to the advantaged—those who benefit from their privileged position in the social status quo. So challenges to the status quo become tantamount to a declaration of war against the prevailing powers.

As a matter of fact, the preservation of normalcy is antithetical to the dynamics of culture as we now know it because *culture is always moving forward.* Any attempt to stall this movement, such as eroding a woman's right to make decisions about her own body, should be seen as regressive. Likewise, preventing the retelling of history to ignore the brutality of our country's existence is also a step backward, regardless of your moral view. Stalling these movements preserves the fallacy of moral uprightness by oppressing another group of people's ability to exist. To acknowledge their existence would require an introspective look at the benefits of one's own privilege due to the place one occupies in the social hierarchy—a privilege that is sustained by erasing the unflattering parts of history and recasting villains as heroes. Furthermore, the acknowledgment of their existence demands accountability from the powerful, if only to mitigate any cognitive dissonance they might feel so that they can sleep well at night.

Indeed, culture is always moving forward. New ideas lead to new realities, which in turn inspire new ways of life, whether technological or social. Can you imagine going back to a world without refrigerators? Can you fathom an existence when bathing wasn't a common ritual? Any attempt to return to a state before these changes were adopted in society would be considered primitive, and that's exactly what's at play in today's social and political discourse. Preserving normalcy is equated with the preservation of power. And it's this preservation that divides us—by race, religion, political affiliation, gender, and every line of demarcation that we use to carve out the place that we occupy in the social world.

According to Collage Group, a consumer research firm that aims to understand the country's diverse consumers, multicultural Americans will constitute the majority of the population by 2050. The growth of multiculturalism fundamentally suggests that there will continue to be new ideas and new perspectives that will challenge the status quo and undermine the power of those who currently benefit from it. This is the root of today's culture wars and the oxygen that breathes life into the battle across the headlines, on social networking platforms, at dinner tables, and throughout the political sphere. But most importantly, these differences will likely widen the gulf that divides us.

Suffice it to say, the culture wars are all about the fear of loss of power. To thwart this loss, these wars are positioned as ideological threats that pit one side against another. The magician's trick in this repositioning is that it flatters our sense of moral uprightness. We're right and they're wrong, so we must be at odds. The use of labels—"them," "they," "those people," "the deep state," "the right," "the left," "liberals," "conservatives," "radicals"—not only helps to distinguish "friend" from "foe" but also helps explain and justify the wedges that separate us. Ingrained myths along party lines help socialize the talking points that evidence our ideological differences—be they conspiracy or conjecture, regardless of whether you're political—and further widen the gap between us.

As disheartening as this may seem, there's hope. In fact, I argue that what's tearing us apart is actually what can bring us together: culture. Although our cultural differences have been weaponized as an instrument of war to divide us, understanding the mechanisms of culture and the subjective nature of our meaning-making systems can be the glue that instead unites us. I don't mean the exclusive "us," as in the networked tribes we explored throughout this book, but rather the inclusive "us" that resides outside our congregations.

By understanding the subjective nature of culture, we quickly realize that the world is not as objective as we would like to believe it to be. Remember, things aren't the way they are; they are the way *we* are. So our senses of morality and judgment are not a product of scientific law or a subject of absolutism. Instead, they arise from the beliefs and ideologies that have been introduced to us by our people and through our sociocultural institutions.

If the world is not objective, then the subjective truths that we hold about the world can, therefore, coexist—even in opposition to each other. Things become problematic only when we impose our truth on someone else. Imposing our subjective truths on others is not an act of morality; it is a performance of power. It doesn't make one's truth any truer but merely subjugates a group of people through marginalization as an act of absolutism. As the Jedi knight Obi-Wan Kenobi once said, "Only a Sith deals in absolutes."

That's the truth about the "truth": my truth is no more valid than someone else's truth because they are both constructed on subjective building blocks of identity, beliefs, and ideologies—the foundations of culture. The only thing that makes my truth truer than someone else's truth is the extent to which I believe it and my resistance to accepting another perspective. Either way, my truth, like yours, is merely an interpretation. Therefore, they can coexist.

For years, I have held up Michael Jackson's *Thriller* as the best album of all time, and I still stand by this. Among the collection of perfectly curated songs is one midtempo ballad that has always stood out for me as a unique reflective and introspective addition: the Rod Temperton–penned "Human Nature."

There's so much to love about this song. From Michael's soaring falsetto during the outro to the interplay between the lead vocal and the staccato of the plunky guitar playing over the verses, the song is exquisitely orchestrated. However, the part I always gravitate toward is the inquiry of the refrain: "Why? Why? Tell 'em that it's human nature. Why? Why?" And Michael's response to the question is simple: "'Cause it do be that way."

I've been singing this lyric for as long as I can remember. However, on one occasion, my wife and my close friend Mike Muse heard me singing it aloud and both asked, in unison, "What did you just say?" I spoke the lyrics instead of singing them this time: "'Cause it do be that way." They looked puzzled. "'Cause it do be that way?" they asked, again in unison. To which I replied, this time indignantly, "Yes, 'cause it do be that way." They laughed, and I didn't understand why.

Unbeknownst to me, the lyric is actually "does he do me that way," not a reply to the question "Why?" but a continuation of the original inquiry of the chorus: "Why? Why does he do me that way?" Go figure. However, that's not how I heard it. Even after listening to the song again, that wasn't what I heard Michael singing. Plus, "does he do me that way" didn't make any sense to me. Who the heck is "he," and what exactly is "he" doing? None of this seemed to compute. I've been singing it one way for forty years, and that made the most sense to me, so I continue singing it that way to this day—even with this new knowledge.

Here's the funny thing: every time the song comes on, I sing the chorus at full volume, "'Cause it do be that way," and my wife just looks at me and smiles as if to say, "Here he goes; loud and wrong." Or maybe she's impressed with my singing voice. It's hard to tell. Regardless, my interpretation of the lyric has no bearing on how she experiences the song. She thinks I'm wrong. I think I'm right, yet we can enjoy the song together. And that's the point: our two truths can coexist despite being at odds, which enables the two of us to coexist, because neither of us is imposing our interpretation of reality on the other. In actuality, the fact that we see things differently has led us to discuss other songs that we've likely been singing "incorrectly," which typically results in the kind of laugher that brings us closer together.

Of course, disagreements over song lyrics do not bear the same weight as disagreements about abortion, trans rights, the omission of history, or any of the other hot-button issues that fuel the social discourse of our contemporary culture wars. However, the principle of the idea still stands. The world is not objective; it is subjective because our realities are translated through the biases of our cultural lenses.

As I reflect on the writing of this book, I realize that this idea has been the biggest learning of my work, and its realization has changed the way I see myself, how I traverse the world, and the manner in which I interact with the diverse array of people I get to meet throughout my comings and goings. This lens through which I view culture has helped me understand why I consume what I consume, why I do what I do, who I am, whom I want to be, and, moreover, why I aspire to these things in the first place. As revelatory as it has been to better see myself, the most eye-opening revelation is that it has helped me to see other people more vividly as well—and, in some ways, to see myself in them.

The mechanisms that have enabled me to create the reality I inhabit day to day are the same ones that have created the subjective reality that you, too, inhabit. It's the same—same but different. And the similarities that constitute our differences actually do more to connect us than to separate us. They help us see the world more vividly. I liken social living to a basketball game, where we're all watching the same objective game, but those sitting courtside experience it completely differently than those with nosebleed seats. So if you want the most holistic view of the game, you must sit in many different seats.

That's the beauty of our realities. Our diverse perspectives contribute to a mosaic that creates a more holistic view of life. The same game, different perspectives. The same world, different truths. And the best part is that our truths can coexist so long as your truth does not mean my marginalization, eradication, subjugation, or oppression.

This perspective has completely changed me, and if you've been following along up to this point, I think it can change you, too. Accepting the truth about the subjective nature of the truth not only bonds us over our similarities (the things that make us say, "Wow, you felt that way, too?") but also helps us learn from the differences that make us—as a species—so similar. Our ability to shape worlds in our minds is nothing short of fantasy, straight out of a George Lucas film. It feels real because, for us at least, it is real. But for someone else, it's just that: fantasy.

Be that as it may, their fantasy does not undermine yours. Their reality does not diminish the validity of your own. In fact, the two interpretations are more like jazz musicians playing their versions of the same song. I might prefer my rendition over yours, but they both have a place so long as we're both able to play. And who knows, you just might like mine better than yours and vice versa.

The rhetoric of the "culture wars" suggests two monoliths trading blows across neutral terrain in hopes that one will prevail by convincing the other that they're wrong—or, what's worse, altogether vanquishing them by use of force. However, surrendering the assumptions of absolutism is what enables transcendence and drives connection. The notion that equity for others undermines one's own prosperity is a scarcity fallacy, and the use of power to marginalize those who see the world differently is an act of tyranny. We don't have to agree, but we must realize the subjectivity of our humanity. Doing so, despite our differences, will help us uncover our entwined desires to be seen, to be heard, and to belong. Through this lens, we might discover more that binds us than separates us. That's a reality I dream of, and I hope you do, too.

Now, go preach the gospel.

# Acknowledgments

I NEVER SET OUT TO WRITE A BOOK. PERHAPS IT LIVED SOMEwhere, subconsciously, on my "oh, that would be cool" list, but it certainly wasn't on my bucket list. However, when I decided to do it, I promised myself that I would write the book that I wish was available to me when I first started exploring the social sciences over a decade ago. I truly hope that I succeeded with this undertaking. Nevertheless, none of this would have been possible without the help of so many brilliant, generous, and challenging people whom I've come to know between then and now. Writing a book can be a lonely process, but I never felt alone. For that, and so much more, I am incredibly thankful.

To my closest thought partner and dear friend, John Branch. My academic pursuits have been inspired by you, fueled by you, and achieved thanks to you. From my early days as an MBA student to my present days as an "academic practitioner," you have been a teacher and a mentor. I could not imagine any of this being possible without your support and friendship. Thank you a million times over.

To my doctoral committee members at the Fox School of Business, Temple University (Susan Mudambi, Lynne Andersson, and Matt Wray), thank you for investing in me and helping me to become a better researcher and scholar. Your guidance and encouragement gave me the confidence to think that my ideas were worth reading. I will never see the world the same way again.

To Jeff Shreve and the entire team at the Science Factory, thank you for taking a chance on me and helping to make all this possible. To Colleen Lawrie, thank you for seeing the vision when it wasn't so clear for me and for helping me toe the line between academic rigor and digestibility. To all the many people at PublicAffairs who are responsible for turning my writing into something material and meaningful, as I consider all that it takes to make a book happen, my appreciation for you grows every day.

To the people who took a chance on me early in my career when I was finding my way, I am incredibly thankful. Derrick Scott, Clifton Brent, Soojin Kwon, Matt Fischer, Ed Suwananjer, Thuy-An Julien, Mathew Knowles, Avi Savar, Steve Stoute, Laura Sawyer, Melanie Barnett Weaver, Puneet Manchanda, and Jeff DeGraff, you saw something in me that wasn't reflected in my résumé. The experiences with which you provided me collectively gave birth to this book.

To my Wieden+Kennedy squad, the work we do every day is a case study. Thank you for helping me feel at home and for making the thinking in this book seem more tangible and applicable than ever. This just might be the best work of my life to date, but I do believe that the very best is yet to come.

To my collaborators and thought partners throughout the years, thank you for helping me see the world more clearly—Russell Pinke (my longest and closest partner in advertising), John Greene,

John McBride, Chaucer Barnes, Charles Wright, Susanna Swartly, Ben Gladstone, Joel Rodriguez, John Petty III, Geoff McHenry, Sandi Preston, Abigail Weintraub, Iyana Sarrafieh, Roby Egan, Tiffany Hardin, Becka Vigorito, Michael Stoopack, Nils Peyron, Patience Ramsey, Lauren Gamsey, Chris Wallace, Leanne Leahy, John Norman, Chris Cereda, Adam Carl, Will Cady, Jason Gaboriau, Caitlin Delaney, Olivia Roth, Kelsey Randsdell, Matt McDonnell, James Ward, Brad Emmett, Rob Strasberg, Rob Legato, Andrew Lamar, Hajj Flemings, Lincoln Stephens, Jada Black, Joe Kantor, Alima Trapp, Eric Thomas, Justine Norman, Marlowe Stoudamire, Josh Luber, Khartoon Weiss, Mark Pollard, Toby Daniels, Michael Ventura, Katie Longmyer, Ken Muench, Cedric Rodgers, Mark Comerford, Hazel Swayne, Inaki Escudero, Andrew Zolty, Lauren Puglia, Jacklyn Ciamilo, Stefan Wendin, Jessalin Lam, Heather LeFevre, Lisa Pertoso, Matt Lemay, Mark Altman, Tiffany Warren, Christena Pyle, Dhani Jones, Stefen Welch, Alicia Jefferys, Charlie Metzger, Charlie Kondek, Cal Hunter, Lindy Greer, Rohit Bery, April Davis, Joy Johnson, Zekeya Ewing, Mitch Brooks, Eric Schwartz, Mike Muse, Paul Johnson, Bryan Johnson, Chad Hughes, Steven Snead, Kristopher Crosby, Ro Adebiyi, John Rhodes, Darius Matthews, David Brown Jr., Jodi Detjen, Rob Kozinets, Grant McCracken, Susan Fournier, Barb Bickart, Rebekah Modrak, Fred Feinberg, Lindy Greer, Brad Killaly, Paula Caproni, Gene Mage, Scott Rick, Rajeev Batra, and Jeffrey Sanchez Burks. To my Music World family, my Translation crew, my "ride or dies" at BigSpeak, my "familj" at Hyper Island, my friends at the American Advertising Federation (special shout out to AHOA Class of 2020), my colleagues at the Ross School of Business, my brothers of Phi Beta Sigma Fraternity, Inc., my supporters at Section4, and my "peeps" at Adweek, thank you for creating the benchmark by which I continue to measure myself.

To my parents, Hershel and Jeannette Collins, words cannot express my gratitude for all that you have done for me. Dad, you are the entrepreneur who taught me to dream. Mom, you are the academic who taught me to be pragmatic in my pursuits. Together, you instilled in me a spirit of grit and gratitude, realizing that all my help and strength comes from God's grace and mercy. To my wife, Alex, and our daughters, Georgia and Ivy, thank you for your love, your support, and all your sacrifices—but most of all, thank you for believing in me. To my natural family and my spiritual family at the Israel of God's Church, thank you for your many prayers and words of encouragement. I hope that I make you all proud.

To my many clients, teammates, colleagues, friends, and students (both past and present), thank you for inspiring me. I have learned so much from you all. This book is not only an articulation of my research and practice but also a by-product of the many conversations, debates, and creative work I have experienced with you throughout the years.

Truly, I am grateful.

# Bibliography

**INTRODUCTION**

McCracken, Grant D. *Chief Culture Officer: How to Create a Living, Breathing Corporation*. New York: Basic Books, 2011.

Hiscott, Rebecca. "The Real Reason Hipsters Love PBR." HuffPost. December 7, 2017. https://www.huffpost.com/entry/pbr-coolness-study_n_5399109.

Walker, Rob. "The Marketing of No Marketing." *New York Times*. June 22, 2003. https://www.nytimes.com/2003/06/22/magazine/the-marketing-of-no-marketing.html.

Passy, Charles. "Opinion: How Did Pabst Blue Ribbon Become a Hipster Favorite?" MarketWatch. July 18, 2015. https://www.marketwatch.com/story/whatll-you-have-not-a-pabst-blue-ribbon-2015-07-16.

Warren, Caleb, and Margaret C. Campbell. "What Makes Things Cool? How Autonomy Influences Perceived Coolness." *Journal of Consumer Research* 41, no. 2 (2014): 543–563.

De Mooij, Marieke. "The Future Is Predictable for International Marketers: Converging Incomes Lead to Diverging Consumer Behavior." *International Marketing Review* 17, no. 2 (2001): 103–113.

Ebony, David. "Oldest Photograph of a Human Is Back in the Spotlight." Artnet News. November 27, 2014. https://news.artnet.com/art-world/oldest-photograph-of-a-human-is-back-in-the-spotlight-159766#:~:text=Taken%20in%201838%2C%20Louis%20Daguerre's,extant%20photograph%20of%20human%20figures.

Peacock, James L. "Durkheim and the Social Anthropology of Culture." *Social Forces* 59, no. 4 (1981): 996–1008. https://search-proquest-com.libproxy.temple.edu/docview/839149378?accountid=14270.

Weaver, Mark. "Weber's Critique of Advocacy in the Classroom: Critical Thinking and Civic Education." *PS: Political Science and Politics* 31, no. 4 (1998): 799–801. https://doi.org/10.2307/420720.

Al-Attili, Aghlab. "1.1 What Is a Market? Unit 1: Small Agribusinesses and Markets." SOAS University of London. Accessed May 1, 2022. https://www.soas.ac.uk/cedep-demos/000_P538_MSA_K3736-Demo/unit1/page_06.htm.

Alsafran, Maryam. "Biology." Sites at Penn State. Accessed May 1, 2022. https://sites.psu.edu/isea/wp-content/uploads/sites/12499/2014/09/MIO-Biology.pdf.

Shutt, Eric. "Cultural Strategy Battle School—iStrategyLabs." SlideShare. April 24, 2015. https://www.slideshare.nlt/ericshutt/cultural-strategy-battle-school.

Ginosar, Shiry, Kate Rakelly, Sarah Sachs, Brian Yin, and Alexei A. Efros. *A Century of Portraits: A Visual Historical Record of American High School Yearbooks*. arXiv.org. November 9, 2015. https://arxiv.org/abs/1511.02575v1.

Hakes, Heather. "The History of Dental Hygiene: Development Through the Years." Today's RDH. June 16, 2020. https://www.todaysrdh.com/the-history-of-dental-hygiene-development-through-the-years/.

Jeeves, Nicholas. "The Serious and the Smirk: The Smile in Portraiture." The Public Domain Review. September 18, 2013. https://publicdomainreview.org/essay/the-serious-and-the-smirk-the-smile-in-portraiture.

Anthony, Scott D. "Kodak's Downfall Wasn't About Technology." *Harvard Business Review*. July 15, 2016. https://hbr.org/2016/07/kodaks-downfall-wasnt-about-technology.

Kotler, Philip. "Dr. Philip Kotler Answers Your Questions on Marketing." Kotler Marketing Group, Inc. Retrieved May 1, 2022. https://kotlermarketing.com/phil_questions.shtml.

Richter, Felix. "Infographic: The U.S. Wireless Headphone Market." Statista Infographics. February 8, 2017. https://www.statista.com/chart/7993/headphone-market-share/.

"World Selfie Day: Who Took the First-Ever Selfie?" *Economic Times*. Last updated June 21, 2018. https://economictimes.indiatimes.com/magazines /panache/world-selfie-day-who-took-the-first-ever-selfie/articleshow /64676143.cms?from=mdr.

Gundlach, Gregory T., and William L. Wilkie. "The American Marketing Association's New Definition of Marketing: Perspective and Commentary on the 2007 Revision." *Journal of Public Policy & Marketing* 28, no. 2 (2009): 259–264.

Jones, Robert Alun. *Emile Durkheim: An Introduction to Four Major Works*. Beverly Hills, CA: Sage Publications, 1986, 60–81.

Wray, Matt, and Michèle Lamont, eds. *Cultural Sociology: An Introductory Reader*. New York: W. W. Norton & Company, 2014.

Christensen, Clayton M. *The Innovator's Dilemma: The Revolutionary Book That Will Change the Way You Do Business*. New York: Harper Business, 2011.

Collins, Marcus. *Exploring Social Contagion Within a Tribe Called Hip Hop: Mechanisms of Evaluation and Legitimation*. Philadelphia, PA: Temple University Press, 2021.

## CHAPTER 1

"Budweiser—The Story of Whassup?!" This Is Not ADVERTISING. September 1, 2011. https://thisisnotadvertising.wordpress.com/2011/09/01 /budweiser-the-story-of-whassup/.

National Standards for Foreign Language Education Project. *Standards for Foreign Language Learning in the 21st Century*. Lawrence, KS: Allen Press, 1999.

Williams, Raymond. *Keywords: A Vocabulary of Culture and Society*, new ed. Oxford, UK: Oxford University Press, 2014.

Williams, Raymond. *Culture and Society, 1780–1950*. New York: Columbia University Press, 1983.

Reed, Americus, Mark R. Forehand, Stefano Puntoni, and Luk Warlop. "Identity-Based Consumer Behavior." *International Journal of Research in Marketing* 29, no. 4 (2012).

Vyain, Sally, Gail Scaramuzzo, Susan Cody-Rydzewski, Heather Griffiths, Eric Strayer, Nathan Keirns, and Ron McGivern. "Chapter 15. Religion." *Introduction to Sociology*, 1st Canadian ed. BCcampus Open Publishing. November 6, 2014. https://opentextbc.ca/introductiontosociology/chapter /chapter-15-religion/.

Burton, Tara I. *Strange Rites: New Religions for a Godless World*, 1st ed. New York: PublicAffairs, 2020.

Fiske, John. "Culture, Ideology, Interpellation." In *Literary Theory: An Anthology*, edited by J. Rivkin and M. Ryan, 305–311. Malden, MA: Blackwell, 1998.

McCracken, Grant. "Culture and Consumption: A Theoretical Account of the Structure and Movement of the Cultural Meaning of Consumer Goods." *Journal of Consumer Research* 13, no. 1 (1986): 71–84.

History.com editors. "Christianity." History. October 13, 2017. https://www.history.com/topics/religion/history-of-christianity.

"The Art of Fika." Swedishness. June 3, 2021. https://swedishness.ch/blogs/news/fika.

"Fika Like a Swede." Visit Sweden. Last updated March 26, 2021. https://visitsweden.com/what-to-do/food-drink/swedish-kitchen/all-about-swedish-fika/.

McCann Worldgroup. "Immunity Charm." Integrated Global Network of Specialty Marketing Agencies. Accessed May 1, 2022. https://www.mccannworldgroup.com/work/immunity-charm.

"Making Immunization into a Tradition." The Immunity Charm. Accessed May 1, 2022. http://www.theimmunitycharm.org/.

A&E Television Networks. "Thanksgiving." History. August 21, 2018. https://www.history.com/topics/thanksgiving.

"Our story." Jimmy's Red Hots. Accessed May 1, 2022. https://www.jimmysredhotchicago.com/our-story.

Hafner, Josh. "Ketchup on Hot Dogs? Heinz's 'Chicago Dog Sauce' Tricks Purists." *USA Today*. July 19, 2017. https://www.usatoday.com/story/money/nation-now/2017/07/19/heinzs-new-chicago-dog-sauce-just-ketchup/491928001/#:~:text=Enter%20Heinz%2C%20the%20brand%20synonymous,It's%20%22Chicago%20Dog%20Sauce.%22.

Montell, Amanda. *Cultish: The Language of Fanaticism*, 1st ed. New York: Harper Wave, an imprint of HarperCollins Publishers, 2021.

National Standards for Foreign Language Education Project. *Standards for Foreign Language Learning in the 21st Century*. Lawrence, KS: Allen Press, 1999.

Collins, Marcus. *Exploring Social Contagion within a Tribe Called Hip Hop: Mechanisms of Evaluation and Legitimation*. Philadelphia, PA: Temple University Press, 2021.

Chang, Jeff. *Can't Stop Won't Stop: A History of the Hip-hop Generation*. London: Picador.

## CHAPTER 2

"Our Company History—Patagonia." Patagonia Outdoor Clothing & Gear. Accessed May 1, 2022. https://www.patagonia.com/company-history/.

Paumgarten, Nick. "Patagonia's Philosopher-King." *New Yorker.* September 12, 2016. https://www.newyorker.com/magazine/2016/09/19/patagonias-philosopher-king.

Holder, Andrew. "Patagonia: Yvon Chouinard." *How I Built This.* NPR. December 25, 2017. https://www.npr.org/2018/02/06/572558864/patagonia-yvon-chouinard.

Etymology. Etymonline. Accessed May 1, 2022. https://www.etymonline.com.

Crossman, Ashley. "How Do You Study the Sociology of Religion?" ThoughtCo. July 3, 2019. https://www.thoughtco.com/sociology-of-religion-3026286#:~:text=Since%20religion%20is%20such%20an,how%20they%20see%20the%20world.

Peck, Brielle. "Why Do Sociologists Study Religion?" Living by Example. October 3, 2021. https://www.livingbyexample.org/why-sociologists-study-religion/.

Nelson, C. Ellis, ed. *Congregations: Their Power to Form and Transform.* Louisville, KY: Westminster John Knox Press, 1988.

Chaves, Mark, Mary Ellen Konieczny, Kraig Beyerlein, and Emily Barman. The National Congregations Study: Background, Methods, and Selected Results. *Journal for the Scientific Study of Religion* (1999): 458–476.

Mishan, Ligaya. "What Is a Tribe?" *New York Times.* April 13, 2020. https://www.nytimes.com/interactive/2020/04/13/t-magazine/tribe-meaning.html.

Hardt, Michael, and Antonio Negri. *Empire.* Cambridge, MA, and London: Harvard University Press, 2000.

"Industrial Revolution." History. https://www.history.com/topics/industrial-revolution/industrial-revolution.

Dunbar, Robin. *Grooming, Gossip, and the Evolution of Language.* Cambridge, MA: Harvard University Press, 1998.

Dunbar, Robin. *How Many Friends Does One Person Need? Dunbar's Number and Other Evolutionary Quirks.* Harvard University Press, 2022.

Maffesoli, Michel. *The Time of the Tribes: The Decline of Individualism in Mass Society.* London: Sage Publications, 1996.

Maffesoli, Michel, and Charles R. Foulkes. "Jeux de masques: Postmodern Tribalism." *Design Issues* (1988): 141–151.

Reed, Americus, II, Mark R. Forehand, Stefano Puntoni, and Luk Warlop. "Identity-Based Consumer Behavior." *International Journal of Research in Marketing* 29, no. 4 (2012): 310–321.

Ross, Ivan. "Self-Concept and Brand Preference." *Journal of Business* 44, no. 1 (1971): 38–50.

Beer, Jeff. "One year later, what did we learn from Nike's blockbuster Colin Kaepernick Ad?" *Fast Company*. September 4, 2019. https://www.fastcompany.com/90399316/one-year-later-what-did-we-learn-from-nikes-blockbuster-colin-kaepernick-ad.

Morris, Charles W. *Mind, Self and Society from the Standpoint of a Social Behaviorist*. Chicago, IL: University of Chicago Press, 1934.

Goffman, Erving. "Presentation of Self in Everyday Life." *American Journal of Sociology* 55 (1949): 6–7.

Yoo, Ryan. "The Origin of the Ohio-Michigan Rivalry." *Observer*. April 12, 2019. https://observer.case.edu/the-origin-of-the-ohio-michigan-rivalry/#:~:text=Since%20their%20first%20game%20in,states%20of%20Michigan%20and%20Ohio.

Sommers, Sam. *Situations Matter: Understanding How Context Transforms Your World*. New York: Riverhead Books, 2011.

Marshall, William J., Marta Lapsley, Andrew P. Day, and Ruth M. Ayling, eds. *Clinical Biochemistry: Metabolic and Clinical Aspects*, 3rd ed. London: Churchill Livingstone/Elsevier, 2014.

Zhang, Ming, Yuki Zhang, and Yazhuo Kong. "Interaction Between Social Pain and Physical Pain." *Brain Science Advances* 5, no. 4 (2019): 265–273. https://doi.org/10.26599/BSA.2019.9050023.

Fogel, Alan. "Emotional and Physical Pain Activate Similar Brain Regions." *Psychology Today*. April 19, 2012. https://www.psychologytoday.com/us/blog/body-sense/201204/emotional-and-physical-pain-activate-similar-brain-regions.

Wanshel, Elyse. "Beyoncé Fans Hilariously Slam Kid Rock for Making Offensive Comments About Her." *HuffPost*. November 30, 2018. https://www.huffpost.com/entry/beyonce-fans-kid-rock_n_5c016262e4b0249dce7487fc.

Friskics-Warren, Bill. "A Church Service Inspired by Beyoncé, No Halo Required." *New York Times*. October 21, 2019. https://www.nytimes.com/2019/10/21/arts/music/beyonce-mass.html.

"Beyoncé Mass." Accessed May 1, 2022. https://www.beyoncemass.com /#:~:text=Beyonc%C3%A9%20Mass%20is%20a%20womanist,their %20bodies%2C%20and%20their%20voices.

Smith, Wendell R. "Product Differentiation and Market Segmentation as Alternative Marketing Strategies." *Journal of Marketing* 21, no. 1 (1956): 3–8. https://doi.org/10.2307/1247695.

Williams, Madison. "Super Bowl Commercial Cost in 2022: How Much Money Is an Ad for Super Bowl 56?" *Sporting News.* February 13, 2022. https:// www.sportingnews.com/us/nfl/news/super-bowl-commercials-cost -2022/v9ytfqzx74pjrcdvxyhevlzd.

Ives, Nat. "Facebook to Advertise in the Super Bowl for the First Time." *Wall Street Journal.* December 19, 2019. https://www.wsj.com/articles/facebook -to-advertise-in-the-super-bowl-for-the-first-time-11576728775.

Dua, Tanya "Inside the Making of Facebook's $11.2 Million Super Bowl Ad, an Epic Undertaking Spanning Several Months and Locations." *Business Insider.* February 4, 2020. https://www.businessinsider.com/inside -facebooks-first-ever-super-bowl-commercial-promoting-groups-2020-2.

Pentland, Alex. *Social Physics: How Social Networks Can Make Us Smarter.* New York: Penguin Press, 2015.

Christakis, Nicholas A., and James H. Fowler. *Connected: The Amazing Power of Social Networks and How They Shape Our Lives.* New York: Harper-Press, 2011.

Farris, Paul, Phillip E. Pfeifer, and Richard R. Johnson. "The Value of Networks. Darden Case No. UVA-M-0645." SSRN. https://ssrn.com/abstract =1420578 or http://dx.doi.org/10.2139/ssrn.1420578.

Public Broadcasting Service. (n.d.). "About Sarnoff." *American Experience.* PBS. Accessed May 1, 2022. https://www.pbs.org/wgbh/americanexperience /features/bigdream-about-sarnoff/.

Kirsner, Scott. "The Legend of Bob Metcalfe." *Wired.* https://www.wired.com /1998/11/metcalfe/.

Reed, David P. "The Law of the Pack." *Harvard Business Review.* August 1, 2014. https://hbr.org/2001/02/the-law-of-the-pack.

Avery, Jill. *Saving Face by Making Meaning: The Negative Effects of Consumers' Self-serving Response to Brand Extension.* Cambridge, MA: Harvard University Press, 2007.

Gutierrez, Joe. "Debunking the Myth that All Millennials Are the Same." *Fast Company.* August 21, 2014. https://www.fastcompany.com/3034593 /debunking-the-myth-that-all-millennials-are-the-same.

## CHAPTER 3

Mainwaring, Simon "How REI Launched and Built a Movement Far Larger Than the Brand Itself." *Forbes.* January 11, 2017. https://www .forbes.com/sites/simonmainwaring/2017/01/10/how-rei-launched -and-built-a-movement-far-larger-than-the-brand-itself/?sh =714598e16761.

Beer, Jeff. "How REI Is Keeping #OptOutside a Black Friday Tradition." *Fast Company.* 2017, November 9, 2017. https://www.fastcompany.com /40493417/how-rei-is-keeping-optoutside-a-black-friday-tradition.

REI Staff. "The History of #OptOutside." Uncommon Path—An REI Co-Op Publication. October 2, 2018. https://www.rei.com/blog/social/the -history-of-opt-outside.

Rajmohan, V., and E. Mohandas. "The Limbic System." *Indian Journal of Psychiatry* 49, no. 2 (2007): 132–139. https://doi.org/10.4103/0019-5545 .33264.

"The Limbic System." Queensland Brain Institute, University of Queensland. January 24, 2019. https://qbi.uq.edu.au/brain/brain-anatomy/limbic -system#:%7E:text=The%20limbic%20system%20is%20the,and %20fight%20or%20flight%20responses.

"The Concept of the 'Triune Brain.'" The Interaction Design Foundation. January 2, 2021. https://www.interaction-design.org/literature/article/the -concept-of-the-triune-brain.

SoP. "The Triune Brain." The Science of Psychotherapy. April 5, 2021. https:// www.thescienceofpsychotherapy.com/the-triune-brain/.

MacLean, Paul D. "Triune Brain." In *Comparative Neuroscience and Neurobiology.* Boston, MA: Birkhäuser, 1988, 126–128.

"Beyond Emotion: Understanding the Amygdala's Role in Memory." Dana Foundation. D. July 29, 2019. https://dana.org/article/beyond -emotion-understanding-the-amygdalas-role-in-memory/.

Bennett, Bo. Logically Fallacious. 2020. https://www.logicallyfallacious.com.

Nudd, Tim. "Ridiculously Nice Ad for a Crappy 1996 Honda Boosts the Asking Price by 300 Times." *Adweek.* November 5, 2017. https://www.adweek .com/creativity/ridiculously-nice-ad-for-a-crappy-1996-honda-boosts -the-asking-price-by-300-times/.

Sinek, Simon. *Start with Why: How Great Leaders Inspire Everyone to Take Action.* London: Portfolio Penguin, 2011.

Younge, Gary. "Martin Luther King: The Story Behind His 'I Have a Dream' Speech." *Guardian.* March 29, 2018. https://www.theguardian.com /world/2013/aug/09/martin-luther-king-dream-speech-history.

History.com Editors. "Mahalia Jackson Prompts Martin Luther King Jr. to Improvise 'I Have a Dream' Speech." History. January 18, 2022. https://www
.history.com/this-day-in-history/mahalia-jackson-the-queen-of-gospel
-puts-her-stamp-on-the-march-on-washington#:%7E:text=August%2028
-,Mahalia%20Jackson%20prompts%20Martin%20Luther%20King%20Jr.
%20to%20improvise%20%22I,basis%20of%20her%20musical%20legacy.

Chang, Rachel. "How Mahalia Jackson Sparked Martin Luther King Jr.'s 'I Have a Dream' Speech." Biography. July 28, 2021. https://www.biography
.com/news/mahalia-jackson-i-have-a-dream-influence.

"Coca-Cola 'Happiness Machine' Wins Top Honors at the 2010 CLIO Awards." The Coca-Cola Company. May 28, 2010. https://investors
.coca-colacompany.com/news-events/press-releases/detail/28/coca
-cola-happiness-machine-wins-top-honors-at-the-2010.

"Dan Wieden." The One Club for Creativity. Accessed May 1, 2022. https://
www.oneclub.org/adc-hall-of-fame/-bio/dan-wieden-adc.

Montag, Ali. "Nike's Steve Jobs for Apple's 'Think Different' Campaign 20 Years Ago—he Called Them 'the Best Example of All.'" CNBC. September 10, 2018. https://www.cnbc.com/2018/09/10/nikes-ads-inspired-steve
-jobs-for-apples-think-different-campaign.html.

*WeCrashed.* Wondery. Accessed May 1, 2022. https://wondery.com/shows
/we-crashed/.

Thomas, Daniel. "Theranos Scandal: Who Is Elizabeth Holmes and Why Was She on Trial?" BBC News. January 4, 2022. https://www.bbc.com
/news/business-58336998.

Allyn, Bobby. "Elizabeth Holmes Verdict: Former Theranos CEO Is Found Guilty on 4 Counts." NPR. January 4, 2022. https://www.npr.org/2022/0
1/03/1063973490/elizabeth-holmes-trial-verdict-guilty-theranos.

Stein, Joel. "The Great Schlep." *Los Angeles Times.* March 1, 2019. https://www
.latimes.com/archives/la-xpm-2008-sep-19-oe-stein19-story.html.

Pilkington, Ed. "Young Make 'Great Schlep' to Persuade a Sceptical Generation to Vote Obama." *Guardian.* November 27, 2017. https://www
.theguardian.com/world/2008/oct/13/uselection-vote-florida-obama.

*The Great Schlep.* YouTube. May 29, 2009. https://www.youtube.com/watch
?v=PtBGXVKbEv4.

Schneider, Amy Beth. "Conversation for a Change: Power of the Great Schlep." eJewish Philanthropy. July 26, 2010. https://ejewishphilanthropy.com
/conversation-for-a-change-power-of-the-great-schlep/.

Motes, Bart. "Tragedy, Tributes, and Triumph: Griffin Farley's Beautiful Minds." HuffPost. September 16, 2013. https://www.huffpost.com/entry
/disappointment-tragedy-an_b_3600531.

Barro, Josh. "SoulCycle: You Say 'Cult.' I Say 'Loyal Customer Base.'" *New York Times*. August 7, 2015. https://www.nytimes.com/2015/08/09/upshot/soulcycle-you-say-cult-i-say-loyal-customer-base.

Sports Team. "New Jersey Nets Team History." Sports Team History. March 25, 2021. https://sportsteamhistory.com/new-jersey-nets.

Bernays, Edward L., and Mark Crispin Miller. *Propaganda*. New York: Ig Publishing, 2005.

Rovell, D. "Nets' Brooklyn Gear Sales Breaking Team Records." CNBC. June 18, 2012. https://www.cnbc.com/id/47831684.

Akhter, Tabir. "19 Signs You Are from Brooklyn." BuzzFeed. August 20, 2020. https://www.buzzfeed.com/tabirakhter/19-signs-you-are-from-brooklyn.

Swindler, Samantha, and Jeff Manning. "Columbia Sportswear CEO Tim Boyle Cuts Own Salary to $10K, Retail Employees Receive Regular Pay." Oregonlive. April 8, 2020. https://www.oregonlive.com/coronavirus/2020/03/columbia-sportswear-ceo-tim-boyle-cuts-own-salary-to-10k-retail-employees-receive-regular-pay.html.

## CHAPTER 4

Raden, Aja. "Modern Love: The Invention of the Diamond Engagement Ring." HuffPost. December 7, 2017. https://www.huffpost.com/entry/modern-love-the-invention_b_9234280.

Day, Meagan. "Is the $90 Million Lesedi La Rona Diamond Actually Worthless?" Medium. March 19, 2018. https://timeline.com/is-the-90-million-lesedi-la-rona-diamond-actually-worthless-b922eaba5cc1.

"The Incredible Story of How De Beers Created and Lost the Most Powerful Monopoly Ever." *Business Insider*. May 8, 2014. https://www.businessinsider.com/history-of-de-beers-2011-12?international=true&r=US&IR=T#de-beers-forged-new-international-markets-using-similar-advertising-campaigns-in-places-like-japan-germany-and-brazil-6.

De Saussure, Ferdinand. *Course in General Linguistics*. New York: Columbia University Press, 2011.

Nodjimbadem, Katie. "The Trashy Beginnings of 'Don't Mess with Texas.'" *Smithsonian Magazine*. March 10, 2017. https://www.smithsonianmag.com/history/trashy-beginnings-dont-mess-texas-180962490/.

"DMWT Case Study." GSD&M. Accessed May 1, 2022. https://www.gsdm.com/dmwt/.

Schwimmer, Eric. "Is Anthropology a Domain of Semiotics?" In *A Semiotic Landscape. Panorama sémiotique: Proceedings of the First Congress of the International Association for Semiotic Studies, Milan June 1974.* Berlin, Boston: De Gruyter Mouton, 2019, 1060–1063. https://doi.org /10.1515/9783110803327-204.

"Semiotics: The Study of Signs and Symbols in Human Communication." ThoughtCo. March 8, 2020. https://www.thoughtco.com/semiotics -definition-1692082.

McCracken, Grant. "Culture and Consumption: A Theoretical Account of the Structure and Movement of the Cultural Meaning of Consumer Goods." *Journal of Consumer Research* 13, no. 1 (1986): 71–84.

Schneider, Katy. "The Unlikely Tale of a $140 Amazon Coat That's Taken Over the Upper East Side." *Strategist.* March 27, 2018. https://nymag.com /strategist/2018/03/the-orolay-amazon-coat-thats-overtaken-the-upper -east-side.html.

Jennings, Rebecca. "The Orolay Amazon Coat, Explained." Vox. February 25, 2019. https://www.vox.com/the-goods/2019/2/25/18233597/orolay -amazon-coat-upper-east-side.

Desta, Yohana. "The Brand Beyoncé Almost Name-Dropped Instead of Red Lobster." *Vanity Fair.* December 9, 2016. https://www.vanityfair.com /hollywood/2016/12/beyonce-formation-red-lobster.

Morgan, Thaddeus. "How Did the Rainbow Flag Become an LGBT Symbol?" History. June 22, 2020. https://www.history.com/news/how-did -the-rainbow-flag-become-an-lgbt-symbol#:%7E:text=The%20rainbow %20flag%20was%20created,San%20Francisco's%20annual%20pride%20 parade.

Kua, Benson. "History of the Rainbow Flag." These Colors Run Deep. August 5, 2010. https://scholarblogs.emory.edu/lgbtflags/history/.

Riley, Charles. "Red Lobster: Sales Spike 33 Percent After Beyoncé Endorsement." CNNMoney. February 9, 2016. https://money.cnn.com/2016/02 /09/investing/red-lobster-beyonce-formation/.

Milian, Mark. "Apple Triggers 'Religious' Reaction in Fans' Brains, Report Says." CNN. May 19, 2011. http://www.cnn.com/2011/TECH/gaming.gadgets /05/19/apple.religion/index.html#:~:text=The%20neuroscientists %20ran%20a%20magnetic,religious%20people%2C%20the%20report %20says.

Shontell, Alyson. "It's Official: Apple Fanboyism Is a Religion: Neuroscientists Find Both Trigger Same Reaction in Brain." *Business Insider.* May 21, 2011. https://www.businessinsider.com/apple-is-a-religion -neuroscientists-find-it-triggers-the-same-reaction-in-your-brain-2011 -5?international=true&r=US&IR=T.

Belsey, Catherine. *Poststructuralism: A Very Short Introduction*. Oxford, UK: Oxford University Press, 2002.

Seymour, Laura. *An Analysis of Roland Barthes's* The Death of the Author. New York: Routledge, 2017.

Geertz, Clifford, and Robert Darnton. *The Interpretation of Cultures: Selected Essays*, 3rd ed. New York: Basic Books.

Lamont, Michèle. "Toward a Comparative Sociology of Valuation and Evaluation." *Annual Review of Sociology* 38 (2012): 201–221.

Suchman, Mark C. "Managing Legitimacy: Strategic and Institutional Approaches." *Academy of Management Review* 20, no. 3 (1995): 571–610.

*Dating App Wars: Are You Ready to Bumble?* Wondery. Accessed May 1, 2022. https://wondery.com/shows/business-wars/episode/5296-dating-app-wars-are-you-ready-to-bumble/.

Cialdini, Robert B. *Influence: The Psychology of Persuasion*, rev. ed. New York: HarperBusiness, 2006.

"U.S. Adult Tobacco Product Use Decreased from 2019 to 2020." CDC Newsroom. January 1, 2016. https://www.cdc.gov/media/releases/2022/p0318-US-tobacco-use.html#:%7E:text=This%20study%20shows%20that%20adult,reported%20smoking%20cigarettes%20in%202020.

McLuhan, Marshall, and Quentin Fiore. *The Medium Is the Massage: An Inventory of Effects*. Berkeley, CA: Gingko Press, 2001.

Henley, Jon. "'What Is Truly Scandinavian? Nothing': Airline Clarifies Ad After Far-Right Criticism." *Guardian*. July 1, 2020. https://www.theguardian.com/world/2020/feb/13/what-is-truly-scandinavian-nothing-airline-clarifies-ad-after-far-right-criticism.

"Global Athleisure Market Forecast Report 2021–2028—Rising Trend of Sustainable Athleisure, Increased Demand from Millennials, Growing Penetration of e-Commerce—ResearchAndMarkets.com." Yahoo. August 31, 2022. https://www.yahoo.com/now/global-athleisure-market-forecast-report-092100644.html?guccounter=1&guce_referrer=aHR0cHM6Ly93d3cuZ29vZ2xlLmNvbS8&guce_referrer_sig=AQAAAKcC8C1qspTSBgwY0yUNr9Vxl3dRoqUfDL1uhTPcon4jrutIEE13SMncDZikVbTJHUZIsafo38zxWpvFnXztM5mm3_83wZCHIvvXpEnVeLthxrNOcf6rzOp_y_cMTQP8w210SzR8KcPIAzbyhnT2GwGuwqjzYj-bMoaJP0zzhjtI#:~:text=The%20athleisure%20market%20is%20expected,9.9%25%20from%202021%20to%202028.

"Distracted Boyfriend." Know Your Meme. June 30, 2022. https://knowyourmeme.com/memes/distracted-boyfriend.

## CHAPTER 5

"Bobby Vinton Biography." Bobby Vinton. Accessed May 1, 2022. http://www
.bobbyvinton.com/.

"Bobby Vinton." Pittsburgh Music History. Accessed May 1, 2022. https://sites
.google.com/site/pittsburghmusichistory/pittsburgh-music-story/pop
/bobby-vinton.

Puterbaugh, Parke. "The British Invasion: From the Beatles to the Stones, the
Sixties Belonged to Britain." *Rolling Stone.* January 3, 2021. https://www
.rollingstone.com/feature/the-british-invasion-from-the-beatles-to-the
-stones-the-sixties-belonged-to-britain-244870/.

Kamp, David. "An Oral History of the British Invasion." *Vanity Fair.* February
10, 2014. https://www.vanityfair.com/culture/2002/11/british-invasion
-oral-history.

Nilsson, Jeff. "Why Early Critics Hated the Beatles." *Saturday Evening Post.* October 3, 2018. https://www.saturdayeveningpost.com/2014/01/why-the
-beatles-bugged-the-critics/.

Hastorf, Albert H., and Hadley Cantril. "They Saw a Game: A Case Study."
*Journal of Abnormal and Social Psychology* 49, no. 1 (1954): 129–134.
https://doi.org/10.1037/h0057880.

Fish, Bill. "Naïve Realism." Oxford Bibliographies. Last modified March 30,
2017. https://www.oxfordbibliographies.com/view/document/obo-9780
195396577/obo-9780195396577-0340.xml.

D'Addario, Daniel. "Why the Kendall Jenner Pepsi Ad Was Such a Glaring
Misstep." *Time.* April 5, 2017. https://time.com/4726500/pepsi-ad-kendall
-jenner/.

Weaver, Warren, and Claude Elwood Shannon. *The Mathematical Theory of
Communication.* Champaign: University of Illinois Press, 1963.

"Shannon and Weaver Model of Communication." Businesstopia. February
15, 2018. https://www.businesstopia.net/communication/shannon-and
-weaver-model-communication.

Al-Fedaghi, Sabah. "A Conceptual Foundation for the Shannon-Weaver
Model of Communication." *International Journal of Soft Computing* 7,
no. 1 (2012): 12–19.

"Shannon and Weaver Model of Communication." Communication Theory. July
10, 2014. https://www.communicationtheory.org/shannon-and-weaver
-model-of-communication/.

Murray, Mark. "As Howard Dean's 'Scream' Turns 15, Its Impact on American
Politics Lives On." NBC News. January 18, 2019. https://www.nbcnews

.com/politics/meet-the-press/howard-dean-s-scream-turns-15-its
-impact-american-politics-n959916.

Walsh, Kenneth T. "The Battle Cry That Backfired on Howard 'The Scream' Dean." *US News & World Report*. January 7, 2008. https://www.usnews.com/news/articles/2008/01/17/the-battle-cry-that-backfired.

Williams, Juan. "What Happened to Howard Dean?" NPR. February 9, 2004. https://www.npr.org/2004/02/09/1667239/what-happened-to-howard-dean.

Roberts, Joel. "The Rise and Fall of Howard Dean." CBS News. February 19, 2004. https://www.cbsnews.com/news/the-rise-and-fall-of-howard-dean-18-02-2004/.

"Excommunication." Catholic Encyclopedia. Accessed May 1, 2022. https://www.newadvent.org/cathen/05678a.htm.

"What Is Excommunication?" Catholic Straight Answers. A. May 21, 2013. https://catholicstraightanswers.com/what-is-excommunication/.

Witter, Brad. "Tina Fey Used Her Real Life as Inspiration for the Unforgettable Characters in 'Mean Girls.'" Biography. May 19, 2020. https://www.biography.com/news/tina-fey-mean-girls-characters.

Wiseman, Rosalind. *Queen Bees and Wannabes: Helping Your Daughter Survive Cliques, Gossip, Boyfriends, and the New Realities of Girl World*, 2nd ed. New York: Three Rivers Press, 2009.

Ortiz, Aimee. "Peloton Ad Is Criticized as Sexist and Dystopian." *New York Times*. December 4, 2019. https://www.nytimes.com/2019/12/03/business/peloton-bike-ad-stock.html#:%7E:text=Many%20social%20media%20users%20criticized,classes%20costs%20%2439%20a%20month.&text=The%20woman%20in%20the%20commercial,pointed%20out%2C%20was%20already%20fit.

Mautz, Scott. "A Peloton Ad Sparked Huge Controversy over Its Sexism. It's Also Just a Terrible Commercial." Inc.com. February 6, 2020. https://www.inc.com/scott-mautz/a-peloton-ad-sparked-huge-controversy-over-its-sexism-its-also-just-a-terrible-commercial.html.

Steinberg, Brian. "Ryan Reynolds Hijacks 'Peloton Wife,' Wrings New Buzz from Old Ad Trick." *Variety*. December 7, 2019. https://variety.com/2019/tv/news/ryan-reynolds-peloton-wife-aviation-gin-advertising-1203428394/.

Hsu, Tiffany. "Peloton's Cringe-y Ad Got Everyone Talking. Its C.E.O. Is Silent." *New York Times*. December 9, 2019. https://www.nytimes.com/2019/12/09/business/media/peloton-ad-ryan-reynolds.html.

Holcombe, Madeline C. "The Peloton Actress Has Traded a Bike for a Cocktail in New Ryan Reynolds Commercial." CNN. December 7, 2019. https://edition.cnn.com/2019/12/07/us/peloton-ad-ryan-reynolds-gin-trnd/index.html.

Levine, Barry. "Sprite Highlights Hip-Hop Culture with 'Thirst for Yours' campaign." Marketing Dive. June 21, 2019. https://www.marketingdive.com/news/sprite-highlights-hip-hop-culture-with-thirst-for-yours-campaign/557327/#:%7E:text=In%201994%2C%20a%20series%20of,Notorious%20B.I.G.%2C%20Nas%20and%20Rakim.

"Obey Your Thirst Campaign (1998)." Marketing Campaign Case Studies. May 24, 2008. http://marketing-case-studies.blogspot.com/2008/05/obey-your-thirst-campaign-1998.html.

Roque, M. "'Same Same, but Different': An Origin Story." Slumber Party Hostels. April 1, 2019. https://slumberpartyhostels.com/same-same-but-different-origin/.

Wotton, Chris. "'Same Same, but Different': The Origins of Thailand's Tourist Catchphrase." Culture Trip. January 9, 2019. https://theculturetrip.com/asia/thailand/articles/same-same-but-different-the-origins-of-thailands-tourist-catchphrase/.

*KKK Series.* Federal Bureau of Investigation. April 27, 2022. https://www.fbi.gov/history/famous-cases/kkk-series.

History.com Editors. "Ku Klux Klan." History. February 4, 2022. https://www.history.com/topics/reconstruction/ku-klux-klan.

Pfeiffer, Lee. "*The Birth of a Nation.*" *Encyclopædia Britannica.* Accessed May 1, 2022. https://www.britannica.com/topic/The-Birth-of-a-Nation.

History.com Editors. "'The Birth of a Nation' Opens, Glorifying the KKK." History. February 7, 2022. https://www.history.com/this-day-in-history/birth-of-a-nation-opens.

Sobchack, Vivian C. *The Address of the Eye: A Phenomenology of Film Experience.* Princeton, NJ: Princeton University Press, 1992.

Sandlin, Jennifer A., Brian D. Schultz, and Jake Burdick, eds. *Handbook of Public Pedagogy.* New York: Routledge, 2009.

Kahneman, Daniel. *Thinking, Fast and Slow.* New York: Macmillan, 2011.

Zajonc, Robert B. "Attitudinal Effects of Mere Exposure." *Journal of Personality and Social Psychology* 9, no. 2, pt. 2 (1968): 1–27. https://doi.org/10.1037/h0025848.

"Yasmin Green." TED. Accessed May 1, 2022. https://www.ted.com/speakers/yasmin_green.

Roose, Kevin, Daniel Guillemette, Rachel Quester, Eric Krupke, Clare Tonies-
koetter, Rob Szypko, Mike Benoist, Marion Lozano, Dan Powell, and
Brad Fisher. "'We're Going to Take Over the World.'" *New York Times*.
September 10, 2021. https://www.nytimes.com/2021/09/10/podcasts
/the-daily/911-conspiracy-theories-loose-change.html.

Lorenz, Taylor. "Birds Aren't Real, or Are They? Inside a Gen Z Conspiracy
Theory." *New York Times*. December 9, 2021. https://www.nytimes
.com/2021/12/09/technology/birds-arent-real-gen-z-misinformation
.html.

## CHAPTER 6

"Obscene, Indecent and Profane Broadcasts." Federal Communications Commission. January 13, 2021. https://www.fcc.gov/consumers/guides
/obscene-indecent-and-profane-broadcasts.

Ott, T. "How George Carlin's 'Seven Words' Changed Legal History." Biography. May 19, 2020. https://www.biography.com/news/george-carlin
-seven-words-supreme-court.

Schrøder, Kim Christian. "Media Discourse Analysis: Researching Cultural Meanings from Inception to Reception." *Textual Cultures* (2007):
77–99.

McCracken, Grant. "Storytime 1: Fast Culture and Slow Culture on Oprah."
Mapping the Future. September 23, 2021. https://mapping-the-future
.com/2020/08/19/test-case/.

"Make Ethnography Better." CultureBy—Grant McCracken. April 27, 2016.
https://cultureby.com/tag/slow-culture.

Barnes, Kenyette Tisha. "R. Kelly Has Finally Been Silenced. Let's Keep It
That Way." *Time*. September 29, 2021. https://time.com/6102538/r-kelly
-conviction-mute/.

Grady, Constance. "20 Years After Aaliyah's Death, R. Kelly's Shadow Looms."
Vox. August 30, 2021. https://www.vox.com/culture/22621692/aaliyah
-death-20-year-anniversary-r-kelly-trial#:%7E:text=Court%20records
%20show%20that%20Aaliyah,deny%20it%20at%20his%20trial.

Seidel, Jon. "Decades of Abuse Allegations Lead R&B Superstar R. Kelly Back
in Front of a Jury." *Chicago Sun-Times*. August 9, 2021. https://chicago
.suntimes.com/2021/8/8/22608334/r-kelly-trial-starting-decades-abuse
-allegations-lead-rb-superstar-back-front-jury#:%7E:text=Early%20in
%202002%2C%20a%2026,pornography%20charges%20in%20June
%202002.

"Update on the Twitter Archive at the Library of Congress." Library of Congress. December 2017. https://blogs.loc.gov/loc/files/2017/12/2017dec _twitter_white-paper.pdf.

Schouten, John W., and James H. McAlexander. "Subcultures of Consumption: An Ethnography of the New Bikers," *Journal of Consumer Research* 22, no. 1 (1995): 43–61.

Spradley, James P. *The Ethnographic Interview.* Long Grove, IL: Waveland Press, 2016.

Kozinets, Robert V. "'I Want to Believe': A Netnography of the X-Philes' Subculture of Consumption." *Advances in Consumer Research* 24 (1997): 470–475.

Kozinets, Robert V. "On Netnography: Initial Reflections on Consumer Research Investigations of Cyberculture." *NA—Advances in Consumer Research* 25 (1998): 366–371.

Kozinets, Robert V. "Utopian Enterprise: Articulating the Meanings of Star Trek's Culture of Consumption." *Journal of Consumer Research* 28, no. 1 (2001): 67–88.

Kozinets, Robert V. "The Field Behind the Screen: Using Netnography for Marketing Research in Online Communities." *Journal of Marketing Research* 39, no. 1 (2002): 61–72.

Kozinets, Robert V. *Netnography: Doing Ethnographic Research Online.* Thousand Oaks, CA: Sage Publications, 2010.

Kozinets, Robert V. "Marketing Netnography: Prom/ot(ulgat)ing a New Research Method." *Methodological Innovations Online* 7, no. 1 (2012): 37-45.

Kozinets, Robert V., and Rossella Gambetti, eds. *Netnography Unlimited: Understanding Technoculture Using Qualitative Social Media Research.* New York: Routledge, 2020.

Ventura, Michael P. *Applied Empathy: The New Language of Leadership.* New York: Touchstone Books, 2018.

Bariso, Justin. "There Are Actually 3 Types of Empathy. Here's How They Differ— and How You Can Develop Them All." Inc.Com. October 7, 2020. https:// www.inc.com/justin-bariso/there-are-actually-3-types-of-empathy -heres-how-they-differ-and-how-you-can-develop-them-all.html.

"What Is Empathy and Why Do I Need It?" Bungalow. February 1, 2022. https://bungalow.com/articles/what-is-empathy-and-why-do-i -need-it.

Raine, Adrian, and Frances R. Chen. "The Cognitive, Affective, and Somatic Empathy Scales (CASES) for Children." *Journal of Clinical Child & Adolescent Psychology* 47, no. 1 (2018): 24–37.

"Culture of Empathy Builder: Daniel Goleman." Accessed May 1, 2022. http://cultureofempathy.com/References/Experts/Daniel-Goleman.htm.

Goleman, Daniel. *Emotional Intelligence*. New York: Bantam Books, 1995.

Sherry, John F. "Postmodern Alternatives: The Interpretive Turn in Consumer Research," *Handbook of Consumer Behavior* 199 (1991): 548–591.

Tett, Gillian. *Anthro-vision: A New Way to See in Business and Life*. New York: Avid Reader Press, 2021.

Withy, Katherine. "Situation and Limitation: Making Sense of Heidegger on Thrownness." *European Journal of Philosophy* 22, no. 1 (2014): 61–81.

Fraade-Blanar, Zoe, and Aaron M. Glazer. *Superfandom: How Our Obsessions Are Changing What We Buy and Who We Are*, 1st ed. New York: W. W. Norton & Company, 2017.

Ohanian, Alexis. *Without Their Permission: How the 21st Century Will Be Made, Not Managed*. London: Hachette UK, 2013.

Bourdieu, Pierre. *Distinction: A Social Critique of the Judgement of Taste*. London: Routledge, 1984.

Stossel, John. "'Super Size Me' Carries Weight with Critics." ABC News. January 6, 2006. https://abcnews.go.com/2020/Oscars2005/story?id=124265&page=1.

"How W+K Won McDonald's, Then Blew the Doors off with Travis Scott, as Told by Jennifer Healan of McDonald's and Tass Tsitsopoulos of Wieden." Apple Podcasts. February 12, 2021. https://podcasts.apple.com/us/podcast/how-w-k-won-mcdonalds-then-blew-doors-off-travis-scott/id1494056579?i=1000508861492.

Sherwood, I-Hsien. "Jennifer Healan Drove Travis Scott Deal for McDonald's." *AdAge*. June 7, 2021. https://adage.com/article/special-report-agency-list/creativity-awards-brand-manager-jennifer-jj-healan/2341341/.

Levin, Tim "Travis Scott Reportedly Earned $20 Million Through His Partnership with McDonald's." *Business Insider*. December 1, 2020. https://www.businessinsider.in/retail/news/travis-scott-reportedly-earned-20-million-through-his-partnership-with-mcdonalds/articleshow/79520385.cms.

Brown, Abram. "How Hip-Hop Superstar Travis Scott Has Become Corporate America's Brand Whisperer." *Forbes*. December 1, 2020. https://www.forbes.com/sites/abrambrown/2020/11/30/how-hip-hop-superstar-travis-scott-has-become-corporate-americas-brand-whisperer/.

McPherson, Miller, Lynn Smith-Lovin, and James M. Cook. "Birds of a Feather: Homophily in Social Networks." *Annual Review of Sociology* 27, no. 1 (2001): 415–444.

Roberts, Kevin. *Lovemarks: The Future Beyond Brands*, 2nd ed., expanded ed. New York: PowerHouse Books, 2005.

Gecas, Viktor. "The Self-Concept." *Annual Review of Sociology* 8, no. 1 (1982): 133.

Wade, Peter. "The Anti-vaxx Movement Is Taking Over the Republican Party." *Rolling Stone*. September 30, 2021. https://www.rollingstone.com/politics /politics-news/republicans-vaccine-poll-disapprove-biden-mandates -1234921/.

"Data." MIT Election and Data Science Lab. March 17, 2022. https:// electionlab.mit.edu/data.

Jones, Bradley. "The Changing Political Geography of COVID-19 over the Last Two Years." Pew Research Center—U.S. Politics & Policy. April 22, 2022. https://www.pewresearch.org/politics/2022/03/03/the-changing -political-geography-of-covid-19-over-the-last-two-years/.

Merica, Dan. "Trump Met with Boos After Revealing He Received Covid-19 Booster." CNN. December 21, 2021. https://edition.cnn.com/2021/12 /20/politics/donald-trump-booster-shot-boos/index.html.

Collins, Marcus. "NFTs Will Become the Ultimate Marker of Belonging." *Adweek*. February 25, 2022. https://www.adweek.com/commerce/nfts-will -become-the-ultimate-marker-of-belonging/.

Collins, Marcus. "Marketers Are Mistaking Information for Intimacy." *Adweek*. August 9, 2021. https://www.adweek.com/performance-marketing /marketers-mistaking-information-intimacy/.

## CHAPTER 7

Tenreyro, Tatiana. "The Terrifying True Story of How 'The Blair Witch Project' Was Made." Vice. July 16, 2019. https://www.vice.com/en/article /8xzy4p/blair-witch-project-oral-history-20th-anniversary.

"Blair Witch." Fandom. Accessed May 1, 2022. https://blairwitch.fandom .com/wiki/Blair_Witch.

Shelton, Jacob. "Decoding the Backstory of 'The Blair Witch Project.'" Ranker. April 13, 2022. https://www.ranker.com/list/blair-witch-project -backstory/jacob-shelton.

Kidd, Celeste, and Benjamin Y. Hayden, "The Psychology and Neuroscience of Curiosity," *Neuron* 88, no. 3 (2015): 449–460.

Loewenstein, George. "The Psychology of Curiosity: A Review and Reinterpretation." *Psychological Bulletin* 116, no. 1 (1994): 75.

Kring-Schreifels, Jake. "'The Blair Witch Project' at 20: Why It Can't Be Replicated." *New York Times.* August 6, 2019. https://www.nytimes.com /2019/07/30/movies/blair-witch-project-1999.html.

Carvell, Tim. "How the Blair Witch Project Built Up So Much Buzz: Movie Moguldom on a Shoestring." CNNMoney. August 16, 1999. https:// money.cnn.com/magazines/fortune/fortune_archive/1999/08/16/264276 /#:~:text=Its%20title%2C%20of%20course%2C%20is,had%20an %20average%20of%20%249%2C003.

Nauert, R. "Why Do We Anthropomorphize?" Psych Central. March 1, 2018. https://psychcentral.com/news/2018/03/01/why-do-we -anthropomorphize#1.

Vega, Nick. "Here's Why User Reviews on Sites Like Amazon Are Such a Big Deal." *Business Insider.* March 20, 2017. https://www.businessinsider .in/heres-why-user-reviews-on-sites-like-amazon-are-such-a-big-deal /articleshow/57742285.cms.

"This Ancient Cave Art Is the Oldest Known 'Storytelling.'" CBC News. December 12, 2019. https://www.cbc.ca/news/science/cave-art-indonesia -1.5393624.

Guarino, Ben. "The Oldest Story Ever Told Is Painted on this Cave Wall, Archaeologists Report." *Washington Post.* December 12, 2019. https:// www.washingtonpost.com/science/2019/12/11/oldest-story-ever-told -is-painted-this-cave-wall-archaeologists-report/.

Guirand, Felix. *New Larousse Encyclopedia of Mythology.* London: Hamlyn, (1968) 1984.

Dundes, Alan. *Interpreting Folklore.* Bloomington: Indiana University Press, 1980.

Dundes, Alan. "The Study of Folklore in Literature and Culture: Identification and Interpretation." *Journal of American Folklore* 78, no. 308 (1965): 136–142.

Ziff, Bruce H., and Pratima V. Rao, eds. *Borrowed Power: Essays on Cultural Appropriation.* New Brunswick, NJ: Rutgers University Press, 1997.

Rogers, Richard A. "From Cultural Exchange to Transculturation: A Review and Reconceptualization of Cultural Appropriation." *Communication Theory* 16 (2006): 474–503.

"Episode 3: The Birth of American Music." *New York Times.* September 7, 2019. https://www.nytimes.com/2019/09/06/podcasts/1619-black-american -music-appropriation.html.

Simeon, Aimee. "The Beautiful, Black History of Cornrows." Byrdie. Last updated April 28, 2022. https://www.byrdie.com/history-of-cornrows

-5193458#:%7E:text=Cornrows%20dated%20far%20back%20to,slaves%2C%20where%20their%20customs%20followed.

Gabbara, Princess. "Cornrows and Sisterlocks and Their Long History." *Ebony*. January 20, 2017. https://www.ebony.com/style/everything-you-need-know-about-cornrows/.

Scott, Nateisha. "The History and Beauty of Cornrows." Popsugar Beauty. January 18, 2022. https://www.popsugar.com/beauty/cornrows-history-essay-48676516.

Payne, Teryn. "Kim Kardashian West Wore Cornrows to the MTV Movie & TV Awards, Despite Past Criticism." *Glamour*. June 19, 2018. https://www.glamour.com/story/kim-kardashian-cornrows-mtv-movie-tv-awards-2018.

"Census Releases Numbers on the Black Population in the U.S." Michigan Radio. October 25, 2011. https://www.michiganradio.org/arts-culture/2011-09-29/census-releases-numbers-on-the-black-population-in-the-u-s.

"The Origins of Modern Day Policing." NAACP. December 3, 2021. https://naacp.org/find-resources/history-explained/origins-modern-day-policing.

Ramirez, Charles E., "Last Original Blue Pigs Member Retires from Detroit Police Dept." *Detroit News*. September 25, 2019. https://eu.detroitnews.com/story/news/local/detroit-city/2019/09/25/detroit-police-blue-pigs-member-retires/2439327001/.

Varolli, Regina. "My Mom Wrote the Motto 'To Protect and to Serve.'" CulEpi. June 4, 2020. https://www.culinaryepicenter.com/my-mom-wrote-the-motto-to-protect-and-to-serve/.

Sastry, Anjuli, and Karen Grigsby Bates. "When LA Erupted in Anger: A Look Back at the Rodney King Riots." NPR. April 26, 2017. https://www.npr.org/2017/04/26/524744989/when-la-erupted-in-"anger-a-look-back-at-the-rodney-king-riots.

Anderson, Elisha. "25 Years Ago, Malice Green Became the Face of Police Brutality in Detroit." *Detroit Free Press*. November 5, 2017. https://eu.freep.com/story/news/local/michigan/detroit/2017/11/03/malice-green-police-brutality-detroit/823635001/.

Powell, John A. "Us vs Them: The Sinister Techniques of 'Othering'—and How to Avoid Them." *Guardian*. November 30, 2017. https://www.theguardian.com/inequality/2017/nov/08/us-vs-them-the-sinister-techniques-of-othering-and-how-to-avoid-them.

"Early Police in the United States." *Encyclopædia Britannica*. Accessed May 1, 2022. https://www.britannica.com/topic/police/Early-police-in-the-United-States.

Brons, Lajos L. "Othering, an Analysis." *Transcience, a Journal of Global Studies* 6, no. 1 (2015).

Cole, Teju. "The White-Savior Industrial Complex." *Atlantic*. June 6, 2021. https://www.theatlantic.com/international/archive/2012/03/the-white-savior-industrial-complex/254843/.

Canales, Mary K. "Othering: Toward an Understanding of Difference." *Advances in Nursing Science* 22, no. 4 (June 2000): 16–31.

Sandlin, Jennifer A., Brian D. Schultz, and Jake Burdick, eds. *Handbook of Public Pedagogy*. New York: Routledge, 2009.

Crang, Mike. *Cultural Geography*. London: Routledge, 1998.

Mcleod, Saul. "Classical Conditioning: How It Works with Examples." Simply Psychology. Last updated November 22, 2021. https://www.simplypsychology.org/classical-conditioning.html.

Bouton, Mark E., and Erik W. Moody. "Memory Processes in Classical Conditioning." *Neuroscience & Biobehavioral Reviews* 28, no. 7 (2004): 663–674.

"Rethink Shinola." Rethink Shinola. Accessed May 1, 2022. https://rethinkshinola.com/.

Modrak, Rebekah. "Bougie Crap: Art, Design and Gentrification." *Infinite Mile Detroit* 14 (February 2014). https://infinitemiledetroit.com/Bougie_Crap_Art,_Design_and_Gentrification.html.

Duggan, Daniel. "Fossil Founder Digs the D." Crain's Detroit Business. June 6, 2012. https://www.crainsdetroit.com/article/20120527/FREE/305279963/fossil-founder-digs-the-d.

Haddad, Ken. "'Green Book' Director Slammed for Claiming Shinola 'Saving Detroit' at Oscars." WDIV. February 25, 2019. https://www.clickondetroit.com/entertainment/2019/02/25/green-book-director-slammed-for-claiming-shinola-saving-detroit-at-oscars/.

Collins, Marcus. "We Must Redefine—and Deepen Our Sense of—Culture." *Adweek*. February 22, 2021. https://www.adweek.com/creativity/e-must-redefine-and-deepen-our-sense-of-culture/.

## EPILOGUE

Daniels, Cheyanne M. "Multicultural Americans to Become Majority Population by 2050: Report." The Hill. January 17, 2024. https://thehill.com/homenews/4412311-multicultural-americans-majority-population-2050.

# Index

**Marcus Collins** is an award-winning marketer and cultural translator. He is the former head of strategy at Wieden+ Kennedy New York and a clinical assistant professor of marketing at the Ross School of Business, University of Michigan. He is a recipient of Advertising Age's 40 Under 40 award and an inductee into the American Advertising Federation's Advertising Hall of Achievement. Most recently, he was recognized by Thinkers50 and Deloitte among their class of 2023 Radar List of 30 thinkers with the ideas most likely to shape the future. His strategies and creative contributions have led to the launch and success of Google's "Real Tone" technology, the Made In America music festival, and the Brooklyn Nets, among others. Prior to his advertising tenure, Collins worked on iTunes + Nike sport music initiatives at Apple and ran digital strategy for Beyoncé. Collins holds a doctorate in marketing from Temple University, where he studied social contagion and meaning-making. He received an MBA with an emphasis on strategic brand marketing from the University of Michigan, where he also earned his undergraduate degree in Material Science Engineering. He lives in Ann Arbor, Michigan.

PublicAffairs is a publishing house founded in 1997. It is a tribute to the standards, values, and flair of three persons who have served as mentors to countless reporters, writers, editors, and book people of all kinds, including me.

I. F. STONE, proprietor of *I. F. Stone's Weekly*, combined a commitment to the First Amendment with entrepreneurial zeal and reporting skill and became one of the great independent journalists in American history. At the age of eighty, Izzy published *The Trial of Socrates*, which was a national bestseller. He wrote the book after he taught himself ancient Greek.

BENJAMIN C. BRADLEE was for nearly thirty years the charismatic editorial leader of *The Washington Post*. It was Ben who gave the *Post* the range and courage to pursue such historic issues as Watergate. He supported his reporters with a tenacity that made them fearless and it is no accident that so many became authors of influential, best-selling books.

ROBERT L. BERNSTEIN, the chief executive of Random House for more than a quarter century, guided one of the nation's premier publishing houses. Bob was personally responsible for many books of political dissent and argument that challenged tyranny around the globe. He is also the founder and longtime chair of Human Rights Watch, one of the most respected human rights organizations in the world.

.    .    .

For fifty years, the banner of Public Affairs Press was carried by its owner Morris B. Schnapper, who published Gandhi, Nasser, Toynbee, Truman, and about 1,500 other authors. In 1983, Schnapper was described by *The Washington Post* as "a redoubtable gadfly." His legacy will endure in the books to come.

Peter Osnos, *Founder*